History and Human Responsibility

History and
Human Responsibility

The Unbearable Weight of Freedom in a
Dystopian World

MARCEL H. VAN HERPEN

ST. AUGUSTINE'S PRESS

South Bend, Indiana

1 2 3 4 5 6   29 28 27 26 25 24

Library of Congress Control Number: 9781587314360

Paperback ISBN: 978-1-58731-437-7
Ebook ISBN: 978-158731-436-0

∞ The paper used in this publication meets the minimum
requirements of the American National Standard for Information Sciences –
Permanence of Paper for Printed Materials, ANSI Z39.48-1984.

St. Augustine's Press
www.staugustine.net

TABLE OF CONTENTS

INTRODUCTION
THE PRESENT CRISIS MOOD

The world is in crisis. Many people share a deep concern about the times we live in. The Covid-19 pandemic and the war in Ukraine are only the latest catastrophes for which the world wasn't prepared. However, neither the pandemic nor the war created the present crisis mood. It only exacerbated an already existing trend. Let us, for instance, take a look at the headlines of some leading political magazines in the year before the outbreak of the pandemic. What did they tell us? The American magazine *Foreign Affairs* (May-June 2018) ran the headline "Is Democracy Dying?" The July-August 2018 issue of the same magazine was titled "Which World Are We Living In?" *The American Interest* (January-February 2018) had the headline *The End of Work* (without a question mark), while *The National Interest* (May-June 2018) announced *A New Cold War*. The same magazine wrote in the July-August 2018 issue that "today, liberalism appears to be dying in much the same way that Soviet Communism did a generation ago."[1] Demographers joined in this chorus of pessimists, predicting "that by the latter half of the century or possibly earlier, the global population will enter a sustained decline for the first time."[2] This process, due to plunging fertility rates, was said to "take decades, but once it starts, decline ... spirals exponentially, threatening to upend how societies are organized—around the notion that a surplus of young people will drive economies and help pay for the old."[3] An article in the *New York Times* was titled "American optimism, R.I.P." "I thought that we were a sunny people," the author wrote. "I thought that optimism was the fundamental nature of the United States of America, the whole point. We had an endless horizon that encouraged people to dream their biggest dreams."[4] No longer so, he continued: "Anxiety rules. Worry reigns ... we don't see ourselves striding toward a better tomorrow. We see ourselves tiptoeing around catastrophe."[5] The same paper published two months later an article titled, "We need to think about the unthinkable future." This "unthinkable future"—for the U.S.—included "insurrection, secession, insurgency and civil war."[6] It is clear: all this is not really optimistic stuff.

The new crisis mood could not only be observed in the United States. It was also present in Europe, nurtured by different factors such as global warming, the worldwide wave of populism, the British Brexit drama, the long-term consequences of the Great Recession of 2008, structural changes in the economy, the introduction of new technologies with still unknown consequences such as artificial intelligence and genetic manipulation, and changing international power relations which announced the end of the West's global hegemony. The presidency of Donald Trump was an important factor in this change of mood. It was a reason for the French paper *Le Monde* to write that with the presidency of Donald Trump, a new reality was emerging: "this reality is the need to reconfigure a world in which the American giant is no longer a friend of Europe."[7] According to the author, European businessmen and diplomats would "have understood that Donald Trump wasn't a historical incident, but personified a deeper, permanent and structural tendency which could already have been discovered before his election if one had paid more attention to the signs."[8] If America would no longer be a friend of Europe, this would mean a complete reversal of the stable post-World War II order that lasted for 75 years. Although Joe Biden's subsequent restoration of the transatlantic alliance and his firm stance against Russia in the Ukraine conflict have assuaged some of those fears, a deep uncertainty about the future of the alliance still lingers.

This crisis mood colors our view of the future. In a report on global trends, published in 2021 by the American National Intelligence Council, most scenarios presented for the next twenty years are a matter of deep concern. One can, for instance, read that internationally the world will be "more contested, uncertain, and conflict prone,"[9] and that "the risk of interstate conflict is likely to rise because of advances in technology and an expanding range of targets, new frontiers for conflict and a greater variety of actors, more difficult deterrence, and a weakening or a lack of treaties and norms on acceptable use."[10] Tellingly, one of the scenarios is titled *A World Adrift*. It describes the emerging international system as "directionless, chaotic, and volatile as international rules and institutions are largely ignored."[11] According to the *New York Times,* "Experts in Washington who have read these reports said they do not recall a gloomier one," adding, "The gloom, however, should not come as a surprise. Most of what Global Trends provides are reminders of the dangers we know and the warnings we've heard."[12] Of course, these are only scenarios and there is nothing preordained, but the message about what lies ahead is not comforting.

BACK TO THE 1930s?

Often references are made to the 1930s. These references only increased after the brutal Russian assault on Ukraine. Already before the war in Ukraine French President Emmanuel Macron said in an interview: "I don't want simply to observe history. I want … to try to understand the lessons from history. I am struck by the similarities between the period in which we are living and [the period] between the two world wars.…"[13] The American historian Timothy Snyder was also very explicit on the new reality created by the election of Donald Trump: "In my world, where I come from, it's the 1930s … Picking out a group of your neighbours and citizens and associating them with the worldwide threat, that's the 1930s."[14] Some months earlier a similar observation was made by a columnist of *The Economist,* who wrote: "After this bleakest of years for Europe, glib talk of the 1930s is in the air. The bonds of trust between nations are fraying.… Populists are on the march. Britain is on the way out. And Europe's neighbours are either menacing (Russia) or threatening to flood it with refugees."[15]

The 1930s with Hitler's *Machtergreifung* (seizure of power), Hitler's paramilitaries in the streets, the persecution of the Jews and, finally, the Second World War, as a point of reference? Isn't that an exaggeration? Yes, answers the English historian Ian Kershaw, who wrote that "the recent economic crisis and the political response to it demonstrate that today's Europe, for all its problems, is light-years removed from the conditions that once produced fascism."[16] Light-years removed? However, this then begs the question, why is this comparison with the 1930s making its appearance all the time? There must be *something* to explain this comparison. The French philosopher Michaël Foessel might come close to it when he writes: "In the phrase 'return to the 1930s' we find the false impression in the word 'return.' No historical event repeats itself in the form and the conditions in which it took place for the first time."[17] One can agree with that. But Foessel also warns about a second misconception: "Asking oneself whether the '1930s' have a future supposes that one overcomes a misconception which is even more persistent than that of the 'return': the naïve belief in the absolute newness of today's world."[18] Indeed, although we can be reassured that the 1930s with Mussolini's Blackshirts and Hitler's Brownshirts in the streets will not come back, this does not mean that we can be sure that fascist movements have disappeared forever. The violent assault on January 6, 2021, on the United States Capitol by a mob of extreme right Trump supporters and Putin's brutal assault on Ukraine on February 24, 2022, are reminders of this fact.

CRISIS AND FEELINGS OF INSECURITY

We should also not forget that between the 1930s and the 2020s there exists at least an important *psychological* parallel: a similarity in the way the crisis is experienced today and how it was experienced in the interbellum. In 1926, in the time of the Weimar Republic when Hitler's SA troops marched through the streets of Germany, the German philosopher Max Scheler (1874–1928) wrote: "We are in the about ten thousand years of history the first period in which man has fully and completely become 'problematic'; in which he no longer knows who he is, however, at the same time *knows that* he doesn't know."[19] Also, today this sense of a historical fracture—a deep crisis—seems to be felt everywhere and, like Scheler, we know that we no longer know who we are and what our role is in the universe—*if* we have a role in the universe. According to Reinhart Koselleck, who wrote a classical study on the crisis phenomenon,

> "It is part of the essence of a crisis that a decision has to be taken, but that [this decision] has not yet been taken. And it is also part of the crisis that it remains open what kind of decision will be taken. The general feeling of insecurity in a critical situation is therefore mixed with the certainty that—

clearly, while [it is] not clear when, certainly, while [it is] not certain how—an end to the critical situation is imminent. What the solution could be remains uncertain; the end itself, however, a change to the existing situation—threatening and feared, or hopefully welcomed—is certain for the people."[20]

A crisis situation is a situation in which people are waiting for some solution of the crisis—without knowing what the final outcome will be and without being able or feeling able to influence the outcome. These feelings of helplessness and powerlessness are not restricted to the man in the street. Political leaders also are left in limbo and don't know how the dice will roll. In a crisis situation nothing is certain; we all share the unpleasant feeling that we are slowly losing the firm ground beneath our feet and that the floor on which we stand has been changed into a collection of moving ice floes. In such a situation there exists a great need for certainty and—in particular—for predictability, and we hope that history can offer us examples and teach us lessons of how we can handle the situation in order to avoid calamities. But we know that a happy end is far from guaranteed, as was emphasized by a German author who wrote that he "intuitively rejects to believe that crises always must end well.... Normally social systems seem to be fragile and precarious, and unpleasant surprises are always possible.... Problems can be such that there doesn't exist a solution for them or in any case not one that can be realized here and now."[21] And one should add there are even solutions which only aggravate the situation.

OUR INCREASED RESPONSIBILITY FOR PAST AND PRESENT GENERATIONS

The present crisis is felt more acutely than previous crisis situations for still another reason. This is the fact that in the post-World War II period human responsibility, which before used to be mainly limited to the society of the living, i.e., the generations which actually make up society, has shown a tendency to project itself further into the past. This projection into the past is primarily a consequence of international human rights legislation enacted after the horrors of the Holocaust, which made descendants of perpetrators of war crimes and crimes against human-ity—although not personally guilty—responsible for the crimes of their forebears. According to Antoon De Baets:

> "The central idea of human rights is that the living possess dignity and therefore deserve respect. In addition, the living believe that the dead also have dignity and thus deserve re-spect too. When human beings die … some human traces sur-vive and mark the dead with symbolic value. The dead are less than human beings, but still *reminiscent* of them, and they are more than bodies or objects. This invites us to speak about the dead in a language of posthumous dignity and re-spect, and about the living, therefore, as having some defin-able core responsibilities to the dead."[22]

After the Second World War, the responsibility of the living towards the dead—in particular towards the victims of genocides and human rights abuses—has massively increased, as can be seen from the current debates on anti-Black racism and the legacy of slavery and the slave trade. Remembering the dead who were victims of grave human rights abuses is increasingly considered a duty. "Acknowledging and recount-ing their suffering would … posthumously restore the dignity of the vic-tims, a dignity that they were denied during their lives."[23] But it is not only a question of restored dignity. It is also a question of justice. De-scendants of the victims go to court to have court judgments posthu-mously reviewed; they organize commemorations and claim compensations. A striking aspect of this new responsibility for past gen-erations is the fact that it is not only the descendants of the victims who play an active role in this movement, but equally the descendants of the perpetrators.

CAN WE LEARN LESSONS FROM HISTORY?

The responsibility for preceding generations comes on top of an already existing responsibility: the responsibility for the well-being of the present—living—generation. Particularly in crisis situations one often hears that we should learn the lessons from history in order not to repeat past negative experiences. When French President Emmanuel Macron and the historian Timothy Snyder both warn about a return of the 1930s, the implicit message is that we should learn the lessons from this period in order to avoid history repeating itself. But does history teach us "lessons"? This is an old question, already asked in the fifth century BCE by Thucydides when he wrote his history of the Peloponnesian War. Learning lessons from history is perhaps one of the major motives for people writing down important events, and created a new discipline called "history," or rather "historiography." In Cicero's *De Oratore* (On the Orator) one can find the famous statement *historia magistra vitae:* history as a teacher for life.[24] But is it true that history is a teacher for our lives? And has it ever been? In crisis periods this question becomes more urgent: old certainties disappear and—independently from our wishes—a new, unknown world is emerging which seems to be at odds with our established ways of thinking and our existing value patterns. However, it is not the first time this is happening. The ways in which our forebears reacted to changes and adapted themselves, or failed to adapt themselves, can offer models to emulate or to avoid.

OUR INCREASED RESPONSIBILITY
FOR FUTURE GENERATIONS

The present crisis is felt more acutely than previous crisis situations for yet another reason. This is the fact that in the post-World War II period human responsibility was also projected further into the future. With the development of nuclear weapons, mankind for the first time in history acquired the capability for virtually decimating all life on the planet— with catastrophic consequences not only for us, but also for future generations. Of course, our forebears equally felt a responsibility for their children and grandchildren. But this responsibility was a *short-term* responsibility, restricted to the descendants they knew and with whom they had a relationship. A new development is that our generation is not only concerned about the fate of the two next generations, but of generations which will live hundreds, if not thousands of years from now. The reason is that man's grip on future developments has exponentially increased—due to the fact that modern technological innovations can have unknown long-term consequences for future generations. Certainly, our unprecedented technological prowess can bring many benefits. That said, it has also an important downside: it creates longer causal chains than previous innovations and inventions, which led to increased risks for future generations. Climate change is only one of them. Willy-nilly, if one likes it or not, modern technology has imposed on mankind a completely new moral imperative: a *long-term* moral responsibility, a responsibility for future generations—*including not yet born generations* who will be living hundreds of years from now.

Unlike the more common concept of judicial responsibility, which is a responsibility *after* the facts, this new *long-term* moral responsibility for future generations is a responsibility *before* the facts—the responsibility to avoid future generations becoming the victims of extravagant risk-taking by preceding generations. For this reason, we cannot leave the future to itself and satisfy ourselves with the knowledge that the future is a black box and that we have no other choice than to wait and see what will happen. We, ourselves, are the creators of the future, and although we don't control the outcome, we have a duty to mitigate the risks and negative consequences of our actions for future generations by developing different scenarios and calculating future trends. This new moral responsibility for future generations has not only made it necessary to develop probabilistic scenarios, but also "worst case scenarios," because the survival of the human species, as well as the animal world, is at stake.

WHO IS RESPONSIBLE?

We are increasingly responsible for the past, the present, and the future. But who is "we"? And are we all *equally* responsible? According to Jean-Paul Sartre we are. He wrote that "man, condemned to be free, carries the weight of the whole world on his shoulders: he is responsible for the world and for himself, as a way of life."[25] Sartre even speaks about an "absolute responsibility" and explains: "if I am mobilized for a war, this war is *my* war, it is made in my image and I deserve it. I deserve it because I could always escape, by suicide or desertion ..."[26] Sartre makes the individual—*each* individual—responsible for "the world." But is this reasonable? Or has Otfried Höffe a point, when he warned that "because the concept of 'responsibility' has become an intellectual fad there is a danger of a lack of clarity which permits to make almost everyone responsible for everything."[27] If everyone is responsible for everything, one risks coming into a situation—described by Hans-Georg Gadamer, a German philosopher—in which "one no longer can indicate who is responsible and to whom one is responsible. No one of us is."[28] Sartre's "responsibility for the world" seems, indeed, to be such a vague notion. By making everyone responsible for everything, one runs the risk of making everyone responsible for nothing.

It seems more appropriate to distinguish *different levels of responsibility* and share the burden of responsibility in such a way that those with the broadest shoulders bear the heaviest burdens. But who has the broadest shoulders? They are in the first place those who consciously and willingly *assume* functions which carry a specific responsibility. Here one should mention, in the first place, politicians. It is they who take decisions which shape the future, it is they who decide on war or peace, and it is they who try to impose their views on past, present, and future events. Max Weber (1864–1920) emphasized the importance of a politician's ethics of responsibility (*Verantwortungsethik*). It is not enough for a politician, he wrote, to have noble intentions. According to Weber, a politician who is acting on the basis of an ethics of responsibility,

> "doesn't feel capable to pass the consequences of his own actions, as far as he could anticipate them, on to others.... No ethical system in the world can get around the fact that achieving 'good' goals often implies that one accepts morally questionable or at least dangerous means, as well as the probability of bad side effects, and no ethical system in the world can decide when and to what extent the morally good goal 'justifies' ethically dangerous means and side effects."[29]

Although politicians are increasingly held to account for their actions when in government and for this reason sometimes even risk ending up in jail, in the nineteenth century the sociologist Herbert Spencer (1820–

1903) pointed out a problem: the intellectual unpreparedness of many politicians for an adequate fulfilment of their function.

> "This best knowledge of the time with which legislators are said to come prepared for their duties," he wrote, "is a knowledge of which the greater part is obviously irrelevant and that they are blameworthy for not seeing what is the relevant knowledge. No amount of the linguistic acquirements by which many of them are distinguished will help their judgements in the least; nor will they be appreciably helped by the literatures these acquirements open to them."[30]

A politician can be a gifted debater and he can have an excellent knowledge of literature and philosophy, but this is not enough to make him a good decision-maker.

> "That which is really needed," continued Spencer, "is a systematic study of natural causation as displayed among human beings socially aggregated." He emphasized that "causal relations may be expected to continue longest unrecognized; yet in our days, the existence of such causal relations has become clear enough to force on all who think, the inference that before meddling with them they should be diligently studied."[31]

Spencer's plea for the study of causal relations "before meddling with them," in order to take the right decisions and to avoid unnecessary risks, is rather modern. Today ministries employ thousands of skilled professionals, and governments are increasingly assisted by think tanks and planning bureaus. This means that the political decision-makers are dependent on the expertise of scientists, who have their own professional responsibility, which is to pursue the truth and to conduct their work with integrity. Scientists are not only working for governments. They are working in universities and in the laboratories of private firms. They are not only expected to develop new policies and new products, but also to present realistic risk assessments and develop different scenarios, identifying eventual negative consequences of new inventions. Politicians and—to a lesser degree—professionals can be said to have a *high intensity* responsibility. In the relationship between politicians and scientific experts, two pitfalls should be avoided: the populist pitfall on the one hand, arguing that one cannot trust the experts, which leads to neglecting their advice—and the technocratic pitfall on the other hand, a blind overreliance on the opinion of experts. When seeking expert advice, the best way to avoid both pitfalls is to be open to a plurality of opinions. However, the politician's reliance on expert advice does not mean that he can hide behind the expert and abrogate his own responsibility. Ultimately it is he who makes the decision and has to bear the final responsibility.[32]

Does the fact that some categories of the population carry greater responsibilities mean that the average citizen can quietly lean backwards, feeling reassured that he has delegated his responsibility to politicians, scientists, CEOs, and other professionals? Certainly not. The French philosopher Patrick Viveret rightly remarked:

> "One cannot build the responsibility of the parliamentarians on the global irresponsibility of the citizens. Because the irresponsibility of the citizens pushes democratic society necessarily towards simplism, demagogy, populism, and it will, at one moment or another, exert a strong pressure on those responsible to move backward. There exists, therefore, a dialectic between the responsibility of the politician and the average quality of the responsibility of the citizens of a population."[33]

The average citizen may not carry the same burden of responsibility as the politician or the scientist. However, this does not mean that he can completely give up his responsibility, "outsourcing" it as it were. In the end it is his civic behavior—his interest in societal problems, his readiness to inform and educate himself, and his active participation in the democratic process—which will guarantee that a system of shared responsibility can be maintained and upheld.

There remains one question. It is clear that we have a responsibility for actions in the past which harmed the interests of preceding generations and their descendants. And it is equally clear that we have a responsibility for actions in the present which possibly harm the interests of our contemporaries. But what about the interests of future generations, generations who are not yet living? Do we also have a responsibility towards them? I think we have, and this responsibility is, as such, not new. The time necessary for a human child to be educated and to become independent is about eighteen to twenty years. During this period the human child is fragile and dependent on parental protection. The parents are responsible for giving the child this protection. In case the parents are absent or deceased, it is the family or the state which takes over this responsibility. The fact that in this case *the state* takes over the responsibility proves that this responsibility is considered a *collective* duty and not the exclusive responsibility of the parents.

The question is: is this responsibility towards their offspring only valid in the world of the living, and can we say, "After us the deluge" with regard to the generations who live after us? According to the philosopher Derek Parfit,

"On one view, moral principles cover only people who can *reciprocate,* or harm and benefit each other.... I assume that we should reject this view. Some writers claim that, while we ought to be concerned about effects on future people, we are morally justified in being less concerned about effects in the further future.... On this view, we can *discount* the more remote effects of our acts and policies, at some rate of *n* percent per year. This is called the *Social Discount Rate.* Suppose we are considering how to dispose safely of the radio-active matter called *nuclear waste.* If we believe in the Social Discount Rate, we shall be concerned with safety only in the nearer future.... On this view, catastrophes in the further future can now be regarded as morally trivial. As this case suggests, the Social Discount Rate is indefensible."[34]

Generations further away in the future need no less our consideration than generations more nearby. But these generations more nearby—the generations of our children and grandchildren—can function as a reminder that we have a responsibility not only towards them, but also to *their* children and grandchildren, as well as to generations in a more distant future. It is worth mentioning in this context that today's younger generation—those who will be the first to live in a future in which we, the older generation, will no longer be around—seem to be the harbingers of this new moral sensibility towards future generations. It is this generation, for instance, who takes the lead in the climate debate. It would, therefore, be recommendable to strengthen the voice of this generation by lowering the voting age to sixteen.[35] But that is not enough. Shouldn't future generations be represented more directly? There are interesting initiatives, such as Finland's parliamentary "Committee for the Future," established in 1993, or Sweden's "Council on the Future," led by Kristina Persson, who became the world's first "Minister of the Future."[35] Initiatives like these can help develop a long-term perspective. In this book I will analyze the three forms of responsibility and show how they impact modern man. Part I will analyze our new responsibility for the past. Part II will explore the responsibility for the present and give a tentative answer to the question whether it is possible to learn lessons from history (I think we can). In Part III and Part IV, I will analyze the responsibility for the future.

STRUCTURE OF THE BOOK
PART I: OUR RESPONSIBILITY FOR THE PAST

Chapter 1.

Our forebears did not feel themselves responsible for crimes committed in the past by their co-nationals. This changed after the Second World War when an international human rights regime was created which emphasized the responsibility of states to uphold human rights. An example is the German atonement for the Holocaust, which is considered "exemplary." However, the recognition by Germany of the Herero genocide in Namibia in the beginning of the twentieth century was a less smooth process. Other questions in this chapter: should the United States pay reparations to descendants of enslaved people? And why was it so hard for the Dutch to apologize for the slave system in their colonies?

Chapter 2.

In this chapter six conditions are mentioned for a successful apology process. The hardest part is to recognize the (ugly) facts. How should these facts be integrated into the national narrative? Is changing street names and toppling statues a good method? And what about reparations? Should individual reparations be paid to descendants of enslaved people, or should one prefer other methods? Another example is the Spanish case: offering citizenship to descendants of Sephardic Jews who were expelled in 1492.

PART II: OUR RESPONSIBILITY FOR THE PRESENT: CAN WE LEARN LESSONS FROM HISTORY?

Chapter 3.

Our responsibility for the present expresses itself in the ability to learn lessons from history. The question of whether "history teaches us lessons" arises particularly during crisis periods. *Can* one learn lessons? Historians and social scientists tend to disagree. Arguments for and against are presented in this chapter. The author analyzes the Munich Conference of September 1938 as an example of a "historical lesson" for posterity. However, one should avoid "the historical metaphor trap": the danger in seeing everything through the prism of a particular event.

Chapter 4.

"Learning lessons from history" leads to the question "What exactly *is* history?" Does there exist one "history" or are there several histories? What if there are different historical narratives about the same events which diverge from each other or even contradict each other? And what about when national governments want to influence historical narratives, as in the case of Russia and in other authoritarian countries? How does one judge the objectivity of these narratives?

Chapter 5.

It would be impossible to learn lessons from history if history were a completely random, chaotic process without any structure. An essential task for historians and social scientists is, therefore, to explore the existence of historical causalities. How does one find these causalities? How does one disentangle and "weigh" the determining factors out of a multitude of factors? And, finally, what are the values that should lead the historian in making his choices?

Chapter 6.

Does history teach us "lessons"? The preliminary answer is that this is in principle possible, although these lessons will not necessarily be the same for everyone. In this chapter different examples are given. They include the lessons learned from the French Revolution by the conservative Austrian statesman Klaus von Metternich, who created a geopolitical system of checks and balances which guaranteed the peace in Europe for about a century. Another example compares the way defeated Germany was treated after the First World War with the way it was treated after the Second World War. In the latter case the Allied countries learned the lessons of the disastrous approach taken after the First World War.

Chapter 7.

In this chapter the author analyzes different factors which stand in the way of learning lessons from history. One of these is "The Three Generation Trap," the fact that the collective memory of dramatic historical events tends to be rather short and, in general, will not last much longer than three generations. These are the generations who have a direct or indirect personal experience of the events. This means that the ability to learn lessons from the past—although possible in principle—remains limited.

Part III: HOW OUR VISION OF THE FUTURE INFLUENCES OUR SENSE OF RESPONSIBILITY FOR FUTURE GENERATIONS

Chapter 8.

Views of the future are colored by the optimism or pessimism of the historians. Optimistic Enlightenment philosophers, such as Turgot and Condorcet, considered history to be a process of linear progress. For these philosophers history is moving in a predetermined positive direction. A special case is represented by dialectical thinkers, such as Hegel and Marx, who considered history as a dialectical process in which negative developments were necessary for a positive result.

Chapter 9.

This chapter analyzes the "prophets of doom," of which Friedrich Nietzsche and Oswald Spengler are the most famous representatives. Their underlying philosophies of history are equally deterministic. Differing from the Enlightenment philosophers and the dialectical philosophers, who depict human history as a process of necessary progress, they depict human history as a cyclical process in which the present is mostly presented as a period of decline.

Chapter 10.

This chapter offers a critical assessment of both the Enlightenment philosophers of progress and the prophets of doom. It is argued that both an unbridled historical optimism, as well as an unbridled historical pessimism, should be avoided and that one should instead adopt an attitude of "cautious optimism" which avoids blind historical optimism and defeatist pessimism. This means that one should consider history not as a predetermined and teleological process, but as an essentially *open* process.

Chapter 11.

Historical optimism and historical pessimism are both influenced by the *Zeitgeist* of a given period. This *Zeitgeist* is often different for different generations. The sociologist Karl Mannheim analyzed how the period in which a generation is growing up shapes its world view and determines how members of this generation view the future. So-called "lost generations," who grow up in crisis periods, tend to develop a more pessimistic view of the future. The question is, will this also be the case for the "Covid-19 generation"?

Chapter 12.

A modern group of "future watchers" consists of the so called "collapsologists," who consider that global warming will lead to the end of human civilization. They are the prophets of doom of the twenty-first century. The author analyzes parallels with the members of an American sect who were waiting for the end of the world, as described in Leon Festinger's famous study *When Prophecy Fails*. Festinger analyzed how these members reacted when the prophecy, that the end of the world was imminent, did not materialize.

PART IV: OUR RESPONSIBILITY FOR FUTURE GENERATIONS

Chapter 13.

This chapter explores in more detail the main reasons why for our generation the future has become a more important issue: modern man's growing awareness of risk. Not only global warming and climate change have contributed to this awareness, but also "black swan" events: rare events—such as the Fukushima nuclear disaster—which have catastrophic consequences and make it necessary to develop worst case scenarios rather than probabilistic scenarios. This chapter analyzes in detail the emergence of this new moral responsibility for future generations.

Chapter 14.

In the past, thinking about the future often took the form of utopias and dystopias, such as the utopias of Thomas More, Campanella, and Francis Bacon, and the twentieth-century dystopias of George Orwell and Aldous Huxley. Karl Popper and Ralf Dahrendorf considered utopias to be dangerous. Are they? The author does not reject utopias outright, but pleads for "mini-utopias" instead of detailed blueprints.

Chapter 15.

Kant was skeptical about the possibility of predicting the future. Nevertheless, there are historians and political scientists who made striking predictions. Tocqueville predicted the Revolution of 1848, Jean Monnet the Second World War, and Arthur Schlesinger Jr. a cyclical 30-year alternation in American politics. These predictions were based on observed causal trends. However, the author argues that such extrapolations can only be made for limited areas. It is easier to predict a demographic trend than a political development. Predictions always remain tentative, because of unexpected events which can give history a completely different turn. One should also be aware of the occurrence of "system breaks" which cause predicted events not to happen.

Chapter 16.

An example of an interesting cyclical predictive model is Nikolay Kondratiev's "long wave" theory. Kondratiev observed after the French Revolution two and a half economic cycles of 47-60 years, characterized by economic growth and price inflation, followed by collapse of prices and crisis. Joseph Schumpeter explained these cycles by waves of innovation—the railroad in the nineteenth century and the automobile in the early twentieth century. Will these "long waves" be reproduced in the future and become predictable, or are they unique events?

Chapter 17.

A case study of a prediction which came true is the demise of the Soviet Union. Different scientists made this prediction many years before it happened. These predictions were based on the ramshackle economy of the Soviet Union on the one hand, and on its colonial structure on the other hand.

Chapter 18.

In the time of the nuclear arms race Hannah Arendt already pointed to the ambiguous, double-edged character of technological innovations. Do we suffer from a "sorcerer's apprentice syndrome," fearing the negative consequences of our technological prowess? And can we put the genie back into the bottle—not only to protect ourselves, but also to protect future generations? The author pleads for a broad public debate before the introduction of new technologies, such as artificial intelligence and gene editing.

NOTES

N.B. All quotes from French, German, Russian, Italian, and Dutch sources have been translated by the author.

1   Daniel McCarthy, "Did Liberalism Fail?" *The National Interest*, No. 156, July/August 2018, p. 87.
2   Damien Cave, Emma Bubola, and Choe Sang-Hun, "World faces startling shift in population," *The New York Times,* May 24, 2021.
3   Ibid.
4   Frank Bruni, "American optimism, R.I.P." *The New York Times,* November 9, 2021.
5   Ibid.
6   Jonathan Stevenson and Steven Simon, "We need to think about the unthinkable future," *The New York Times,* January 14, 2022.
7   Sylvie Kauffmann, "Faire sans les Etats-Unis," *Le Monde,* July 12, 2018.
8   Ibid.
9   "Global Trends 2040 – A More Contested World," *National Intelligence*

Council, March 2021, p. 6. https://www.dni.gov/files/ODNI/documents/assessments/GlobalTrends_2040.pdf

10   Ibid., p. 90.

11   Ibid., p. 5.

12   The Editorial Board, "Why Spy Agencies Say the Future Is Bleak," *The New York Times,* April 15, 2021. https://www.nytimes.com/2021/04/15/opinion/global-trends-intelligence-report.html

13   Stéphane Vernay, "Le moment que nous vivons ressemble à l'entre-deux-guerres," Interview with Emmanuel Macron, *Ouest-France,* October 31, 2018.

14   Peter Walker, "Donald Trump is behaving like 1930s fascist dictator, explains Yale historian," *The Independent,* March 27, 2017. https://www.independent.co.uk/news/world/americas/us-politics/donald-trump-1930-thirties-fascist-dictator-adolf-hitler-reichstag-fire-trick-yale-historian-timothy-a7651766.html

15   Charlemagne, "A warning from the past," *The Economist,* December 24, 2016.

16   Ian Kershaw, "Ghosts of Fascists Past," *The National Interest,* No. 112, March/April 2011, p. 12.

17   Michaël Foessel, *Récidive 1938* (Paris: Presses Universitaires de France, 2019), p. 11.

18   Ibid., p. 15.

19   Max Scheler, "Mensch und Geschichte," in Max Scheler, *Philosophische Weltanschauung* (Bern and Munich: Francke Verlag, 1968), p. 62. (Emphasis in original, MHVH).

20   Reinhart Koselleck, *Kritik und Krise – Eine Studie zur Pathogenese der bürgerlichen Welt* (Frankfurt am Main: Suhrkamp Verlag, 1973), p. 105.

21   Wolfgang Streeck, *Gekaufte Zeit – Die vertagte Krise des demokratischen Kapitalismus* (Berlin: Suhrkamp Verlag, 2013), p. 8.

22   Antoon de Baets, "A Declaration of the Responsibilities of Present Generations Toward Past Generations," *History and Theory,* Issue 43, No. 4, December 2004.

23   Ibid.

24   The complete quote reads as follows: "Historia vero testis temporum, lux veritatis, vita memoriae, magistra vitae, nuntia vetustatis, qua voce alia, nisi oratoris, immortalitati commendatur?" (History, which is a true witness of [past] times, a light of truth, the life of memory, the teacher of life, the messenger of times past, by what other voice, if not the orator's, can it be entrusted to eternity?). (Cicero, *De Oratore Libri tres,* with an introduction and notes by Augustus S. Wilkins (Hildesheim, Zurich, and New York: Georg Olms Verlag, 1990), p. 245.

25 Jean-Paul Sartre, *L'être et le néant – Essai d'ontologie phénoménologique* (Paris: Éditions Gallimard, 1943), p. 639. In the same vein Emmanuel Lévinas wrote: "It happened that I said somewhere … that I am responsible for the persecutions which I undergo." Emmanuel Lévinas, "La responsabilité pour autrui," in Emmanuel Lévinas, *Éthique et infini* (Paris: Fayard, 1982), p. 95.

26 Ibid.

27 Otfried Höffe, *Moral als Preis der Moderne – Ein Versuch über Wissenschaft, Technik und Umwelt* (Frankfurt am Main: Suhrkamp Verlag, 1995), p. 20.

28 Hans-Georg Gadamer, "Angst und Ängste," in Hans-Georg Gadamer, *Über die Verborgenheit der Gesundheit* (Frankfurt am Main: Suhrkamp Verlag, 1994), p. 197.

29 Max Weber, "Politik als Beruf," in Max Weber, *Schriften 1894 – 1922,* Selected by Dirk Kaesler (Stuttgart: Alfred Kröner Verlag, 2002), pp. 545–46.

30 Herbert Spencer, *The Man Versus the State* (Indianapolis: Liberty Classics, 1981), p. 96.

31 Ibid., p. 97.

32 On the responsibility of respectively the politician and the scientific expert see Laura Münkler, "Demokratie und Expertise – Ambivalenzen und rechtliche Lösungsansätze," *Aus Politik und Zeitgeschichte,* Bundeszentrale für politische Bildung, 2022. https://www.bpb.de/shop/zeitschriften/apuz/wissenschaft-oeffentlichkeit-demokratie-2022/509587/demokratie-und-expertise/

33 Patrick Viveret, "Le pouvoir, l'expertise, la responsabilité," in Monique Vacquin (ed.), *La responsabilité – La condition de notre humanité* (Paris: Éditions Autrement, 1994), p. 240. See also Olivier Abel, "La responsabilité incertaine," *Esprit,* No. 206, November 1994, p. 20: "The 'organized flight' from the political and public sphere into private life should not liberate the individuals from every political responsibility."

34 Derek Parfit, *Reasons and Persons* (Oxford and New York: Oxford University Press, 1987), p. 357.

35 Lowering the voting age to sixteen is Proposal #15 in my book *The End of Populism – Twenty Proposals to Defend Liberal Democracy* (Manchester: Manchester University Press, 2021), pp. 201–05.

36 Roman Krznaric, *The Good Ancestor – How to Think Long-Term in a Short-Term World* (London: Penguin, 2020), pp. 176–77.

PART I

OUR RESPONSIBILITY FOR THE PAST

CHAPTER 1

OUR INCREASED RESPONSIBILITY FOR CRIMES OF THE PAST

Do we have a responsibility for events which took place in the past? This is an important question which in recent decades has become a topic of heated public debate. But if we answer this question in the affirmative, what, exactly, do we mean by "the past" and what do we mean by the word "we"? "The past"—to begin with—is not an indeterminate past, in the sense of "everything that happened." It refers to certain events which have taken place in certain periods in certain contexts. These events are characterized, firstly, by the fact that they are *man-made* (people are less likely to feel responsible for natural disasters, such as floods, droughts, earthquakes, or volcanic eruptions).[1] Second, these events are mostly considered to be *morally reprehensible*; and, third, descendants or representatives of the perpetrators, as well as of the victims of these acts, are still around. This brings us to the question of the "we"—the subject of this responsibility. The word "we" refers to people who are living today. But why should people who are living today feel responsible for the actions and the (mis)deeds of people who were living in the past, sometimes even centuries ago? The key concept to explain this phenomenon is identification. Later generations *identify* themselves with earlier generations because there exists (or one assumes that there exists) a common bond which unites these generations. This common bond can consist of family ties, of being members of the same tribe or ethnic group, or it can be based on the fact that one shares the same nationality. Particularly, national identity is an important factor which creates intergenerational bonds. However, identification is not enough. An additional, necessary condition is an increased sensitivity to human rights violations. This new kind of sensitivity developed before and during the

Second World War. Its principles are enshrined in the Universal Declaration of Human Rights, adopted on 10 December 1948 by the General Assembly of the United Nations.[2] This Declaration has rightly been called by legal specialists a revolution in international law.

> "The human rights developments over the last three decades have assumed a revolutionary character in international law. The individual is now a subject of the law, and the traditional theory of international law, according to which only states were the subjects of the law, has had to undergo a fundamental change. Not only is the individual now a subject of the law, but under certain treaties he has even been granted procedural access to international tribunals in order to seek his own remedies. It is difficult to exaggerate the profundity of these changes in legal terms."[3]

THE "EXEMPLARY" GERMAN ATONEMENT FOR THE NAZI CRIMES

Let us, for instance, take the case of Germany. After the Second World War Germans had to come to terms with the crimes of Hitler's regime. There were different theories. One of these was the theory of "collective guilt" that held that *all* Germans were guilty of Hitler's crimes. However, it is clear that not all Germans had committed crimes (the truth was that Germans were among Hitler's first victims), and one can only speak about "guilt" in the case of someone who is personally accountable for a crime. The question became even more pressing when after the war a new generation grew up. Could this new generation be blamed for the crimes committed by their parents or their co-nationals? They *felt* blamed, as former Chancellor Helmut Schmidt—who himself fought in the war—reminds us, writing that, "All later-born Germans also have to live with the terrible stigma of the Holocaust."[4] But he added, "Out of conviction ... I have always rejected the theories of 'collective guilt' of the Germans."[5] The German philosopher Karl Jaspers took a similar position. "Should we Germans be made responsible for the crimes which Germans committed against us?" he asked. And he answered: "Yes—

for the fact that we have tolerated that such a regime could emerge in our country. No—because many of us were in their deepest selves adversaries of all this evil and need not acknowledge, by any act, or by any motivation, a moral complicity. *Making [someone] responsible doesn't mean to acknowledge that one is morally guilty.*"[6] Schmidt and Jaspers are right: "collective guilt" does not exist, and one may not hold the children accountable for the sins of their parents. The problem in post-war Germany was rather that the former Nazis themselves didn't feel personal guilt, as Peter Sichrovsky found out—he published a book which included interviews of children from Nazi families. "Almost no one spoke about personal guilt, embarrassment, or even shame of the parents in the interviews," he wrote.[7] And he added, "The ugly Germans became mostly lamenting Germans, who couldn't understand that after all those many years they were still considered responsible for the horrors of the Nazi period."[8]

However, this does not mean that later generations can neglect or be indifferent to the crimes committed by their forebears. Helmut Schmidt spoke about "the terrible stigma of the Holocaust" with which later generations of Germans had to live. Although they were not personally guilty, he argued, there was a stigma and—as Germans—they had to carry it. Later generations have the collective responsibility to assume this negative national heritage and to take a moral position vis-à-vis events which happened in the past. Note, however, that in this case we no longer speak about collective *guilt*, but about collective *responsibility*. According to Hannah Arendt,

> "Two conditions have to be present for collective responsibility: I must be held responsible for something I have not done, and the reason for my responsibility must be my membership in a group (a collective) which no voluntary act of mine can dissolve, that is, a membership which is utterly unlike a business partnership which I can dissolve at will." (9)

Family bonds are, as a rule, characteristic of a group "which no voluntary act of mine can dissolve." One cannot change one's family relationships. But what about nationality? You can give up your nationality and adopt a new one. This is, maybe, not as easy as dissolving a business partnership, but it is possible. Would the simple fact of changing your nationality, i.e., your legal status, be enough to "escape" the stigma of your nationality of origin? Would a 20-year-old German who migrates to the United States and becomes naturalized as a U.S. citizen, giving up his German nationality, be "liberated" from the historical heritage of his country of origin? One may doubt it. Because a nationality is more than a passport. The Germans have a special word for this. They call a nation a *Schicksalsgemeinschaft*—a community of fate. If you have shared this fate in your formative years, it will have a lasting influence on who you are, how you define yourself, and how others will see you. Hannah Arendt gave an additional reason why the term "collective guilt" should be rejected. She spoke about "the fallacy of the concept of collective guilt as first applied to the German people and its collective past—all of Germany stands accused and the whole of German history from Luther to Hitler—which in practice turned into a highly effective whitewash of all those who had actually done something, for where all are guilty, no one is."[10] By declaring *all* Germans guilty, the real culprits could hide themselves behind the collective, avoiding being held to account.

Germans, including those born after the war, have very well understood their responsibility vis-à-vis the past. On December 7, 1970, Chancellor Willy Brandt fell famously to his knees at the memorial to the Warsaw Ghetto, a gesture which was a powerful symbol of German atonement for the crimes committed in World War II—even more so if one takes into consideration that during the Nazi dictatorship Willy Brandt lived as a refugee in Norway and Sweden. He was a living example of someone who was not guilty, but who felt responsible for the crimes of his fellow compatriots. The German atonement for the crimes of the Nazi regime is generally considered exemplary. The Jewish American philosopher Susan Neiman wrote that "no country in the world has, even approximately, confronted the crimes of its history as Germany [has done]."[11] Brandt's gesture was very effective. "Brandt's Warsaw genuflection," wrote Axel Honneth, "was an internationally visible gesture which made it for years almost impossible for the Polish government to stir up once again the prejudices against the Federal Republic of Germany which existed before in its own population."[12] However, in Germany this atonement was not appreciated by everyone. The conservative politician Franz Josef Strauß, for instance, called Willy Brandt "a failed prophet and the founder of a political religion."[13] Others feared that too much self-flagellation could have an adverse effect on the younger generation.[14]

On September 10, 1952, the German government signed the so called "Luxembourg Agreements" with the government of Israel on the one hand and the "Claims Conference"—an organization of 23 Jewish organizations—on the other. Reparations were made to pay the cost of resettling uprooted Jewish refugees in Israel and to compensate individual Jews for losses in livelihood and property during the Nazi period. The Claims Conference stressed, however, that no amount of money "can make good the destruction of human life and cultural values."[15] There were not only critics of this agreement on the German side. "During the meetings of the Claims Conference, the Federal Republic, and the State of Israel in Luxembourg in 1952, the position of claimant was sometimes experienced as embarrassing in Jewish circles in Europe and particularly in Israel. For some people contact with the hangman evoked impurity and provoked repulsion. 'Blood money' [English in text], was one of the terms with which the German money was stigmatized."[16]

THE HERERO GENOCIDE:
A CRIME GERMANY WANTED TO FORGET

Despite these reservations, the German reparations became an example of reparative justice in which victims on the one hand, and descendants (or representatives) of the perpetrators on the other hand, created the conditions for reconciliation. This reparations regime soon became a model for other groups which had been subjected to a policy of systematic extermination. To these belonged the Herero and Nama peoples, living in Namibia, the former South West Africa. In 1883 this territory, rich in diamonds, was declared a German protectorate by chancellor Bismarck—a unilateral step which was ratified one year later, in 1884, at the Berlin Conference, when European countries divided up the African continent. The first governor of this *Deutsch Südwestafrika* (German

South West Africa) was Heinrich Göring, the father of the Nazi leader Hermann Göring. The Herero and Nama, nomad peoples living for generations in South West Africa, gradually lost the land on which their cattle grazed and they were forced to become the ill-treated farmhands of the white settlers. This led, to a revolt on January 12, 1904. This revolt became a pretext for the colonial government to implement its project to reserve the colony only for a white population and to chase out and exterminate the original black inhabitants. On October 2, 1904, General Lothar von Trotha, the military commander of the protectorate, issued a *Vernichtungsbefehl,* an "extermination order."[17] In a letter sent on October 4, 1904, to General Von Schlieffen, the German Chief of the Defense Staff, Von Trotha left no doubt as to his intentions. He wrote that "the Herero nation must be exterminated, or, if this proved to be militarily impossible, thrown out of the country ... I have given order to execute the prisoners, to send the women and children into the desert.... The revolt is and remains the beginning of a race war."[18] Members of the Herero and Nama peoples were tortured and executed. Many were forced to flee into the Omaheke desert, where they died from hunger and thirst (water wells were poisoned by the German occupants). Those who tried to return were put in concentration camps or killed. The results of this genocidal policy were catastrophic. "The population census of 1911 indicates that of 80,000 Herero ... there remained no more than 15,000; as concerns the Nama, they passed from 20,000 to 10,000."[19]

The German government, which was widely praised for its policy of *Wiedergutmachung* (coming to terms with the crimes committed during the Second World War), had more problems recognizing the mass killings of the Herero and Nama as a genocide. According to the paper *Süddeutsche Zeitung,*

"Germany's colonial government in Namibia ended with the First World War. The atrocities committed there in the name of the German Empire were forgotten—especially after the horrors of the Holocaust and the Second World War. For a long time the federal government avoided calling the fate of the Herero and Nama a 'genocide.'"[20]

How long could the German government continue to deny the facts? Already in 1985, in the "Whitaker Report" on genocide, commissioned by the UN Commission on Human Rights, the verdict was clear: the report labeled the mass killings of the Herero and Nama peoples between 1904 and 1908 in Namibia unequivocally as "genocide."[21] In June 2001 a newly created Herero People's Reparation Corporation (HPRC) filed a lawsuit in the Court of Appeals of the District of Columbia (USA) against the state of Germany and the companies Deutsche Bank and Woermann Line (which, under its new name Deutsche Afrika-Linien (DAL), presents itself on its website as "one of the most highly respected liner shipping companies operating with a focus on Africa").[22] The HPRC claimed $2 billion in damages. The Herero Chief Kuaima Riruako also requested a "Mini-Marshall Plan" for community development.[23] On June 11, 2004, the case was dismissed for failure to state an actionable claim. The plaintiffs appealed to the US Supreme Court, which declined to hear the case. (24) The German government refused to pay reparations, despite the fact that in 1998 Roman Herzog, the German president, had admitted that "incorrect acts" had been committed during this period. However, Herzog also insisted that the Herero could not claim reparations because at the time of the events, he argued, "there did not yet exist international law concerning the protection of civilians."[25] Herzog was right: the UN Convention on the Prevention and Punishment of the Crime of Genocide was enacted in 1948—more than forty years after the facts. But was this not equally the case for the Holocaust which took place *before* this Convention entered into force?[26] Herzog's purely juridical arguments didn't seem to make political sense.

In order to get out of this impasse, in 2015 Germany started negotiations with the Namibian government. Herero and Nama were not satisfied, because the Namibian government is dominated by the Ovambo people, Namibia's largest ethnic group. As representatives of the victims, they wanted direct negotiations with the German government. To obtain this goal, in January 2017 they filed a lawsuit in the federal court of New York against Germany in which they invoked the 2007 UN Declaration on the Right of Indigenous Peoples to participate in negotiations which concern their rights. In March 2019 the case was dismissed. The plaintiffs appealed to the Supreme Court, which—again—declined to hear the case.[27] On May 28, 2021, after more than five years of negotiations, the Namibian and German governments finally signed an agreement. The German Foreign Minister spoke about the German responsibility for the *Greueltaten* (atrocities) committed by the German colonizers. "We will call these events now also officially as what they were from today's perspective: a genocide," he said.[28] The German government agreed to pay $1.1 billion for development aid, requesting "forgiveness." However, the German government still refused to use the term "reparation." In a jointly written op-ed published in the *New York Times*, a descendant of Holocaust survivors and a descendant of Herero survivors called the agreement "an insult." "We have a personal sense of the devastation Germany has wrought," wrote the authors. "To begin to atone for its Namibian genocide, it must negotiate directly with descendants of survivors— and commit to wide-ranging reparations." In addition, "Germany could also integrate the Namibian genocide into its national narrative, through public education and commemoration, and build memorials at the sites of former concentration camps."[29] It is clear that Germany's reconciliation process with the Herero and Nama peoples—which it initiated only late and reluctantly—progressed less smoothly than its atonement for the Holocaust, which included the payment of reparations which continue to this day.[30]

SHOULD THE UNITED STATES PAY REPARATIONS TO DESCENDANTS OF SLAVES?

Taking responsibility for the crimes of one's ancestors is not easy. It is always a painful process—and not only for the financial consequences. In recent years the payment of reparations to help to right the wrongs of slavery have become a burning question in the United States, and not only there. The idea of compensation for slavery is not new. In 1865, at the end of the Civil War, General William Sherman proposed to redistribute land on the Atlantic coast to the recently freed slaves. This project, known as "40 acres and a mule," was accepted by President Lincoln. After its adoption by Congress, about 40,000 "freedmen" began a new life as a small farmer. However, after Lincoln's assassination the project was abandoned by Lincoln's successor Andrew Johnson, who returned the land to the former owners. When Congress made another proposal, it was vetoed by Johnson.[31] In the present debate it is argued that not only the forebears of African Americans suffered from the slave system, but that still today their descendants feel the consequences of this system in their daily lives. In a report of the Brookings Institution, for instance, one can read that,

> "Today, the average white family has roughly 10 times the amount of wealth as the average Black family. White college graduates have over seven times more wealth than Black college graduates. Making the American Dream an equitable reality demands the same U.S. government that denied wealth to Blacks restore that deferred wealth through reparations to their descendants in the form of individual cash payments in the amount that will close the Black-white racial wealth divide."[32]

Who should receive reparations? According to the report, "In short, a Black person who can trace their heritage to people enslaved in U.S. states and territories should be eligible for financial compensation for slavery. Meanwhile, Black people who can show how they were excluded from various policies after emancipation should seek separate damages."[33] This means, explain the authors, "that President Obama (Kenyan immigrant father and white mother), may only seek redress for housing and/or education segregation. Sasha and Malia Obama (whose mother Michelle is a descendant of enslaved Africans), would qualify."[34]

Would such an elaborate system of reparations be the solution? This was the key topic for discussion in a Congressional hearing, organized on June 18, 2019, by the Commission to Study and Develop Reparation Proposals for African Americans, a commission tasked "to examine slavery and discrimination in the colonies and the United States from 1619 to the present and recommend appropriate remedies."[35] In the hearing two experts, both African Americans, were asked their opinion on this matter. The first speaker, the author Ta-Nehisi Coates, spoke out in favor of paying reparations. He referred to Senate Majority leader Mitch McConnell's statement that "America should not be held liable for something

that happened 150 years ago, since none of us currently alive are responsible." "This rebuttal," said Coates, "proffers a strange theory of governance—that American accounts are somehow bound by the lifetime of
its generations."[36] Coates pointed out the apparent inconsistency in this
kind of reasoning, arguing that "well into this century, the United States
was still paying out pensions to the heirs of Civil War soldiers…. We are
American citizens, and thus bound to a collective enterprise that extends
beyond our individual and personal reach."[37] The testimony of the second
expert, Coleman Hughes, an African American who spoke out against
paying reparations to descendants of slaves, deserves to be quoted at full
length:

> "In 2008," he said, "the House of Representatives apologized
> for slavery and Jim Crow. In 2009 the Senate did the same.
> Black people don't need another apology. We need safer
> neighborhoods and better schools. We need a less punitive
> criminal justice system. We need affordable healthcare. And
> none of these things can be achieved through reparations for
> slavery…. If we were to pay reparations today, we would only
> divide the country further…. What we should do is pay repa-
> rations to Black Americans who actually grew up under Jim
> Crow and were directly harmed by second-class citizenship,
> people like my grandparents. But paying reparations to all
> descendants of slaves is a mistake. Take me, for example. I
> was born three decades after the end of Jim Crow into a priv-
> ileged household in the suburbs. I attend an Ivy League
> school. Yet I'm descended from slaves who worked on
> Thomas Jefferson's Monticello plantation. Reparations for
> slavery would allocate federal resources to me but not to an
> American with the wrong ancestry, even if that person is liv-
> ing paycheck to paycheck and working multiple jobs to sup-
> port his family. You might call it justice. I call it justice for
> the dead at the price of justice for the living."[38]

Coleman Hughes's argument that paying reparations to the descendants of slaves would divide the country further should be taken seriously.

A Gallup poll, conducted in the summer of 2019 revealed that 67 percent of Americans said the government should not make cash payments. Only 29 percent said it should (including 73 percent of Black Americans).[39] It is no surprise that most opponents could be found among Republicans (92 percent). However, even among Democrats almost half (47 percent) of respondents were against. Hughes's second argument was that cash payments would be made to people who eventually wouldn't need them, while those who did need them but had no enslaved ancestors, would be left behind empty-handed. This is clear in the case of Obama's two daughters, mentioned in the report of the Brookings Institution. According to this report President Obama, who had a Kenyan father (no descendant of slaves) and a white mother (no descendant of slaves) would not qualify as a descendant of slaves. He would only qualify for reparations for damages suffered due to discrimination caused by Jim Crow laws which enforced racial segregation from the end of the Reconstruction period to the middle of the twentieth century. The question of reparations remains very sensitive. Frantz Fanon, the Black freedom fighter from the French Caribbean island of Martinique, was a skeptic. In his 1952 book *Black Skin, White Masks* he wrote:

"I as a man of color do not have the right to hope that in the white man there will be a crystallization of guilt toward the past of my race. I as a man of color do not have the right to seek ways of stamping down the pride of my former master. I have neither the right nor the duty to claim reparation for the domestication of my ancestors."[40] "Am I going to ask the contemporary white man to answer for the slave ships of the seventeenth century?"[41]

His reservations about reparations were shared by Aimé Césaire, the initiator of the French *négritude* movement[42] who, in 2001, said in an interview:

"It is already important that Europe has come so far to admit the reality of the slave trade, this trade in human beings which is a crime. But I am not so much in favor of repentance or reparations. I think there is a danger in the idea of reparations. I don't want that Europe one day says: OK, here is your money or check and we no longer speak about it. There is no reparation possible for something which is irreparable and not quantifiable. What remains is that the countries, responsible for the slave trade, need to become aware that it is their duty to help the countries which through their actions plunged into misery."[43]

In the United States there are historical precedents for reparations payments. After the Second World War, for instance, Congress installed the Indian Claims Commission, tasked to pay compensation to Indian tribes for land that had been seized by the United States. However, "the results were disappointing for Native Americans. The commission paid out about $1.3 billion, the equivalent of less than $1,000 for each Native American in the United States at the time the commission dissolved in 1978."[44] Moreover, "the government took a paternalistic view and kept Native Americans from having direct control of the funds in the belief they were not 'competent to receive such large amounts of money.'"[45]

THE RELUCTANT DUTCH: WHY IS IT SO HARD TO APOLOGIZE?

The discussion on the moral implications of slavery and the slave trade, including the question of whether one should pay compensation, also takes place elsewhere. In 2001, for instance, France adopted a law which defined slavery as a crime against humanity.[46] Crimes against humanity include a wide range of violations, such as extermination, murder, enslavement, rape, torture, imprisonment, sexual violence, and persecution on political, racial, religious, and gender grounds. According to a United Nations definition,

"Crimes against humanity have not yet been codified in a dedicated treaty of international law, unlike genocide and war crimes, although there are efforts to do so. Despite this, the prohibition of crimes against humanity, similar to the prohibition of genocide, has been considered a peremptory norm of international law, from which no derogation is permitted and which is applicable to all states."[47]

In French law there were provisions to give slavery a more prominent place in school curricula and to make funds available to promote historical and social research. However, there were no provisions for financial reparations to descendants of slaves. In the Netherlands the debate started much later, although the Dutch had been an active actor in the transatlantic slave trade. They transported 5 percent of about 12 million slaves[48] and for centuries exploited slave labor through a plantation system in Suriname. This slave system was, according to an expert, "known … as the cruelest form of slavery by a Western power."[49] Voltaire described the Dutch slave system in Suriname in his satirical novel *Candide,* published in 1759. Candide, the main character of the novel, met in Suriname "a negro stretched upon the ground … the poor man had lost his left leg and his right hand." The man said that it was his Dutch slave master who treated him in this way: "When we work at the sugarcanes, and the mill snatches hold of a finger, they cut off the hand; and when we attempt to run away, they cut off the leg; both cases have happened to me. This is the price at which you eat sugar in Europe."[50] Did Voltaire in his satirical zeal exaggerate? Maybe. But a Dutch historian reminds us that "the Dutch ships compared with the ships of other slave trading nations took the greatest toll on slaves' lives."[51] In his book *Slaven van Suriname* (Slaves of Suriname), published in 1934, the Surinamese author Anton de Kom, a descendant of slaves, wrote:

"When one considers that more than one hundred thousand, I repeat: one hundred thousand Surinamese people have worked hard for Holland as slaves during three and a half centuries and were paid nothing, who would deny the Surinamese people the right to make demands on the country that owed the prosperity of its colony to this inhuman system?"[52] And he continued: "What would have been the value of Suriname without the work of the slaves? Nevertheless, one has done nothing for these Surinamese on the occasion of the

so-called emancipation [the abolition of slavery in 1863]....
While the colonists received three hundred guilders for each
[freed] slave, the freed slaves didn't even have a single
penny.... They didn't receive land, like European colonists
in the past."[53]

De Kom was arrested by the colonial authorities for agitation. Accused
of being a communist (although he was not a member of the Communist
Party), he was exiled to the Netherlands, where he was arrested by the
German occupiers in August 1944 for illegal activities. On April 24,
1945, he died in a German concentration camp at 47 years old—a few
days before the end of the war. However, one cannot say that his book
has been an inspiration for the Dutch government which, until recently,
was utterly reluctant to recognize the Dutch role in the slave trade and
was unwilling to apologize. In February 2021, Mark Rutte, the Dutch
Prime Minister, justified his refusal to apologize with the argument that
"a debate on this subject would exacerbate divisions in the Netherlands,"
and that "as a historian" he was reluctant to apologize for something that
happened 150 years ago. He added that he also didn't want to criticize
his predecessors on moral grounds,[54] suggesting that one didn't have the
right to condemn practices of the past because our forebears had different
value systems. In one respect, however, Rutte was right: the Dutch population was, indeed, divided on the subject. Although 56 percent agreed
that the Netherlands had played a "serious role" in the slave trade, almost
the same percentage—55 percent—was against an official apology.[55]

In fact, the reluctance of the Dutch government and a majority of
the Dutch population to apologize was an expression of a deeply in-
grained Dutch complacency. The Dutch consider their country to be an
example of freedom and tolerance—an exaggerated rosy view which
leads to an inability to face up to reality. This complacency dates back
to the period between the two world wars, when the Dutch proudly
touted the "ethical course" (*ethische koers*)—a supposedly enlightened
method of colonial governance, which would be in the interest of the
colonized peoples. According to the Dutch sociologist Van Doorn, "this
sense of mission, the feeling of being 'responsible' for Indonesia grew
between the world wars to almost mythical proportions."[56] And the

Dutch were not alone. They were also praised by outsiders—even by Americans, who, as a rule, were critical of colonial rule:

> "In the 1920s American perceptions of Dutch colonial rule had been positive, even if such assessments were colored by paternalistic, racial overtones. Consul-General Chas Hoover spoke approvingly of Dutch colonial rule over the 'apatheti- cally conservative people of these islands [of Indonesia].' His successor argued that 'the whites—particularly the 30,000 Dutch who are doing it—are experts in the art of government' who were willing to 'discuss with friendly interest the aspi- rations of the brown people to learn how to govern them- selves.'"[57]

However, the Dutch "experts in the art of government" had great difficulty in coming to terms with atrocities committed by Dutch troops in Indonesia during the two colonial wars (euphemistically called "police actions") in the period 1945–1950. A critical interview with a Dutch whistleblower in 1969 led to a preliminary investigation,[58] but there was no follow-up. David Van Reybrouck, a Belgian author who wrote a book on the Indonesian anti-colonial revolution, observed that "more than half of the Dutch population is still proud of the colonial past, much more than in other countries."[59] He added that he had observed a characteristic of the Netherlands which had disappointed him, namely "looking away and ignoring history ... As a neighboring country of Germany, the Netherlands should know that you become greater when you don't ig- nore the black pages of history."[60] We can observe here the post-colonial syndrome which is also present in other nations which were powerful in the past but had lost their former supremacy. According to Norbert Elias and John Scotson, "Their members can suffer for centuries under this situation, because the charismatic We-Ideal of the group ... will live on for many generations ... and their dream of a special charisma will be kept alive in many ways—in history classes, by old buildings, mas- terpieces of the nation in its glory days, or by actual achievements which, again, seem to confirm past greatness."[61]

However, despite the apparent reluctance of the Dutch Prime Minister to apologize, in 2020 things suddenly began to change. In July 2020 the Ministry of the Interior installed a mixed advisory "dialogue group" on the history of the Dutch slave trade and the Dutch slave system. In July 2021 this group published its report, titled "Ketenen van het verleden" (Chains of the Past).[62] The authors of the report recommended that the Dutch government recognize the Dutch role in the slave system, admit that it constitutes a crime against humanity, and offer its excuses. Although the authors didn't speak out in favor of individual reparations, they recommended taking structural measures, funded by a national fund, in order to repair the negative cultural, psychological, and economic consequences of the slave system which can still be observed today.[63] On July 1, 2021, Femke Halsema, the mayor of Amsterdam, offered her excuses for Amsterdam's role in the slave system. With her initiative she was the first in the Netherlands—following the example of London and Liverpool in the UK and Chicago and Charleston in the US.[64] Descendants of slaves hope that the Dutch government will follow suit.

NOTES

1   We should add here: *modern* people, because pre-modern peoples tend to explain natural disasters as a punishment by the gods for man's sins, thereby creating an indirect causal nexus between human behavior and the disaster.

2   The adoption of the Universal Declaration of Human Rights is often explained as a reaction to the horrors of the Holocaust. However, this theory is criticized by Hans Joas, who writes: "During the war the world was not aware of the scale of the Holocaust; the aspirations concerning a declaration of human rights didn't emerge only after the end of the war. They were at the latest an explicit part of American politics since the State of the Union Address of President Roosevelt on January 6, 1941, and, since January 1, 1942, also [a part of] of the allied war objectives." Hans Joas, "Wertegeneralisierung—Die Allgemeine Erklärung der Menschenrechte und die Pluralität der Kulturen," in Hans Joas, *Die Sakralität der Person—Eine neue Genealogie der Menschenrechte* (Berlin: Suhrkamp Verlag, 2015), p. 267.

3   Dennis J. Driscoll, "The Development of Human Rights in International Law," in Walter Laqueur and Barry Rubin (eds.), *The Human Rights Reader* (New York: New American Library, 1979), p. 52.

4   Helmut Schmidt, *Ausserdienst—Eine Bilanz* (Munich: Siedler Verlag, 2008), p. 84. Schmidt repeated this during a visit to Auschwitz in November 1977, where he said that "the crimes of Nazi fascism, the guilt of the German Reich under Hitler's leadership are the reasons for our responsibility. We, Germans who are living today, are not guilty as persons, but we have to carry the political heritage of those who are guilty, this is our responsibility." Helmut Schmidt, "Ansprache in Auschwitz-Birkenau, Gehalten am 23. November 1977," in Helmut Schmidt, *Der Kurs heisst Frieden* (Düsseldorf and Vienna: Econ Verlag, 1979), p. 53.

5   Helmut Schmidt, *Ausserdienst—Eine Bilanz,* op. cit., p. 85.

6   Karl Jaspers, "Die Schuldfrage," in Karl Jaspers, *Die Schuldfrage—Für Völkermord gibt es keine Verjährung* (Munich: R. Piper & Co. Verlag, 1979), pp. 44–45. (Emphasis in the original, MHVH.)

7   Peter Sichrovsky, *Schuldig geboren—Kinder aus Nazifamilien* (Cologne: Kiepenheuer & Witsch, 1987), p. 24.

8   Ibid., p. 25.

9   Hannah Arendt, *Responsibility and Judgment* (New York: Schocken Books, 2003), p. 149.

10   Ibid., p. 21.

11   Susan Neiman, "Von den Deutschen lernen?—Essay," *Aus Politik und Zeitgeschichte,* October 1, 2021.

12   Axel Honneth, "Anerkennung zwischen Staaten," in Axel Honneth, *Das Ich im Wir* (Berlin: Suhrkamp Verlag, 2010), p. 199.

13   Franz Josef Strauß, *Deutschland Deine Zukunft* (Stuttgart: Seewald Verlag, 1975), p. 13. In 1975 Franz Josef Strauß warned his followers: "Wir dürfen nicht die Dauerbüßer der Geschichte sein" (We may not be the permanent repentants of history). ("Worte des Kandidaten Franz Josef Strauß," 6/7, *Die Zeit,* 1979/28.)

14   Bernhard Schlink expressed his fear that the insistence with which the German baby-boom generation over the years had been criticizing the preceding war generation could have a boomerang effect. When "no one had to be convinced any longer that the past should not be forgotten and repressed.... The result is a certain banalization ... [which explains] the cynical tone with which the next generation often speaks about the past...." (Bernhard Schlink, "Epilog: Die Gegenwart der Vergangenheit," in Bernhard Schlink, *Vergangenheitsschuld und gegenwärtiges Recht* (Frankfurt am Main: Suhrkamp Verlag, 2002), p. 147).

15   "History," Claims Conference—Conference of Jewish Material Claims Against Germany, no date. https://www.claimscon.org/about/history/

16   Ariel Colonomos, "L'exigence croissante de justice sans frontières—le cas de la demande de restitution des biens juifs spoliés," *Les Études du CERI,*

No. 78, July 2001, p. 29. https://www.sciencespo.fr/ceri/sites/sciencespo.fr.ceri/files/etude78.pdf

17   Quoted by Joël Kotek, "Le génocide des Herero, symptôme d'un *Sonder-weg* allemand?" *Revue d'Histoire de la Shoah,* 2008/2 (No. 189). https://www.cairn.info/revue-revue-d-histoire-de-la-shoah-2008-2-page-177.htm

18   Ibid. Referring to von Trotha's letter, Von Schlieffen wrote to German Chancellor Bernard von Bülow: "One can agree with [von Trotha's] plan of annihilating the whole people or driving them from the land.... The intention of General von Trotha can therefore be approved. The only problem is that he does not have the power to carry it out." (Quoted in Daniel Jonah Goldhagen, *Worse than War—Genocide, Eliminationism, and the Ongoing Assault on Humanity* (New York: Public Affairs, 2009), p. 220). For reasons of expediency Von Trotha's annihilation order was rescinded by the German Kaiser. However, wrote Goldhagen, "The Germans' formal halt of mass killing, because it was born out of practicality, was only partial. They continued their annihilationist practices...." (Ibid., p. 221).

19   Nadja Vuckovic, "Qui demande des réparations et pour quels crimes?" in Marc Ferro, *Le livre noir du colonialisme – XVIe–XXIe siècle: de l'extermination à la repentance* (Paris: Robert Laffont, 2003), p. 775.

20   "US-Gericht weist Klage zu deutschen Kolonialverbrechen ab," *Süddeutsche Zeitung,* March 7, 2019. https://www.sueddeutsche.de/politik/herero-nama-namibia-deutschland-voelkermord-1.4359508

21   "Revised and updated report on the question of the prevention and punishment of the crime of genocide prepared by Mr. B. Whitaker," United Nations Commission on Human Rights—Subcommission on Prevention of Discrimination and Protection of Minorities, July 2, 1985, p. 9. https://digitallibrary.un.org/record/108352?ln=en

22   Website Deutsche Afrika-Linie. https://www.dal.biz/

23   Nadja Vuckovic, "Qui demande des réparations et pour quels crimes?" in Marc Ferro, op. cit., p. 777.

24   "Herero People Reparations Corporation v. Deutsche Bank," United States Court of Appeals, District of Columbia, No. 03-7110, June 11, 2004. https://caselaw.findlaw.com/us-dc-circuit/1054653.html

25   Nadja Vuckovic, "Qui demande des réparations et pour quels crimes?" in Marc Ferro, op. cit., p. 777.

26   The UN Convention on the Prevention and Punishment of the Crime of Genocide was signed on December 9, 1948, and became effective on January 12, 1951. https://www.un.org/en/genocideprevention/genocide-convention.shtml

27   "Völkermord an Herero und Nama: Abkommen zwischen Deutschland und Namibia," *Bundeszentrale für politische Bildung,* June 22, 2021.

https://www.bpb.de/politik/hintergrund-aktuell/335257/abkommen-zwis-chen-deutschland-und-namibia#:~:text=Die%20deutsche%20und%20die%20namibische,1%20Milliarden%20Euro%20Wiederaufbauhilfe%20leisten.

28 "Außenminister Maas zum Abschluss der Verhandlungen mit Namibia," *Pressemitteilung,* Ministry of Foreign Affairs, May 28, 2021. https://www.auswaertiges-amt.de/de/newsroom/-/2463396

29 Kavena Hambira and Miriam Gleckman-Krut, "Germany apologized for a genocide. It's nowhere near enough," *The New York Times,* July 9, 2021.

30 In October 2020, for instance, the Claims Conference announced "that $662 million in COVID-19 relief aid will be divided among about 240,000 of the poorest Holocaust survivors. The survivors are located primarily in Israel, North America, the former Soviet Union and Western Europe." (Sophie Lewis, "Germany to give $662 million to Holocaust survivors struggling during the coronavirus pandemic," *CBS News,* October 15, 2020. https://www.cbsnews.com/news/holocaust-survivors-germany-reparations-coronavirus-pandemic/).

31 Patricia Cohen, "What Reparations for Slavery Might Look Like in 2019," *The New York Times,* May 23, 2019. https://www.nytimes.com/2019/05/23/business/economy/reparations-slavery.html

32 Rashawn Ray and Andre M. Perry, "Why we need reparations for Black Americans," *Brookings,* April 15, 2020. https://www.brookings.edu/policy2020/bigideas/why-we-need-reparations-for-black-americans/

33 Ibid.

34 Ibid.

35 H.R. 40—Commission to Study and Develop Reparation Proposals for African-Americans Act, 116th Congress (2019–2020). https://www.congress.gov/bill/116th-congress/house-bill/40

36 Ta-Nehisi Coates and Coleman Hughes, "Should America pay reparations for slavery? Ta-Nehisi Coates v Coleman Hughes," *The Guardian,* June 19, 2019. https://www.theguardian.com/commentisfree/2019/jun/19/reparations-slavery-ta-nehisi-coates-v-coleman-hughes_

37 Ibid.

38 Ibid.

39 Mohamed Younis, "As Redress for Slavery, Americans Oppose Cash Reparations," *Gallup,* July 29, 2019. https://news.gallup.com/poll/261722/redress-slavery-americans-oppose-cash-reparations.aspx

40 Frantz Fanon, *Black Skin, White Masks* (London: Pluto Press, 1986), p. 228.

41 Ibid., p. 230.

42 The *négritude* movement was an emancipation movement which aimed at the acceptance of being black and embracing black history and black culture.

43 Quoted in Élisabeth Roudinesco, *Soi-même comme un roi – Essai sur les derives identitaires* (Paris: Seuil, 2021), pp. 195–96.

44 Adeel Hassan and Jack Healy, "America Has Tried Reparations Before. Here Is How It Went," *The New York Times,* June 19, 2019. https://www.nytimes.com/2019/06/19/us/reparations-slavery.html

45 Ibid.

46 "Loi no. 2001-434 du 21 mai 2001 tendant à la reconnaissance de la traite et de l'esclavage en tant que crime contre l'humanité," *Légifrance.* https://www.legifrance.gouv.fr/loda/id/JORFTEXT000000405369/

47 "Crimes Against Humanity," UN Office on Genocide Prevention and the Responsibility to Protect. https://www.un.org/en/genocideprevention/crimes-against-humanity.shtml

48 H. L. Wesseling, "Schuld en boete," in H. L. Wesseling, *Daverende dingen dezer dagen* (Amsterdam: Prometheus, 2018), p. 35.

49 Duco van Oostrum, "De adem der vrijheid. Wij slaven van Suriname als literatuur," in Anton de Kom, *Wij slaven van Suriname* (Amsterdam and Antwerp: Uitgeverij Atlas Contact, 2021), p. 19.

50 Voltaire, *Candide,* Introduction by Philip Littell (New York: Boni and Liveright, Inc., 1918), p. 90. https://www.gutenberg.org/files/19942/19942-h/19942-h.htm#Page_89

51 Willem Flinkenflögel, *Nederlandse slavenhandel (1621 – 1803)* (Utrecht and Antwerp: Kosmos – Z & K Uitgevers, 1994), p. 72.

52 Anton de Kom, *Wij slaven van Suriname,* op. cit., p. 134.

53 Ibid., pp. 136–37.

54 Esther Lammers, "Rutte: Dit kabinet maakt geen excuses voor de slavenhandel," *Trouw,* February 12, 2021. https://www.trouw.nl/politiek/rutte-dit-kabinet-maakt-geen-excuses-voor-de-slavenhandel~b8ecba92/

55 Eric Brassen, "Nederlanders vinden slavernijverleden ernstig, maar achten excuses niet op zijn plaats," *Trouw,* February 12, 2021. https://www.trouw.nl/nieuws/nederlanders-vinden-slavernijverleden-ernstig-maar-achten-excuses-niet-op-zijn-plaats~bacd9e55/

56 J. A. A. van Doorn, *Indische lessen: Nederland en de koloniale ervaring* (Amsterdam: Bert Bakker, 1995), p. 38.

57 Hendrik Spruyt, *Ending Empire: Contested Sovereignty and Territorial Partition,* (Ithaca: Cornell University Press, 2005), p. 57.

58 The conclusions of this investigation, titled *Excessennota* (Memorandum of Excesses), were presented to the Dutch parliament on June 2, 1969. https://start7mei.files.wordpress.com/2013/01/excessennota.pdf

59 "Interview. David Van Reybrouck over Revolusi," *Vrij Nederland,* 81/#10, 2020, p. 97.

60 Ibid.

61 Norbert Elias and John L. Scotson, *Etablierte und Außenseiter* (Frankfurt am Main: Suhrkamp Verlag, 1993), p. 45.

62 "Ketenen van het verleden," met bijlagen, *Rijksoverheid,* July 26, 2021. https://www.rijksoverheid.nl/documenten/rapporten/2021/07/01/ketenen-van-het-verleden

63 The Dutch historian Piet Emmer asked: "Why could descendants of the victims of the Dutch slave trade and slave system not be compensated for lost wages?" (P. C. Emmer, *De Nederlandse slavenhandel 1500 – 1850* (Amsterdam and Antwerp: De Arbeiderspers, 2000), p. 238). He gave the example of former forced laborers in Nazi Germany who received payments for lost wages. However, Emmer mentioned two practical problems: first, that due to the great time interval each slave had many descendants, and, second, that the slave traders and slave owners were mainly private enterprises which, in the meantime, had disappeared. For this reason he preferred a symbolic gesture, such as organizing official commemorations on July 1, the day on which slavery in the Dutch colonial empire was abolished.

64 Maartje Geels and Joram Bolle, "'Eindelijk excuses' van Amsterdam voor slavernij. Nu de staat nog, zeggen de nazaten," *NOS,* July 1, 2021. https://nos.nl/artikel/2387567-eindelijk-excuses-van-amsterdam-voor-slavernij-nu-de-staat-nog-zeggen-nazaten

CHAPTER 2

SIX CONDITIONS FOR A SUCCESSFUL APOLOGY PROCESS

The Dutch example shows that it is not easy to take responsibility for past crimes. Political leaders are, as a rule, reluctant to apologize for crimes committed by their predecessors. Even today it remains a rare phenomenon. However, after the Nuremberg trials, which revealed the atrocities committed by the Nazi regime and defined new rules of international humanitarian law, the practice has gradually become more common. In this respect one can speak, with Norbert Elias, of a *civilizing process*. But for a successful apology process, a number of conditions have to be fulfilled.

THE HARDEST PART: RECOGNIZING THE (UGLY) FACTS

In the *first* place one has to *recognize the facts*. This is the hardest part. History can be written in different ways. One can emphasize the positive facts and neglect the negative facts, or one can describe the negative facts in such a way that they are presented as the consequences of the actions of others, thereby exonerating the behavior of one's co-nationals. Therefore, an objective, scientific, and independent historiography is a *sine qua non* without which no historical responsibility can be established. Such an objective description of the facts is—in principle—possible in open and democratic societies where freedom of research is guaranteed, but it will be more difficult, and often even impossible, in countries with authoritarian and semi-authoritarian regimes. The unwillingness, for example, of the government of Russia, the successor state of the Soviet Union, to recognize the Ukrainian Holodomor (Great Famine) of 1932 and 1933, which numbered between three and six million victims, as a man-made genocide engineered by Stalin, is a case in point.[1] The reluctance of the Turkish government to recognize the Armenian genocide, which in 1915 and 1916 took the lives of between 600,000 and 1.2 million people, is another example.[2] One should also not forget China's "killing of more than half a million and perhaps as many as 1.2 million Tibetans since their imperial occupation of Tibet in 1950,"[3] which the Chinese never recognized. The chance that the Chinese government will take responsibility for this crime is dim if one considers the gruesome fact that "from October 1949 to 1987, the Chinese Communist Party (CCP) probably killed more than 35,200,000 of its own subjects."[4] The portrait of Mao Zedong, the perpetrator of most of these killings, is still depicted on Chinese banknotes.

Although democratic states offer better conditions for pursuing historical truth, this is not enough. A *second* condition is a certain *time distance*. It is easier to apologize for crimes of the past when the perpetrators of these crimes are no longer alive. One may object that this time distance was absent in the case of the German apologies for the Holocaust, but this was because Germany, as a defeated country, had no choice but to apologize, and because of the extreme horror of the events which led Germans to spontaneously atone for the Holocaust.

A *third* condition is that the apology should not be a one-way street. It is not enough for the offender to offer an excuse; he has to make sure that the excuse will be accepted by the offended party. This means that offering an apology is an interactive, reciprocal process, in which one party apologizes and the other party accepts the apology, thereby enabling a process of *catharsis* in which the parties reconcile themselves, and, by repairing their relationship, make it possible to work together in the future without resentment or hard feelings. An African author grasped this reciprocal character of an apology very well when he wrote: "European countries, stop being afraid. Don't get defensive. Ask for forgiveness. You will be forgiven."[5] Jacques Derrida asked: "Is forgiveness a personal face to face or does it need some institutional mediation?" And he answered: "Forgiveness should engage two individuals: the person who is guilty ... and the victim. The moment a third party intervenes one can speak of amnesty, reconciliation, reparation, etc. But certainly not of forgiveness in a strict sense."[6] He gave the example of a woman whose husband had been murdered during the Apartheid regime. When she appeared before the Truth and Reconciliation Commission, headed by Bishop Desmond Tutu, she said: "A commission or a government cannot forgive. I alone, eventually, could do it. *(And I am not ready to forgive)*."[7]

A *fourth* condition is that the party who apologizes doesn't think that after it has made its excuses the case is "closed"—or *erledigt* as the Germans say. Apologies concern not only the past, but they concern equally the present and the future. Part of the apology process is the promise by the offender that these crimes will not happen again, and ideally he has a debt of honor to fight similar crimes when they take place in other parts of the world. According to Martin Karnitschnig, Germany failed to live up to this present- and future-oriented part of the apology process.

> "Under Angela Merkel," he wrote, "Germany has faced the raw reality of its past like never before, winning admiration and praise for what has come to be known as *Erinnerungskultur,* or the 'culture of remembrance.' However," he continued, "Germany's no-holds-barred reckoning has had another profound, if unexpected, consequence: a near-crippling loss of purpose and direction in its dealings with the rest of the world … as German leaders never miss an opportunity to proclaim the importance of a global 'rules-based order,' as soon as it's truly threatened, you'll either find them hiding deep in the skirts of their allies … or on the sidelines…. It's striking how quickly Germany looks the other way when it suits its economic interests, whether in China, Russia, or Iran." And he concludes, "*Erinnerungskultur* has become a diplomatic ripcord that gets tugged whenever the outside world nudges Berlin to do something that could harm its industrial core. It allows Berlin to claim the high ground, to believe it is drawing on the lessons of its own history, when, in reality, it's just copping out."[8]

Is Karnitschnig's judgment too harsh? Maybe. But the German attitude in 2022 in the first month of the Russian war against Ukraine, when

Germany not only reacted late and hesitatingly, but also refused to send heavy weapons to Ukraine, seemed to confirm Karnitschnig's view. Germany's treatment of Russia and China tends to be too soft-handed, taking into account the flagrant violations of international law by the former and the treatment by the latter of the Uyghur Muslim minority of Xinjiang, which probably amounts to genocide.

INTEGRATING APOLOGIES
INTO THE NATIONAL NARRATIVE

A *fifth* condition for a successful apology process is that the apology should become an integral part of the national historical narrative. This means that the incriminating facts must be integrated into school curricula and that they get a prominent place in national commemorations. This can, for instance, be done by creating a new holiday. An example is "Juneteenth" in the United States. Juneteenth is a combination of June and 19th—and refers to June 19, 1865, the day on which General Gordon Granger arrived in Galveston, Texas, to deliver General Order No. 3, ending slavery in that state.[9] On June 15, 2021, President Joe Biden signed a bill in which the Juneteenth National Independence Day was established as a federal holiday. In the same vein the authors of the Dutch "dialogue group" proposed to make July 1 a national holiday (slavery in the Dutch colonies was abolished on July 1, 1863).

Other possibilities to give the past a more prominent place in the public conscience is to open a Memorial Museum, such as the Shoah Memorial Museum in the center of Paris, which has a Wall of Names with the names of the 76,000 Jews who were deported from France during the Second World War and of whom only 2,500 survived.[10] Renaming streets is also a powerful instrument, because street names carry both an overt and a hidden message. The overt message is that they tend to perpetuate the supposed glory of "great men" (mostly they are men!) and national heroes, even after their reputation has come under attack. The hidden message is the absence of the names of personalities who were influential but didn't belong to the mainstream culture. Renaming street names can, therefore, be used as an instrument to restore the balance. This was, for instance, the case after the murder of Martin Luther

King. "Nearly 1,000 American streets have been renamed after King since his assassination in 1968, many of them in the Southeast."[11] How far should this renaming process go and should it also include the removal of statues? This has become an important issue. On June 7, 2020, for instance, during a Black Lives Matter rally in the English city of Bristol, the statue of Edward Colston, a seventeenth-century slave trader and philanthropist, was toppled and thrown into the water of the harbor. The presence of Colston in Bristol is ubiquitous. "His philanthropy has meant the Colston name permeates Bristol. Besides the statue, there is Colston's, an independent school, named after him, along with a concert hall, Colston Hall, a high-rise office block, Colston Tower, Colston Street, and Colston Avenue."[12] Demonstrators argued that the statue "was an affront."[13] However, Prime Minister Boris Johnson condemned the action, describing it as a "criminal act." "If people wanted the removal of the statue," he said, "there are democratic routes which can be followed."[14] Labour leader Keir Starmer took a middle position. He said he could not condone the act, but accused the municipal authorities of a lack of understanding; the statue, he said, should have been removed "a long, long time ago."[15] Starmer had a point, because the statue was toppled after years of trying to have it removed and placed in a museum.[16]

But what about the graffiti found in June 2020 in London on the base of a statue of Winston Churchill on Parliament Square with the text: "Churchill was a racist"? There exists, indeed, historical evidence that Churchill had racist and white supremacist ideas.[17] For this reason, should the statue of this great statesman, who played a major role in the Allied victory over Nazi Germany, be removed? The same question has been asked concerning George Washington,[18] Thomas Jefferson,[19] and James Madison,[20] who possessed plantations which depended on slave labor. Should therefore the statues of these American Founding Fathers and Presidents of the young republic be removed? This question became even more pertinent when, in June 2020, students at the University of Wisconsin-Madison called for the university to remove the statue of Abraham Lincoln which had a prominent place on the campus. People didn't believe their ears. Removing the statue of Abraham Lincoln, the "Great Emancipator" of enslaved African Americans, the man who said: "As I would not be slave, I would not be master"?[21] For what reason should *his* statue be removed? The reason the students gave was that in 1862 Lincoln allowed the execution of 38 Native Americans in the aftermath of the United States–Dakota War.[22] The demands of the students led to accusations of "cancel culture," and an article in *Forbes* was titled "Abe Lincoln Is Next On The Cancel Culture Chopping Block."[23] It is clear that the removal and destruction of statues, a practice which evokes memories of the iconoclastic rage of sixteenth-century wars of religion, is not the solution. Rather one should have recourse to a process of *contextualization,* in which one connects historical personalities and their actions to the specific circumstances of the time in which they lived. This contextualization should take into account both the positive and negative sides of their actions. Panels with explanatory texts can be added to monuments and statues. However, this process of contextualization obviously has its limits and it is absolutely *off limits* for monuments and statues of slave traders, (war) criminals, and the perpetrators of genocides. For this reason, you cannot find monuments for Nazis in Germany.

> "In Germany," wrote Joshua Zeitz, "you won't see neo-Nazis converging on a monument to Reinhard Heydrich or Adolf Hitler, because no such statues exist. The country long ago came to grips with the full weight of its history.... In 1949, the Federal Republic of Germany (West Germany) criminalized the display of swastikas; the symbol was also scraped and sometimes blown off buildings. The federal state systematically destroyed statues and monuments, razed many Nazi architectural structures, and buried executed military and civilian officials in mass, unmarked graves so that their resting grounds would not become Nazi shrines."[24]

HOW TO SOLVE THE PROBLEM OF REPARATIONS?

There exists, finally, a *sixth*, and last condition for a successful apology process. This is a satisfactory solution to the problem of *reparations.* It is clear that victims of slavery, torture, rape, sexual violence, expropriation, forced labor, racial discrimination, and violations to the right to life, have a right to reparation. For the direct victims this poses no problem.[25] Also, descendants of a victim should be able to pursue claims of reparations, which means that the right to reparations does not end with the death of the victim. However, through how many generations can such claims be upheld? This is a crucial question in the case of slavery which in the US was abolished in 1865, and in the case of Britain (1833) and France (1848) even later.[26] Should one be able to claim rights for what happened to one's ancestors six or more generations ago? Stuart E. Eizenstat, the Special Representative on Holocaust-era issues of U.S. Presidents Clinton and Obama, expressed his doubts:

> "What I learned as chief negotiator for both the U.S. government ... and for the Jewish Claims Conference ... is that reparations are complicated, contentious, and messy, and work best when the crime was recent and the direct victims are still alive. Based on my experience, I believe that trying to repay descendants of slaves could end up causing more problems than reparations would seek to solve, and that there are better ways to end racial disparities.... The fact that slavery is so much farther in the past makes the logistics of reparations next to impossible."[27]

Charles Tilly mentioned some additional problems.

> "Categories of people who have suffered call for just compensation that requires today's members of oppressing groups to feel some measure of the pain they or their predecessors have inflicted," he wrote.[28] "No doubt these outcomes do sometimes occur," he continued. "But reparations politics involves two great dangers. First, it provides incentives for people including lawyers and advocates to hoard rewards for themselves rather than redistributing them to genuine victims. Second, it reinforces us-them boundaries instead of dissolving them. When, for example, Native Americans receive compensation for past wrongs in the form of property rights, exemption from taxes, and direct government subsidies, both effects often happen. Lobbyists and lawyers make money as

differences between Native Americans and other Americans sharpen."[29]

Another author, Paul Starobin, argued that the Union soldiers fallen in the Civil War should be taken into account:

> "In America, at least 360,000 Union soldiers died in a war that was caused by the South's insistence on keeping slavery and that became, as the fighting ground on, largely about the emancipation of the slaves. This expended blood represents a kind of reparations, America's cemeteries stocked with the bones of the fallen payers."[30]

Additionally, there is the problem that many white migrants arrived after the abolition of slavery, often themselves the victims of repression:

> "Twenty-first century America is largely the product of waves of immigration which mounted in the years after the war was fought and which came from virtually every corner of the planet. The Jews seeking refuge in the United States from the Tsar's Russia and later the Soviet Union, the boat people fleeing Communist Vietnam, the migrants coming across the southern border from crime-plagued Honduras, Guatemala, and El Salvador—none of these peoples, and many others, like them, has any moral or historical tie to the practice or institution of slavery in America."[31]

It seems, therefore, that paying reparations should be reserved for the *direct* victims of abuse, their children, and—eventually—grandchildren. Claims which are based on the simple fact of having a distant ancestor who was a victim should not qualify. This means that paying reparations to descendants of slaves is not the solution. Taking into account the time distance it is rather a Pandora's Box. Does this mean that the question of reparations for slavery can be pushed aside? No, because there are better methods than issuing checks to individuals who have the "right" ancestors. The slave system still has negative consequences today, and these negative consequences do not only concern the descendants of slaves but also other African Americans. Reparations should therefore instead aim to alleviate the still-existing cumulative negative effects of Jim Crow laws, segregation, discrimination, and redlining (the fact that services are denied or absent because one lives in a "wrong" neighborhood), by long-term investments in education, employment, housing, and health care, measures by which the whole Black community will profit.

THE SPANISH CASE: OFFERING CITIZENSHIP TO DESCENDANTS OF SEPHARDIC JEWS

Reparations concern not only cash payments. A special case is a reparation procedure recently initiated by Spain. The abuse which the Spanish government wanted to repair was even older than the slave trade. It concerned the expulsion of the Jews from Spain in 1492, an expulsion which was preceded by a period of violent persecution by the Spanish Inquisition. "From 1478 to 1492, and beyond, dependent on the personalities of the inquisitors, the courts burned several thousand individuals at the stake or condemned them to prison sentences...."[32] In March 1492 the decision was taken to expel the Jews. They had the choice of becoming Christians, leaving the country before July 31, or risk being killed. It led to an exodus of an estimated 200,000 Jews. In 1992—five hundred years after the facts—the new, democratic Spain wanted to make amends.

"On March 31, 1992, King Juan Carlos of Spain went to the great synagogue of Madrid, asking the Great Rabbi to pardon him in the name of his ancestors, and repealed the expulsion Edict of March 21, 1492. All over Spain Jewish and Jewish-Christian ceremonies were organized, commemorating the sad exodus which took place five hundred years earlier, particularly in Toledo, where all those who had the name Toledano came together; they received the keys of the city. Torches were lit and brought to the host countries of 1492, Morocco, Italy, Greece, Turkey, France, England, Holland ... seven havens for the Jews of Spain during the 16th and 17th century."[33]

But was offering excuses enough to reconcile Spain with the Jewish community? There was a feeling that something was still missing, a gesture which would go beyond a verbal excuse. In 2015 the Spanish government moved from words to deeds, when Spain adopted a law offering Sephardic Jews, who could prove their descent from expelled Jews, Spanish citizenship.[34] Due primarily to the time distance of 500 years, the application process was not easy. Kiku Adatto, a Sephardic Jew and the wife of Harvard philosopher Michael Sandel, who was one of the applicants, together with her brother and her two sons, was disappointed.

> "The application process is daunting and difficult," she wrote. "Requirements include proofs of Sephardic lineage (one need not be a practicing Jew); a rigorous, four-hour Spanish-language test; and a citizen test. Every document—from birth certificates to criminal-background checks—must be translated, notarized, and certified with an apostille seal. Applicants are required to travel to Spain to sign with a Spanish notary, and many people, including our family, hire a Spanish lawyer to help navigate the citizenship process."[35]

As Charles Tilly had predicted, the reparation procedure was a boon for Spanish lawyers. But even they could not solve the problems. In July 2021 it became known that although since the adoption of the law 34,000 people had obtained Spanish citizenship, "3,000 applications have been suddenly rejected in the past few months and 17,000 others have received no response."[36] One of the applicants, Maria Sánchez, 60, of New Mexico, whose application was rejected, said: "It felt like a punch in the gut.... You kicked my ancestors out. Now you're doing this again."[37] It is a sign of how difficult and complex reparations procedures tend to be. Even when they are started with the best intentions, they can easily backfire if not all the consequences are thought through.

NOTES

1   Marcel H. Van Herpen, Putinism—*The Slow Rise of a Radical Right Regime in Russia* (Houndmills and New York: Palgrave Macmillan, 2013), pp. 63–65.

2   According to Daniel Jonah Goldhagen (*Worse than War—Genocide, Elim-inationism, and the Ongoing Assault on Humanity,* op. cit., p. 38): "The Turks eliminated almost all of the 2 million Armenians living in Turkey, exterminating 1.2 million, expelling most of the rest." And David Fromkin wrote: "Rape and beating were commonplace. Those who were not killed at once were driven through mountains and deserts without food, drink, or shelter. Hundreds of thousands of Armenians eventually succumbed or were killed; Armenian sources have put the figure as high as 1,500,000, and though the figures are still the subject of bitter dispute, there can be no disputing of the result: Turkish Armenia was destroyed, and about half of its people perished." (David Fromkin, *A Peace to End All Peace—The Fall of the Ottoman Empire and the Creation of the Modern Middle East* (New York: Henry Holt and Company, 2001), p. 212).

3   Daniel Jonah Goldhagen, *Worse than War—Genocide, Eliminationism, and the Ongoing Assault on Humanity,* op. cit., p. 42.

4   R. J. Rummel, *Death by Government* (New Brunswick and London: Trans-action Publishers, 2004), p. 98.

5   Yarri Kamara, "Dear the West, why do you find it so hard to say sorry?" *African Arguments,* January 1, 2019. https://africanarguments.org/2019/01/african-heritage-dear-west-why-hard-sorry/

6   Jacques Derrida, "Le siècle et le pardon," in *Foi et savoir suivi de Le Siècle et le Pardon* (Paris: Éditions du Seuil, 2000), p. 117.

7   Ibid., p. 118. (English in the original, MHVH).

8   Matthew Karnitschnig, "Why Angela Merkel can't stop apologizing," *Politico,* July 15, 2021. https://www.politico.eu/article/why-angela-merkel-cant-stop-apologizing-germany-foreign-policy/

9   Michael Davis, "National Archives Safeguards Original 'Juneteenth' General Order," *National Archives,* June 19, 2020. https://www.archives.gov/news/articles/juneteenth-original-document

10   http://www.memorialdelashoah.org/en/the-memorial/the-spaces-of-the-museum-memorial/the-wall-of-names.html

11   Malia Wollan, "How to Rename a Street," *New York Times Magazine,* June 23, 2020. https://www.nytimes.com/2020/06/23/magazine/how-to-rename-a-street.html

12   Martin Farrer, "Who was Edward Colston and why was his Bristol statue toppled?" *The Guardian,* June 8, 2020. https://www.theguardian.com/uk-news/2020/jun/08/who-was-edward-colston-and-why-was-his-bristol-statue-toppled-slave-trader-black-lives-matter-protests

13   "Edward Colston: Bristol slave trader statue 'was an affront'," *BBC,* June 8, 2020. https://www.bbc.com/news/uk-england-bristol-52962356

14   Ibid.

15   Ibid.

16 Naomi Fowler, "Britain's Slave Owner Compensation Loan, reparations and tax havenry," *Tax Justice Network,* June 8, 2020. https://taxjustice.net/2020/06/09/slavery-compensation-uk-questions/

17 Richard Toye, "Yes, Churchill was a racist. It's time to break free of his 'great white men' view of history," *CNN,* June 10, 2020. https://edition.cnn.com/2020/06/10/opinions/churchill-racist-great-white-men-view-toye-opinion/index.html

18 Erin Blakemore, "Did George Washington Really Free Mount Vernon's Enslaved Workers?" *History.com,* October 11, 2017 (updated February 18, 2020). https://www.history.com/news/did-george-washington-really-free-mount-vernons-slaves

19 "Jefferson's Attitude Toward Slavery," *Monticello.org.* https://www.monticello.org/thomas-jefferson/jefferson-slavery/jefferson-s-attitudes-toward-slavery/

20 James Madison owned over one hundred slaves on his Virginia plantation. In the Federalist Papers he criticized the slave trade, but not slavery, calling the slave trade a "barbarism of modern policy," which the United States would abolish in a period of twenty years (i.e., in 1808). He added: "Happy would it be for the unfortunate Africans if an equal prospect lay before them of being redeemed from the oppressions of their European brethren," expressing the wish that European countries would follow the American example. (James Madison, Paper No. 42, in Alexander Hamilton, James Madison, and John Jay, *The Federalist Papers* (New York, Ontario, and London: New American Library, 1961), p. 266).

21 Erik H. Erikson, *Insight and Responsibility* (New York and London: W. W. Norton & Company, Inc., 1964), p. 221.

22 Kelly Meyerhofen, "University of Wisconsin students call for removal of Abraham Lincoln statue on Madison campus," *Chicago Tribune,* June 30, 2020. https://www.chicagotribune.com/midwest/ct-wisconsin-madison-lincoln-statue-bascom-hill-20200630-hhfadge53fethiobylwvklz24q-story.html

23 Evan Gerstmann, "Abe Lincoln Is Next On The Cancel Culture Chopping Block," *Forbes,* October 14, 2020. https://www.forbes.com/sites/evangerstmann/2020/10/14/abe-lincoln-is-next-on-the-cancel-culture-chopping-block/

24 Joshua Zeitz, "Why There Are No Nazi Statues in Germany," *Politico,* August 20, 2017. https://www.politico.com/magazine/story/2017/08/20/why-there-are-no-nazi-statues-in-germany-215510/

25 The main problem in this case is how victims of human rights violations can pursue their claims for reparations. To improve the positions of the victims, the European Commission published the report "Strengthening Victims' Rights: From compensation to reparation—For a new EU victims'

rights strategy 2020–2025," Report of the Special Adviser, J. Milquet, to the President of the European Commission, Jean-Clause Juncker, Luxembourg, March 2019.

26 In France slavery was abolished for the first time in 1794, during the French Revolution—without much effect. It was reinstated in 1802 by Napoleon.

27 Stuart E. Eizenstat, "What Holocaust Restitution Taught Me About Slavery Reparations," *Politico,* October 27, 2019. https://www.politico.com/magazine/story/2019/10/27/slavery-reparations-holocaust-restitution-negotiations-229881/

28 Charles Tilly, *Credit & Blame* (Princeton and Oxford: Princeton University Press, 2008), p. 150.

29 Ibid.

30 Paul Starobin, "Guilty Conscience," *The National Interest,* Number 170, November/December 2020, p. 48.

31 Ibid.

32 Béatrice Leroy, *Les juifs dans l'Espagne chrétienne avant 1492* (Paris: Éditions Albin Michel, 1993), p. 112.

33 Ibid., p. 117.

34 Portugal, which expelled the Jews in 1497, made a similar offer in 2015.

35 Kiku Adatto, "Spain's Attempt to Atone for a 500-Year-Old Sin," *The Atlantic,* September 21, 2019. https://www.theatlantic.com/international/archive/2019/09/spain-offers-citizenship-sephardic-jews/598258/ Michael Sandel tells about the experience of his wife in his speech upon receiving the Princess of Asturias Award for Social Sciences 2018. https://www.fpa.es/en/princess-of-asturias-awards/laureates/2018-michael-j-sandel.html?texto=discurso&especifica=0

36 Toi Staff, "After welcoming Sephardic Jews, Spain rejects thousands of citizenship requests," *Times of Israel,* July 25, 2021. https://www.timesofisrael.com/after-welcoming-sephardic-jews-spain-rejects-thousands-of-citizenship-requests/

37 Ibid.

PART II

OUR RESPONSIBILITY FOR THE PRESENT: CAN WE LEARN LESSONS FROM HISTORY?

CHAPTER 3

CAN WE LEARN LESSONS FROM HISTORY? ARGUMENTS FOR AND AGAINST

We are not only responsible for the crimes of our ancestors, but we are equally responsible vis-à-vis our contemporaries. This is the responsibility not to repeat past mistakes and to learn "the lessons from history." The question of whether "one can learn lessons from history" emerges particularly during crisis periods. The French historian Marc Bloch who, on June 16, 1944, was to be executed by a firing squad for his activities in the resistance against the German occupying forces, wrote in 1942: "Our art, our literary monuments are full of echoes from the past; our politicians talk all the time about their real or supposed lessons."[1] And he continued: "Each time that our gloomy societies, in a continuous growth crisis, start to doubt themselves, one sees them asking themselves if they were right to ask questions about their past or whether they asked the right questions."[2] Bloch spoke about asking the "right" questions about our past in order to learn from history. But the central question is: *can* we learn something from history? That is the question I want to address in the second part of this book.

LEARNING LESSONS FROM HISTORY – BUT HOW?

The Scottish philosopher David Hume (1711–1777) wrote: "The object of eloquence is to persuade, of history to instruct, of poetry to please...."[3] As for Cicero, the role of history was for him "to instruct": history was something one could learn from. This seems to be obvious for an Enlightenment philosopher. However, there were also philosophers who answered this question in a negative way. One of them is Georg Wilhelm Friedrich Hegel (1770–1831), who wrote: "One urges rulers, statesmen, peoples to learn from the experience of history, however, what experience and history teach is that peoples and rulers have never learned anything from history, nor acted on the basis of the lessons they could have learned. Each age has such specific circumstances, is such a particular situation, that one can only and should only take decisions accordingly."[4] Today Hegel's skepticism has become widespread, as the historian David Fischer observed, who wrote: "Many of our contemporaries are extraordinarily reluctant to acknowledge the reality of past time and prior events, and stubbornly resistant to all arguments for the possibility or utility of historical knowledge."[5] However, the Dutch historian Pieter Geyl disagreed fundamentally with this skepticism. "But what is then the benefit [of history]?" he asked. "You know the words of the businessman," he answers, "who considered history a waste of time. It was Ford who expressed it in such a concise way: History is bunk."[6] Geyl gave yet another example of a businessman who did not hide his skepticism about the usefulness of history: the Dutch captain of industry Albert Plesman, the founder of the airline company KLM. In 1948, when Plesman appeared in Parliament for a hearing on the period 1940–1945, he showed himself markedly reluctant.

> "He 'did not like it.' One was looking, he said, 'at a past that no longer existed.' I find this an expression," wrote Geyl, "which as a symptom of a certain mentality deserves to become a classic alongside Ford's. The chairman [of the parliamentary commission] … answered: 'However, it happens that the past sometimes offers us a lesson for the future.'"[7]

Geyl's comment:

> "This answer is going along the right lines, but for me it isn't completely satisfying. *Historia magistra vitae*. That is an old proverb. But modern historians have become hesitant—sometimes, I should add, much too hesitant—about the function attributed to his profession offering lessons for practical life, as a rule the practical life of politics…. Lessons, like: in these circumstances do this or that, no. Because the circumstances

are always, in the most treacherous way, just a bit different. But to stimulate and prepare the imagination, so that in certain circumstances parallels appear, all different from what is the situation at that moment, but suggesting all the possibilities or impossibilities, all helping to understand certain phenomena a bit more deeply in their surprising unicity, all preparing the mind at least a minimum for the always newly arising problem of the suddenly emerging case—that is certainly what history can help us with...."[8]

Against Hegel's apodictic denial of the possibility to learn from history Geyl emphasized that history can help people to orient themselves in unknown situations, although he rightly adds that one cannot expect history to repeat itself or to offer ready-made blueprints. Another historian, who emphasized not only the utility but the necessity of history, is Arthur Schlesinger Jr.

"What is the point of history at all?" he asked. And he answered: "The past is not an irrelevance. 'We cannot escape history,' said Lincoln. History is to the nation what memory is to the individual. As an individual deprived of memory becomes disoriented and lost, not knowing where he has been or where he is going, so a nation without an understanding of its past will be disabled in dealing with its present and its future."[9]

History is knowledge of the collective past and is necessary to orient a nation. The American sociologist Robert MacIver wrote in the same vein, "One reason why man's efforts to shape the future are so often futile or worse is that he is slow to learn the lessons of his own past."[10] MacIver didn't doubt *in principle* man's ability to learn from history, but he ascribed his problems of actually putting this into practice to his intellectual deficiency—man's abstruseness. The German-American historian Fritz Stern was also positive. "Despite all justified doubt that one can learn from history," he wrote, "I have kept this fundamental belief and tried in this sense to put my knowledge into practice."[11] His opinion is shared by former German chancellor Helmut Schmidt, who gave a part of his memoirs the title "Learning from History."[12] In the same vein the German historian Friedrich Meinecke wrote, "Learning lessons from history to see in it an example or a warning, is traditionally one of the indestructible fundamental motives that lead to historiography."[13] However, he cautioned, "this implies the greatest dangers for its scientific character, [namely] that of tendential inflection, idealization, or distortion."[14]

That is why historians should not jump too quickly to conclusions, but should scrupulously analyze causal relations, because "the study of causal relations already offers abundantly practical lessons. Everything that works in history through general, typically returning causes can also return in the present time and then be treated according to the experiences made in the past."[15] Meinecke criticized Hegel in a footnote: "Hegel denied that peoples and rulers ever learned anything from history and would have acted according to the lessons that could have been learned. It is more correct to say that they seldom learned what an observer would have wished that they had learned."[16] Particularly important is Meinecke's remark that the study of historical causalities abundantly offers practical lessons, as we will see in the next chapter. But first we have to signal a problem.

HISTORY DOESN'T OFFER UNEQUIVOCAL LESSONS

The problem is that interpretations of historical events tend to differ. If even professional historians can disagree about causal relations, then it is clear that one cannot learn unequivocal "lessons" from history. "I am skeptical," wrote, for instance, Ian Buruma, "about the idea that we can learn much from history, at least in the sense that knowledge of past follies will prevent us from making similar blunders in the future. History is all a matter of interpretation. Often the wrong interpretations of the past are more dangerous than ignorance."[17] It is, indeed, a fact that the same historical events can be interpreted in different ways by different historians. A classic example is the British historian E. H. Carr (1892–1982), who was a great admirer of the Bolshevik revolution and wrote a fourteen-part study titled *History of Soviet Russia,* in which he described the development of the Soviet Union between 1917 and the early 1930s as a model of historical progress. Until the end of his life Carr remained a convinced supporter of the Soviet system, which he considered an important step forward in the global liberation of the proletariat. It is clear that Carr learned different lessons from the October Revolution than most of his colleagues, who considered it the beginning of a totalitarian nightmare. The question of whether one can learn from history is, therefore, clearly linked with a more fundamental question: whether a more or less *objective* historiography is possible.

HISTORICAL LESSONS CONTAIN A VALUE JUDGMENT

The question of whether one can learn from history is further linked with another question: whether one may make historical value judgments. It is clear that "learning lessons from history" implies per definition also making value judgments. However, postmodernist thinkers —who adhere to a complete value relativism and for whom there are no general value measures with which to judge individual epochs—deny that one can learn from history. According to them, one should judge individual epochs with the value measures which are valid in those epochs. This would mean that an autocratic and unequal society, which is based on slavery and permits torture, would be equivalent to a democratic society in which minorities are protected and human rights are guaranteed. Such a postmodernist value relativism is untenable. It ends in an aporia, a logical contradiction, because it relativizes all opinions except its own, which, in a dogmatic manner, is presented as absolute. However, if one takes postmodernist value relativism to its logical conclusion, then *all* values and opinions are relative, included those of the postmodernists. It is clear that if one wants to learn lessons from history, such a value relativism has to be rejected. The need to learn lessons is a result of the need to avoid the negative experiences of the past, and to use positive experiences of the past as a model to be emulated. This means that periods of peace and prosperity in which rulers govern in a wise and moderate way, and ideals of freedom and equality are increasingly realized, are models to be followed by later generations. The English philosopher A. C. Grayling has expressed the same idea as follows:

"There are those who say that history teaches no lessons, because the present and the future are too different for any such lessons to apply; and there are those who more pertinently point out that to ignore the lessons of the past is to be condemned to repeat them."[18] "But I wish to argue that the ideas which emerged in the eighteenth century about individual autonomy and rights, pluralism, a framework of impartial law impartially administered, privacy, freedom of thought and expression, democratic institutions, secularism, and the importance of education and equality of opportunity, are achievements of history that should be permanent because the principles they embody are universal and right."[19]

For the time being we can formulate three conditions for the possibility of learning lessons from history. In the first place, historiography should guarantee the greatest possible scientific objectivity in order to avoid biased historical narratives. In the second place, it should reject each value relativism and be explicit about its own values and ethical standards. In the third place, it should concentrate on exploring causal relationships in historical processes.

THE MUNICH CONFERENCE OF SEPTEMBER 1938 AS AN EXAMPLE OF A "HISTORICAL LESSON" FOR POSTERITY

The Munich conference of September 1938 is usually considered a major example of a missed historical opportunity and a lesson for future generations. In this conference the English Prime Minister Neville Chamberlain abandoned the Czechoslovak Sudetenland to Hitler. His motive was to preserve the peace in Europe. The contrary, however, was the case: this concession only increased Hitler's territorial appetite.

"What is certain...," wrote the French historian François Paulhac, "is that Munich did a lot for the Führer's popularity in Germany. There was already the *Anschluss,* realized on 12 March 1938 without any bloodshed. Munich was in the eyes of the

Germans a new peaceful victory for Hitler. From this point of view the 'capitulation' of the French and the English had very serious consequences. It made the German people believe that Hitler could realize *without a war* everything that German public opinion had wished for twenty years.... This idea that, anyway, war in the West was impossible, that a last-minute arrangement like the one in Munich could again be made, has one year later largely contributed to undermining the credibility of the French-British declarations concerning Poland...."[20]

Although Chamberlain, on his return from Munich, was loudly applauded in England as a peace apostle, critical voices were also already being heard. Winston Churchill is the most well-known critic. In a debate on October 5, 1938, in the House of Commons, Churchill warned as a twentieth-century Cassandra that after the "spontaneous outburst of joy and relief" the people should know the truth:

"They should know that there has been gross neglect and deficiency in our defences; they should know that we have sustained a defeat without a war, the consequences of which will travel far with us along our road; they should know that we have passed an awful milestone in our history, when the whole equilibrium of Europe has been deranged, and that the terrible words have for the time being been pronounced against the Western democracies: 'Thou art weighed in the balance and found wanting.' And do not suppose this is the end. This is only the beginning of the reckoning. This is only the first sip, the first foretaste of a bitter cup which will be proffered to us year by year unless by a supreme recovery of moral health and martial vigour, we arise again and take our stand for freedom as in the olden time."[21]

Not only Churchill, but ordinary citizens also had their doubts. On October 7, 1938, one week after the Munich conference and two days after Churchill's speech, the French writer André Gide wrote in his diary:

"Since the 22nd of September we have lived through days of anguish…. Even though the events of history seem to me to escape at one and the same time both the will and the foresight of men, it seemed to me that reason (if not justice and right) was winning a victory over force; but I am not so convinced of this that I was not considerably shaken in my optimism by the admirable letter Jef Last[22] wrote me. He is willing to see in the Munich conversations nothing but a shameful defeat, which can only result in a new strengthening of Hitler and new claims; for us, nothing but new withdrawals and with dishonor."[23] And Gide asked: "Would Germany have yielded to a firmer attitude…?"[24]

When, in March 1939, Hitler's troops would invade Prague, the time for illusions was over. In his book *The New German Empire*, published in May 1939 —ust after the German invasion of Prague, but before the outbreak of the Second World War—the Austrian sociologist Franz Borkenau wrote that people outside Germany tended to underestimate the radical character of Hitler's conservative revolution.

"In non-revolutionary countries," he wrote, "the outlines of the revolutionary process dissolved themselves in a tale of meaningless horror; or else, and this is perhaps the more frequent attitude, the politicians of countries not directly affected by the revolutionary process regard it as a thing that really could only be a mistake, a short deviation of history, a nightmare which once over would lead back to the old 'natural' state of things."[25]

He warned that one could not expect such a "back to normal." "Germany to-day," he wrote, "is a boiling cauldron without a safety valve … the only question is in which direction the bomb will explode…. For explosion there must be."[26] In early 1939 Borkenau had no illusions about Germany's war plans, writing that "Germany aims first of all at conquering her nearest neighbours."[27]

It is always easy to criticize in hindsight the shortsightedness of previous generations. However, for those living through a particular period, the difficulty in evaluating their own situation becomes clear from Churchill's book *Great Contemporaries,* which was published in September 1937—exactly one year before the Munich conference. One of the "great contemporaries" described by Churchill in this book is Adolf Hitler. Churchill begins this chapter as follows:

> "It is not possible to form a just judgment of a public figure who has attained the enormous dimensions of Adolf Hitler until his life work as a whole is before us. Although no subsequent political action can condone wrong deeds, history is replete with examples of men who have risen to power by employing stern, grim, and even frightful methods, but who, nevertheless, when their life is revealed as a whole, have been regarded as great figures whose lives have enriched the story of mankind. So may it be with Hitler."[28]

Churchill had written this chapter in 1935, three years before the Munich conference. He clearly already had his doubts. These doubts also appear at the end of this chapter, where he writes:

> "Thus the world lives on hopes that the worst is over, and that we may yet live to see Hitler a gentler figure in a happier age. Meanwhile, he makes speeches to the nations, which are sometimes characterized by candour and moderation. Recently he has offered many words of reassurance, eagerly lapped up by those who have been so tragically wrong about Germany in the past. Only time can show, but, meanwhile, the great wheels revolve; the rifles, the cannon, the tanks, the shot and shell, the air-bombs, the poison-gas cylinders, the aeroplanes, the submarines, and now the beginnings of a fleet flow in ever-broadening streams from the already largely war-mobilized arsenals and factories of Germany."[29]

The prevailing tone of Churchill's portrait of Hitler is one of deep concern. Although in the beginning of the chapter he is prepared to give Hitler the benefit of the doubt, he has major doubts. Churchill doesn't trust Hitler's rhetoric and thinks that one can read his real intentions more reliably from the unparalleled mobilization of the German war industry. His book was published in 1937. That means that shortly before the Munich conference and the *Anschluss* of Austria, Churchill was still leaving all possibilities open—including the possibility that Hitler would develop into a more moderate political leader.[30]

HOW TO AVOID THE "HISTORICAL METAPHOR TRAP"

The fact that even a visionary statesman, such as Winston Churchill, is wrestling with the right evaluation of the events of his time is an indication of how difficult it is to evaluate contemporary events and—even more so—to discover in these events trends, let alone to predict future developments. "Learning from history," therefore, looks easier than it really is, as does all reasoning after the facts. History does not offer a collection of standard blueprints for how to act and behave "in the right way" in particular circumstances. Situations differ and actors differ, apart from unexpected and unforeseen events which can happen and often have their own dynamic. One should also be aware of the danger of the "historical metaphor trap": the danger that one sees everything through the prism of a particular event. "Munich" is a case in point. "Famously," write Gilman and Ganesh, "the debate about what to do about Vietnam in 1965 in Lyndon Johnson's presidential administration was ultimately a dispute between those who described situations as 'more like Munich'—thus demanding escalation rather than peacemaking—or 'more like Korea'—a quagmire to be avoided. Both metaphors were misleading in different ways, and yet they were used extensively in debates and decision-making."[31]

NOTES

1   Marc Bloch, *Apologie pour l'histoire ou Métier d'historien*, Préface de Jacques Le Goff (Malakoff: Armand Colin, 2018), p. 38.
2   Ibid.
3   David Hume, "Of the standard of taste," in David Hume, *Essays—Moral, Political, and Literary* (Indianapolis: Liberty Fund, 1987), p. 240.

4   G. W. F. Hegel, "Vorlesungen über die Philosophie der Geschichte," *Werke,* Volume 12 (Frankfurt am Main: Suhrkamp Verlag, 1970), p. 17.

5   David Hackett Fischer, *Historians' Fallacies: Toward a Logic of Historical Thought* (New York: Harper & Row, 1970), p. 307.

6   Pieter Geyl, "Een historicus tegenover de wereld van nu," in Pieter Geyl, *Historicus in de tijd* (Utrecht: Uitgeversmaatschappij W. de Haan N.V., 1954), p. 158.

7   Ibid., pp. 163–64.

8   Ibid., p. 164.

9   Arthur M. Schlesinger Jr., *The Cycles of American History* (Boston and New York: Houghton Mifflin Company, 1999), pp. viii–ix.

10   R. M. MacIver, *The Challenge of the Passing Years—My Encounter with Time* (New York: Pocket Books, Inc., 1963), p. 112.

11   Helmut Schmidt and Fritz Stern, *Unser Jahrhundert—Ein Gespräch* (Munich: Verlag C.H. Beck, 2010), p. 279.

12   Helmut Schmidt, *Ausserdienst—Eine Bilanz* (Munich: Siedler Verlag, 2008), p. 69.

13   Friedrich Meinecke, "Kausalitäten und Werte in der Geschichte," in *Historische Zeitschrift,* Volume 137 (2), 1928, p. 22.

14   Ibid.

15   Ibid.

16   Ibid.

17   Ian Buruma, *Year Zero—A History of 1945* (New York: The Penguin Press, 2013), p. 10.

18   A. C. Grayling, "History and Progress in the Twentieth Century," in A. C. Grayling, *Liberty in the Age of Terror—A Defence of Civil Liberties and Enlightenment Values* (London, Berlin, and New York: Bloomsbury, 2009), p. 213.

19   Ibid., p. 214.

20   François Paulhac, *Les accords de Munich et les origines de la guerre de 1939* (Paris: Librairie J. Vrin, 1988), pp. 174–75.

21   Quoted in Martin Gilbert, *Churchill—A Life* (London: Heinemann, 1991), p. 600.

22   André Gide had known the Dutch writer Jef Last since June 1936, when both visited the Soviet Union. The visit was a disillusion for Gide, who had communist sympathies. He saw with his own eyes that Stalin's empire was not the communist paradise it was made out to be. In his book *Retouches à mon retour de l'U.R.S.S.* (1937) he settled his accounts with the Soviet Union.

23   André Gide, *Journals, Volume 3, 1928-1939* (Urbana and Chicago: University of Illinois Press, 2000), pp. 405–06.

24 Ibid., p. 406.
25 Dr. F. Borkenau, *The New German Empire* (Harmondsworth: Penguin Books, 1939), p. 14.
26 Ibid., p. 24.
27 Ibid., p. 111.
28 Winston Churchill, "Hitler and His Choice," in Winston Churchill, *Great Contemporaries* (London: Thornton Butterworth Ltd., 1937), p. 261.
29 Ibid., pp. 268–9.
30 Immediately after Hitler's appointment as Chancellor on January 30, 1933, British government circles were concerned about his foreign policy. But according to Ian Kershaw the expectation was "that Hitler was, beneath the rhetoric, ultimately a politician like others who, whatever the distaste for his actions in internal matters, could be dealt with as regards foreign affairs on rational grounds of balancing respective interests, that he would be a 'moderate' once in power, was an illusion which would last through the 1930s." (Ian Kershaw, *Making Friends with Hitler—Lord Londonderry and Britain's Road to War* (London and New York: Penguin, 2005), p. 38).
31 Nils Gilman and Maya Indira Ganesh, "Making Sense of the Unknown," *Berggruen Institute,* July, 2020.

CHAPTER 4

WHAT IS HISTORY?

If one wants to learn from history, this implies that such a thing as "history" does exist. But what is "history" exactly? The word "history" has two meanings. In the first place it refers to "all that has happened" in human society. In the second place it refers to the written records of history which make use of primary sources, interpret these sources, analyze causes and effects, and put together a cohesive and meaningful narrative. The first kind of "history" is only the substrate, the raw material of which history as a discipline is made. For "history," as we know it, we need more—structure, order. The only one who can bring this order is man, especially *writing* man. "History" is per definition *human* history: the development of intelligent creatures who are capable of projecting themselves into the future and act accordingly. Animals don't project themselves into the future and they don't, therefore, "make" history. For this reason, it is not a coincidence that we don't call the development of the animal world "history," but "evolution" (of which we humans, in the family of the primates, are a part). The problem with the first kind of "history"—in the sense of "all that happened"—is that this consists of a vertiginous multitude of facts, acts, movements, and data apparently without form and structure. It is the human intellect and human language—and later the invention of script—which have enabled man to remember, transmit, interpret, and write down historical facts. What we call "history" is in fact mostly what has been written down and revealed in the form of historiography. It is through historiography that "history" as a discipline became possible. The historian is, as it were, a midwife. It is true, he does not *make* the facts, but he gives the facts names, structures them, and places them in broader contexts.

SARKOZY AND "HISTORYLESS" AFRICAN MAN

This leads to a further question: in the case of primitive peoples who don't have script, can one speak of their "history"? This is a pertinent question: the tribes of the Baliem Valley in Indonesian New Guinea, who not so long ago still lived in the Stone Age, objectively had the same "past" as the civilized Dutch colonizers who "discovered" them. However, this past was not considered to be "history" because—apart from some objects found on their territory—the most important instrument to construct this history, written sources, was lacking. Also, the ability of these tribes to project themselves into the future, being hunter-gatherers who lived from day to day, was much more restricted than that of modern Western man.

This idea might have played a role when, on July 26, 2007, French President Nicolas Sarkozy, in a speech at the University of Dakar, Senegal, told his audience that "the drama of Africa is that African man has not sufficiently gone down in history."[1] "The African farmer," he said, "knows only the eternal restarting of time, rhythmically beaten out by the endless repetition of the same gestures and the same words ... Man never launches himself into the future. It never occurs to him to leave repetition behind him in order to take his fate into his own hands."[2] "History" is here restricted by Sarkozy to a *certain kind* of history, namely a history such as the West knows it, a history which is dynamic and turned toward the future, a history that is focused on continuous change and improvement. According to Sarkozy, African history would rather resemble Nietzsche's *ewige Wiederkunft des Gleichen* (the eternal return of the same). Being repetitive and not very dynamic, it wouldn't merit the qualification "history." Sarkozy's speech was not only heavily criticized in Africa, but also in France.[3] It was denounced as "racist" and the diplomatic damage was great. In the autumn of 2007 the Foreign Ministry received reports of 42 French ambassadors in Africa who confirmed that "the image of France in Africa oscillates between attraction and repulsion in our former colonies, that the Africans reject a France which lectures everyone else...."[4] Sarkozy's *dédain* for African history was said to be a continuation of a vision which was popular in nineteenth-century Europe. In 1837 the German philosopher Hegel wrote in his philosophy of history: "We leave Africa here and will not return to it later on. Because it is not a historical continent, it cannot show change and development.... What we actually mean by Africa is the unhistorical and inaccessible, still captured in the spirit of nature, and must be presented here only as standing on the threshold of world history."[5] Hegel's vision was shared by Victor Hugo, who was, differently from Hegel, in many respects a progressive thinker. In a speech delivered on May 18, 1879, he said: "Asia has its history, America has its history, even Australia has its history; Africa has no history."[6]

This polemic indicates how difficult it is to give an unequivocal definition of "history." "History" in principle involves all human activities as its object; human activities can have both repetitive and dynamic patterns, so there exists no reason for reserving the qualification "history" only for the dynamic, Western variant. Moreover, no human society is purely static, as the French philosopher Cornelius Castoriadis rightly remarks. "Historical is essentially *each* society...," he writes, "even if it is 'prehistoric' or 'without history,' in the sense that it changes itself, that it is not once and for all self-creation, but continuous self-creation...."[7] The problem in the case of (sub-Saharan) Africa is not that it wouldn't have a history, but that it had not, until the arrival of the Europeans, a historiography.

The Dutch historian Henk Wesseling, an expert on the history of Africa, also asked the question: "Does Africa have a history?" And he answered: "Not so long ago this question would be answered in the negative. In a passage that has become famous the English historian Hugh Trevor-Roper compared in 1965 the history of Europe with that of Africa and concluded that to tell the truth the second did not exist."[8] But Wesseling indicated that this gap had been partially filled: "As one knows," he writes, "traditional, that means written sources, are in the case of Africa relatively scarce. However, this scarcity has also acted as a stimulus to explore new sources and to apply new methods and techniques. One of the most famous examples of the use of new methods is the analysis of the oral tradition...."[9] "Does this mean that African history has become comparable with European history, that it has reached the same level of exactitude, has acquired a same character?" he asked. "I don't believe so," was his answer, "and I don't believe that this will ever happen, because in this respect there exist great and major differences between Europe and Africa, in particular but not only as concerns the sources."[10] One of these differences was, according to him, the fact that "African cultures … were much less preoccupied with chronology and giving dates than the European culture which, as we know, has a strong historical character."[11] In fact, Sarkozy's remark was a pure product of a nineteenth-century, Europe-centric idea of history in which Africa didn't play a role as an independent subject and only enters (Western) history as an object of imperialist greed after its "discovery" by white explorers. The fact that in sub-Saharan Africa there didn't exist an indigenous historiography only helped to spread this vision. Although historiography is the most important source of history as a science, also oral sources, mentioned by Wesseling, can play a role.

DIFFERENT NARRATIVES

In order to learn lessons from history there is still another problem, which is that historical narratives often don't coincide. This is because a historical narrative consists not only of irrefutable facts and dates, but also of guesses, probabilities, interpretations, and motives that are (rightly or wrongly) ascribed to historical actors. Historical narratives may largely overlap in the reproduction of basic facts—as, for instance, the irrefutable fact that in 1914 Germany invaded Belgium and not Belgium Germany—but different historians will give different interpretations of certain historical events. No one will today deny that the Ribbentrop-Molotov Pact of August 23, 1939, had an additional secret protocol in which Nazi Germany and the Soviet Union agreed to divide up Poland and to recognize mutual spheres of influence that led to the annexation of the Baltic states and parts of Finland and Romania by the Soviet Union. But the interpretations of this pact and the secret protocol differ fundamentally. In the Soviet historiography this protocol is explained as a defensive measure against the intention, ascribed by the Kremlin to France and Britain, to direct German aggression against the Soviet Union, an interpretation still defended in 2015 by the Russian President Vladimir Putin.[12] For the West and for Poland, Finland, Romania, and the Baltic states it was a cynical deal between two totalitarian powers which prepared an act of pure aggression.

The question is: how can we learn from history if there is not one, but several different interpretations, not to say several different "histories?" Because it is clear that different interpretations lead to different evaluations, which lead to different "lessons" which one could learn from past events. This is an indication of the importance of an accurate, objective historiography, which sticks scrupulously to the facts and leaves no room for biased, partisan interpretations. Only by sticking to the facts can a consensual view emerge of what really happened. For this reason, historiography has to be kept out of the hands of states and governments. Particularly in authoritarian states, historiography is often reduced to a political propaganda instrument and subjected to the ideological goals of the regime. In 1935, for instance, the Nazi government founded the "Reichsinstitut für Geschichte des neuen Deutschlands" (State Institute for the History of the New Germany), which was directed by the historian Walter Frank. This institute, which in 1936 opened a "Forschungsabteilung Judenfrage" (Research Department for the Jewish Question), was completely dependent on the regime and helped the regime to prepare its Final Solution.

THE RUSSIAN COMMISSION AGAINST THE "FALSIFICATION OF HISTORY"

Totalitarian and authoritarian states want to keep an iron grip on the interpretation of history and are, therefore, not interested in an objective historiography. For this reason, it is no surprise that on May 15, 2009, Russian President Medvedev installed a presidential commission which had the task of defending Russia against "attempts to damage the interests of Russia by the falsification of history."[13] The task of this commission was to combat supposed "falsifications" in the new post-Soviet states of the nature and extent of Stalin's repression. One of the commission's objectives was to combat Ukraine's attempts to have the *Holodomor*—the artificial famine caused by Stalin's policies in the 1930s which claimed millions of victims—recognized internationally as an act of genocide.[14] The Russian presidential commission which had to uncover and combat these so called "falsifications" consisted of 28 "experts." Of these 28 there were precisely four professional historians.

The most prominent of these was General Vasily Khristoforov, the head of the archives of the KGB and its successor, the FSB.[15]

Another historical "blind spot" was Stalin's Great Terror of 1937 and 1938. In Russia "rather than blame the government, most see the Great Terror as something akin to a natural disaster. Very few Russians privately acknowledge—and fewer still are brave enough to publicly declare—that the mass Soviet political repression of 1937–1938 was a crime, planned and perpetrated by Stalin and his government against the Soviet people."[16] One would have thought that one of the central "lessons" which a Russian historical commission might learn from Russian history is a critical analysis of the crimes of Stalin's regime with the objective of avoiding its repetition. The contrary, however, was the case. Critical voices in the post-Soviet states concerning Stalin's regime are interpreted as attacks on Russia. It was, therefore, no surprise when, in December 2021, the Russian NGO "Memorial"—a human rights group which recorded Stalin-era crimes—was shut down. In essence not much seems to have changed. In the 1930s Leon Trotsky, one of the leading figures of the Russian Revolution and the founder of the Red Army, had already been eliminated from Russian history books as if he had never existed. Such a denial of historical facts goes against the basis of any serious historiography, namely, to tell what actually happened.

In recent years the Kremlin's efforts to deny and suppress historical facts have only increased. Antoon De Baets, a Belgian historian, coined a new term to describe this situation: "crimes against history."[17] De Baets pointed to the fact that "already in 1918 Lenin said that the revolution didn't need historians." In Putinist Russia the situation is no different. Not only are historians denied access to archives and respected NGOs, such as "Memorial," are persecuted, but the government has escalated its attacks on historical truth by directly attacking historians, the producers of historiography. In a report published by the International Federation of Human Rights this "war on history," which has morphed into a war against independent historians, is analyzed in detail.[18] The report mentions many cases of prosecutions and expulsions of independent historians. The persecution of Yuri Dmitriev has become a hallmark of this repressive policy.

"Since the 1990s," one can read, "Dmitriev ... has worked to uncover mass graves from Stalin's Great Terror, and to identify individual victims. The discovery of Sandarmokh, an execution site dating from 1937–1938, where over 9,000 people of more than 58 nationalities were buried, brought him international recognition.... In 2016, Dmitriev was arrested on charges of sexual misconduct and production of child pornography.... In July 2017, Human Rights Center Memorial concluded that the criminal case against Dmitriev was fabricated, and recognized him as a political prisoner."[19]

After a first condemnation to 3.5 years in prison, the appellate court increased his sentence in September 2020 to a draconian 13 years. In December 2021 a court increased his jail sentence to 15 years in a penal colony. For Dmitriev, who turned 65 in 2021, this verdict was essentially a life sentence. "A media investigation has traced Dmitriev's persecution to an adviser of Vladimir Putin, who is the former head of the Karelia FSB, and whose relatives had served in the Soviet security services."[20] A new attack on the independence of historians took place in 2020, when during a revision of the Russian Constitution a new article was added that declared off limits a critical historical reevaluation of the role of the Soviet Union before and during the Second World War, attributing to the state the role to defend historical truth.[21] There are still local efforts and private initiatives which try to bring the truth to light despite all the hurdles put in place by the authorities.

"And yet," wrote Anne Applebaum, "in Russia, a country accustomed to grandiose war memorials and vast, solemn state funerals, these local efforts and private initiatives seem meagre, scattered and incomplete. The majority of Russians are probably not even aware of them. And no wonder: ten years after the collapse of the Soviet Union, Russia, the country that has inherited the Soviet Union's diplomatic and foreign policies, its embassies, its debts, and its seat at the United Nations, continues to act as if it has not inherited the Soviet

Union's history. Russia does not have a museum dedicated to the history of repression. Nor does Russia have a national place of mourning, a monument which officially recognizes the suffering of victims and their families.... More notable than the missing monuments, however, is the missing public awareness. Sometimes, it seems as if the enormous emotions and passions raised by the wide-ranging discussions of the Gorbachev era simply vanished, along with the Soviet Union itself. The bitter debate about justice for the victims disappeared just as abruptly. Although there was much talk about it at the end of the 1980s, the Russian government never did examine or try the perpetrators of torture or mass murder, even those who were identifiable."[22]

The reason is, she added, that "very few people in contemporary Russia feel the past to be a burden, or as an obligation, at all. The past is a bad dream to be forgotten, or a whispered rumour to be ignored. Like a great, unopened Pandora's box, it lies in wait for the next generation."[23]

"Facts are always in danger of disappearing from the world, not only temporarily, but possibly forever," wrote Hannah Arendt.[24] "Once they are lost no effort of the mind or reason can bring them back."[25] However, it is not only in Russia that there exists a tendency to promote an official historiography which is at odds with a critical exercise of this science. Recently decolonized states often feel a strong need to promote a new, "official" historiography that distances itself from that of the former colonial powers. This need is understandable. For the subjected peoples, the colonial history represents a period of exploitation and humiliation. After obtaining independence, governments can exercise pressure on their own historians, who often studied at Western universities, to create a national epic narrative. This narrative can consist of heroic rebellions against the colonial power, or—at a greater historical distance—a reference to a great and glorious pre-colonial past. According to the American sociologist Edward Shils, "The conflict between critical scientific historiography and the eagerness to confirm a newly established tradition by making it appear old, and thereby legitimating the new national state, is resolved in favor of the latter through the allegation of a fictitious 'golden age,' a time of plenitude and glory before the coming of the foreign conqueror."[26] It is clear, however, that this newly created national myth will not, in most cases, satisfy the strict criteria of an objective scientific historiography.

HOW OBJECTIVE CAN HISTORIOGRAPHY BE? HOW TO WEIGH THE DIFFERENT FACTORS?

It is necessary that the historians stick meticulously to the facts—*all* relevant facts, the pleasant as well as the unpleasant ones—and distance themselves from ideological prejudices and political interests. However, even if this is the case and historians do their research in a professional manner independently from national governments, historical narratives will still diverge. Each historian has his own perspective and interest, and these determine the choice of his subject and the way in which he conducts his research. This does not necessarily lead to narratives that contradict each other. These professional narratives may rather complement each other. One historian will analyze the economic development of an epoch, another will focus on its cultural aspects, while a third takes the political or military development as his subject. In this way we get a mosaic of narratives which partly overlap and partly complement each other. The difference between these narratives may be the relative *weight* which they ascribe to the factors they are analyzing. The ongoing debate on the origins of the Second World War is a case in point. Is the Second World War the consequence of the humiliating conditions imposed on Germany in the Treaty of Versailles? Is it the consequence of the crash of 1929? Or is it the consequence of the political polarization in Germany which led to the disappearance of the political center in the German parliament? One can find arguments for all three explanations.

What we are concerned with here is the relative *weighing* of these different factors and how the individual historian makes this weighing plausible. This weighing will also be influenced by the explicit or implicit philosophy of history of the historian. According to Heinrich Rickert (1863–1936) it is not easy

> "... to understand why one researcher treats these events in a detailed way, others only briefly and yet others [these] very

real processes not at all. The historians themselves are not always conscious of the reasons for this. They cannot be, because they often understand nothing of the logical structure
of their activity and don't believe that they work from a value
standpoint. It is even more important to lay bare their value
system and make explicit what they are reliant upon in the
formation of their material. Then it will become clear that
each historian, particularly when he doesn't restrict himself
to specialist research, in fact possesses a kind of 'philosophy
of history' which determines what he considers to be important and what to be unimportant, and it is certainly worth-
while explicitly laying bare the philosophies of history of the
great historians in particular."[27]

Historians—even those who deny it—work on the basis of an implicit or explicit philosophy of history, and Rickert rightly argues that
we should lay bare these underlying philosophies in order to understand
(and eventually criticize) their choice of certain subjects and of certain
interpretations. We may, therefore, conclude that "history as such" does-
n't exist. Rather there exists a multitude of historical narratives side by
side. These need not contradict each other but can complement each
other like the colored stones of a mosaic. What is crucial is that historians
strive for objectivity and base their research on factual data. Direct de-
pendence on national governments is anathema. In this process different
interpretations can stand side by side, dependent on a different weighing
of causal factors. "Learning lessons from history" is only possible when
we accept the existence of causal relationships. In the next chapter we
will have a closer look at how historians define these relationships.

NOTES

1   "Le discours de Dakar de Nicolas Sarkozy," *Le Monde*, November 9, 2007.
     http://www.lemonde.fr/afrique/article/2007/11/09/le-discours-de-
     dakar_976786_3212.html
2   Ibid.
3   Cf. Thomas Hoffnung, "Le jour où Sarkozy stupéfia l'Afrique," *Libération*,
     October 9, 2007.

4   Catherine Coquery-Vidrovitch, *Enjeux politiques de l'histoire coloniale* (Marseille: Agone, 2009), p. 11.

5   G. W. F. Hegel, "Vorlesungen über die Philosophie der Geschichte," op. cit., p. 129.

6   Quoted in Élisabeth Roudinesco, *Soi-même comme un roi – Essai sur les dérives identitaires,* op. cit., p. 85.

7   Cornelius Castoriadis, *Domaines de l'homme (Les carrefours du labyrinthe 2)* (Paris: Éditions du Seuil, 1986), p. 526.

8   Henri Wesseling, *Le partage de l'Afrique 1880 – 1914* (Paris: Denoël, 1996), p. 13. According to Trevor-Roper, Africa had no history, but only "the unrewarding gyrations of barbarous tribes in picturesque but irrelevant corners of the globe." (Quoted in Richard J. Evans, *In Defence of History* (London: Granta Books, 2018), p. 264.)

9   H. L. Wesseling, "Heeft Afrika een geschiedenis?" in H. L. Wesseling, *De draagbare Wesseling* (Amsterdam: Prometheus, 2002), pp. 190–91.

10   Ibid., p. 191.

11   Ibid., p. 192.

12   See "Putin Defends Ribbentrop-Molotov Pact in Press Conference with Merkel," *The Moscow Times,* May 11, 2015. https://themoscowtimes.com/news/putin-defends-ribbentrop-molotov-pact-in-press-conference-with-merkel-46441

13   See "Medvedev sozdal komissiya pri prezidente RF po protivodeystviyu popytkam falsifikatsii istorii v ushcherb interesam Rossii." *Interfaks,* May 19, 2009. http://www.interfax.ru/russia/80400

14   Marcel H. Van Herpen, *Putinism—The Slow Rise of a Radical Right Regime in Russia* (Houndmills and London: Palgrave Macmillan, 2013), p. 70.

15   Ibid., p. 71.

16   Nikita Petrov, "Don't Speak, Memory – How Russia Represses Its Past," *Foreign Affairs,* Volume 97, No. 1, January-February 2018, p. 20.

17   "Le dirigeant russe transforme l'histoire en champ de bataille," Interview of Isabelle Mandraud with Antoon De Baets, *Le Monde,* June 11, 2021.

18   "Russia: Crimes Against History," International Federation of Human Rights, June 2021, No. 770a. https://www.fidh.org/IMG/pdf/russie-_pad-uk-web.pdf

19   Ibid., p. 29.

20   Ibid.

21   "Konstitutsiya Rossiyskoy Federatsii," *Rossiyskaya Gazeta,* July 4, 2020, Art. 67-1, 3. The text of this new article reads as follows: "The Russian Federation respects the memory of the defenders of the Fatherland, [and] guarantees the defense of historical truth. The belittling of the heroic deeds of the people for the defense of the Fatherland is not allowed." https://rg.ru/2020/07/04/konstituciya-site-dok.html

22 Anne Applebaum, *Gulag—A History of the Soviet Camps* (London and New York: Allen Lane, 2003), p. 506.

23 Ibid., p. 512.

24 Hannah Arendt, "Wahrheit und Lüge in der Politik," in Hannah Arendt, *Denken ohne Geländer—Texte und Briefe* (Munich and Zurich: Piper, 2010), p. 121.

25 Ibid.

26 Edward Shils, *Tradition* (Chicago: The University of Chicago Press, 1981), p. 62.

27 Heinrich Rickert, *Die Probleme der Geschichtsphilosophie – Eine Einleitung* (Heidelberg: Carl Winters Universitätsbuchhandlung, 1924), p. 111.

CHAPTER 5

THE SEARCH FOR HISTORICAL CAUSALITIES

If one wants to learn from history, one accepts the existence of causal relationships in history. If in the past situation A has led to situation B, then it is obvious that when there is again a situation in which one recognizes elements of the former situation A, one will ask oneself whether this will lead to a situation which is more or less comparable with the former situation B. If one has experienced the former situation B as negative, voices will quickly be raised asking for the course to be corrected, in order that the supposed causality is cancelled and the development of a situation, similar to the former situation B, will be avoided.

SOCIOLOGISTS VERSUS HISTORIANS

The urge to discover causal relations is as old as historiography. Greek and Roman historians explained certain events by referring to the influence of gods and supernatural forces. The deeds of heroes and exceptional personalities were thought to have been inspired by these celestial powers. These heroes, however, were not pure instruments of these celestial powers, but were considered to possess special, innate qualities. A similar historiography, based on the deeds of extraordinary, "heroic" persons, can still be found in the work of the nineteenth-century British historian Thomas Carlyle (1795–1881), who considered history the work of Heroes (written with capital letters): these were larger-than-life personalities, like Alexander the Great and Napoleon, individuals who had a broad strategic vision and great willpower, which gave them the opportunity to leave their mark on their times.[1] The Swiss historian Jacob Burckhardt (1818–1897), who shared Carlyle's vision, wrote

"The great man is the one without whom the world would look incomplete to us because certain great deeds could only be accomplished by him in his time and environment and would otherwise be unthinkable; he is an essential element in the great stream of causes and consequences. The proverb goes: 'No man is irreplaceable.' But the few who are, are great."[2]

Great personalities have certainly left their mark on the course of history. They waged wars, expanded territories, made laws, and introduced new political systems. These great personalities, however, were and remain unique phenomena. Their advent and their actions are unpredictable and often sudden. In 1789 no one had predicted the advent and rise of Napoleon Bonaparte, possibly himself included. Although there will always be "Heroes" in the sense of Carlyle—positive, as well as negative heroes—they remain in the realm of historical incidents.

In the last hundred years in modern historiography a change has taken place. One emphasizes less the influence of personal factors and emphasizes instead the influence of *supra-personal*, structural factors. This new approach is related to the emergence of the social sciences in which social phenomena are explained by underlying trends and tendencies which are invisible to the human eye. In his essay *History and Sociology,* the American sociologist Robert A. Nisbet described how both disciplines slowly moved closer together and began to influence each other.

"Until recent years," he wrote, "the relationship between history and sociology was a distant one.... Sociologists were only too likely to regard historians as theory-dreading, fact-worshipping, data-collecting antiquarians...."[3] "For historians, on the other hand," he continued, "sociology took on more and more the character of a science of Never-Never Land, what with its bland disregard of particularity and its preoccupation with universalist schemes of development that seemingly could never be precisely located in time or space."[4]

Nisbet was right. While sociologists accused the historians of emphasizing too one-sidedly the uniqueness and singularity of historical events, historians, from their side, accused the sociologists of being too fond of discovering "general laws" and causal chains whose existence was far from certain and therefore had to be questioned. Both images were of course caricatures. However, behind these caricatural descriptions a real problem was hidden. And had the sociologists not a point? If historiography was nothing else than the description of unique, singular events, would the result not be an enumeration of sterile facts? Of course, such a collection of facts could in itself be interesting and also have its usefulness as basic material, but it lacked an important quality, namely the discovery of connections and causal relations through which a deeper understanding of the historical process becomes possible.

Historiography as a science can and may not be satisfied by only producing a chronology of facts and events. It has also the task of discovering the relationships which exist *between* these facts and events. Nisbet pointed to the fact that the mutual prejudices between historians and sociologists slowly disappeared, making place for a growing consensus and mutual recognition, which had led to an increasing cooperation with fruitful results in the field of comparative studies of uniformities. The professional historian studied the specific, historical singularity of a phenomenon, while the sociologist used his material to develop causal models with which it was possible to compare certain historical phenomena, such as feudal systems, modern state formation, revolutions, etc.

FERNAND BRAUDEL AND "LONG TERM" HISTORY

This cross-fertilization between the social and historical sciences found an eminent expression in the French *Annales* group. In 1929 a group of French historians, led by Lucien Febvre and Marc Bloch, founded the magazine *Annales d'histoire économique et sociale*. In this magazine they introduced a completely new approach. The group distanced itself from the dominant, particularly political, historiography, which was based on the comings and goings of "great personalities." They wanted to lay bare the underlying socio-economic tendencies, which as invisible undercurrents influenced the course of history. A famous representative of this group was Fernand Braudel (1902–1985). To characterize his method, he used the concept of the *longue durée* (long term), because instead of focusing on rapidly changing political situations in which events continually alternate, Braudel and his colleagues were interested in long-term developments. "The traditional historiography," he wrote, "which concentrates on the short term, the individual, the event, has accustomed us for a long time to a quick, dramatic portrayal which is short of breath."[5] However, he argued, another approach has also developed, "which treats periods of centuries: the history of the long, even of the very long period of time ('longue durée')."[6] Braudel applied this method in his *magnum opus,* a book on the historical development of the Mediterranean region. This book consists of three parts. In the first part he dealt with "the almost motionless history" of man in his relationship with his natural environment.[7] In the second part he looked at man's social history, the history of groups, which he called "a history of the slow rhythm." Finally, on top of these two layers, in the third part, comes traditional history, the history of the individual and the singular historical event. This history is for Braudel an "agitation on the surface, the waves thrown up by the tides in their powerful movement. A history with short, quick, nervous, oscillating movements."[8]

However, Braudel is mostly interested in exploring "the great underlying currents, often quiet, whose importance only becomes clear when one takes great time periods. The sensational events are often only moments, mere manifestations of these great movements and can only be explained by these."[9] Braudel's method is to explore historical material stored in libraries and archives: merchants' tables, shipping documents, baptismal registers, etc. His objective is to discover causal relations between these underlying "slow" movements and the quickly changing events on the surface. Did he succeed? He himself is positive, but he also expressed some doubts in the Foreword to the second edition. "The essential problem still remains the same," he wrote. "It is the same for each historical enterprise: is it possible to capture at the same time, in one way or another, a history which is changing quickly, [which] attracts attention precisely because of these changes and the spectacle that is accompanying it—and an underlying history which is rather silent, certainly discreet, almost unnoticed by its witnesses and actors, which maintains itself at all cost despite the continuous erosion of time?"[10] For the historian of the *Annales* group the question of causality is even more pressing than for a traditional historian. Because how can one connect the "surface history" of the political events with the slow movement, the *longue durée* of the "underlying history?"

THE SPECIFIC CHARACTER OF HISTORICAL CAUSALITY

Historical causality is a central problem with which already many historians, sociologists, and philosophers have dealt with. Against the danger that history is considered as a loose collection of unconnected facts there is an opposite danger, namely that of an arbitrarily *hineininterpretieren* (reading too much into the facts), in which historical facts are erroneously endowed with a causal relationship. How can the historian navigate between this Scylla and Charybdis? He must take some precautionary measures. In the first place he must distance himself from the model of causality used by the physical sciences and in particular of the positivist view that one may only talk about causality when one can observe a *recurring* relationship between two phenomena, as, for instance, the fact that water boils at 100 degrees Celsius.[11] Historical causality can be the case even when an event takes place only once— what is common in history. Although sometimes events seem to happen twice—as Marx famously said: first as tragedy, second as farce.[12] But even if an event will never reproduce itself in the same way, one may hold on to the existence of causal relationships.

In the second place the historian should guard against the urge to equate *post hoc* with *propter hoc:* an event which takes place *after* another event (*post hoc*), is not necessarily caused by the first (*propter hoc*). But even if the historian manages to avoid both obstacles, a new problem emerges. This is the fact that in history one can find an infinite multitude of potential causal factors. The question is, how is it possible to distill from this multitude of potential causal factors exactly those factors which have been decisive? This problem was for some historians, for instance the Italian historian Benedetto Croce, insurmountable and a reason to abandon the search for causal relations altogether. Croce asked, "what happens if one connects one fact with another as its cause and in this way constructs a chain of causes and consequences...?"[13] His conclusion was: "One falls prey to an endless regression...."[14] Other authors also have pointed to this problem. The American political scientist Francis Fukuyama calls it "the turtle problem." If one wants to explain a historical fact by another historical fact, then the problem is that this underlying fact (Fukuyama calls this "the turtle") is caused by another fact. "There is, moreover, the turtle problem," writes Fukuyama, "the turtle one chooses as an explanatory factor is always resting on another turtle farther down."[15]

This means that looking for explanatory causal factors, as Croce said, is a virtually endless process; it is a labyrinth in which one risks getting lost. Croce and Fukuyama are not the first to point to this problem. Voltaire had already written: "Let us be clear about this. Every effect obviously has its cause, which can be retraced from cause to cause into the abyss of eternity; but every cause does not have its effect to the end of time.... All things have fathers, but not all things have children."[16] This is an important observation. While in history there exists, in principle, a multitude of factors which might serve as the cause of a certain phenomenon, only a small number actually fulfill this function. It is as Voltaire said: "All things have fathers, but not all things have children." There clearly exists a hierarchy, and the task of the historian is to distill from the huge multitude of potential explanatory factors those factors which, according to him, have played a decisive role in the production of a historical fact. Croce's trepidation, recoiling from exploring causal relations, seems therefore to be unjustified. Exploring causal relations is and remains a basic feature of every science, and history should not be an exception.

THE "WEIGHING" OF CAUSAL FACTORS IS VALUE-RELATED

The historian who explores historical causalities is not a *tabula rasa,* a clean slate. Still less is he a "neutral observer"—even if he considers himself to be one. Every historian has a philosophy of history, whether he is conscious of this fact or not, and also every historian works on the basis of certain values. These values can remain implicit or made explicit by him, but finally it is his theory of history and his value system which determine his choices, and when one looks for causal factors, it is clearly a question of choice. According to Heinrich Rickert, "everyone should accept that history does not take *all* the individual [events] in its representation, but only the 'important,' 'interesting,' in short the essential."[17] But who determines what is "essential"? It is clearly the individual historian who makes this decision, even if he insists that it is not he, but "history" itself that imposes these choices. According to Rickert, one should "reject a widespread opinion as not sustainable. [Namely that something] … is historical that has or has had an effect. This [opinion] does not solve the problem, but only displaces it. Because *everything* in the world has an effect, the historian is in most effects not interested. Only 'essential' effects are represented by him."[18] Similarly, Georg Simmel (1858–1918) draws our attention to the fact that for a historian there exist "innumerable *possible* research objects, which one ignores because knowledge of them would have no value—value, which in many cases rests on another [value], but ultimately this consists of a valuation which cannot be further rationalized."[19] Facts and events, continues Simmel, "which we call 'important,' are on reflection those whose consequences are for us more visible [and] quantitatively estimable than those of 'unimportant' events."[20]

The fact that a historian is led by his own theory of history and his own values in the choice of his subject has the consequence that there are in principle many different historical narratives. A historian who considers history as a protracted process of decline will write a different history than the historian who considers history as a process of continuous progress. A third historian, who considers history as the movement of ebb and flow in which periods of progress and decline alternate, will write yet another history. In all these cases this implicit or explicit theory of history is related to values. Ultimately it is the historian's values which determine whether he considers a certain epoch as a period of progress or decline.[21]

THE VALUE RELATIVISM OF HISTORICISM: EACH EPOCH HAS ITS OWN *ZEITGEIST*

However, there are also historians who deny that the historian should judge facts from the past and historical epochs with his own value system. This theory, which was very influential in nineteenth-century Germany, was called historicism (in German, *Historismus*). According to this theory historical epochs cannot be compared. They stand completely apart and can only be understood on the basis of their own standards, because each epoch would have its own *Zeitgeist* ("spirit of the age"). This means not only that one cannot speak about progress or decline in history, but also that objective value measures are lacking with which to evaluate past epochs. Historicism—a forerunner of contemporary postmodernism—leads therefore to a complete value relativism. Making its stance against the eighteenth-century philosophy of progress, it is in fact more optimistic than this because for the latter, progress is only a perspective that realizes itself slowly in history, while for the adept of historicism all that exists and existed is per definition good. It is clear that this theory *in extremis* leads to a total nihilism: for a consequent follower of historicism, it would be impossible to evaluate and compare Roosevelt's "New Deal" with Hitler's "Third Reich." The radical historicist would insist that both would have to be understood from their own, local *Zeitgeist,* using their own values. The result would be, as the French proverb goes, *tout comprendre c'est tout pardonner* (to understand all is to forgive all). For this reason, Heinrich Rickert made a scathing judgment on historicism. He called it "rubbish" (*ein Unding*) and continued: "As a view of the world it makes the lack of principles to be its principle and should therefore be challenged fundamentally by philosophy as well as philosophy of history."[22] For the historicist, all ideas are historically determined and relative. This leads in fact to a paradox. If all ideas are related to a specific historical epoch and doomed to disappear, does this not equally apply to the ideas of historicism, which, therefore, cannot claim to be universally valid?[23]

German historicism has its roots in the *Sturm und Drang* (Storm and Stress), a literary youth movement of which Johann Wolfgang Goethe (1749–1832) and Johann Gottfried Herder (1744–1803) were the leading figures.[24] In particular Herder's book *Auch eine Philosophie der Geschichte zur Bildung der Menschheit* (Another Philosophy of History of the Formation of Mankind), published in 1774, played an important role. Criticizing the Enlightenment philosophers, Herder wrote that "each nation has the center of its happiness in itself, like each sphere its point of gravity."[25] This idea was already present five years earlier in his travel diary of 1769, in which he wrote: "The human race has reached happiness in all epochs, only in each [of them] in a different way."[26] Herder's conclusion is that one should evaluate each epoch and each nation according to the value criteria of that epoch and nation. "Clearly in this theory are contained the roots of relativism, because it supposes that knowledge content and value concepts are bound to cultural and historical entities. Such an idea could make an anarchy of values possible."[27]

It is clear that historicism as a theory is untenable. Historians make choices which are based on their philosophies of history and their value systems. Different historians can apply different criteria for what they consider progress or decline in history, and these criteria will influence the choice of the causal relationships in which they are interested. The historian must make a choice from what Friedrich Meinecke calls the "plurality of causes." "This 'plurality of causes,' which can be observed everywhere," Meinecke writes, "doesn't mean anything other than that, strictly speaking, each causal theory requires a kind of theory which first provides the criteria for what, in a particular field, can be considered a cause and what not."[28] For this reason, it is important that the historian makes his philosophy of history and value system explicit.

However, it isn't exclusively the historian's philosophy of history and value system that determines his choices. His professional background also plays a part. "For the historical science also at least a clearly defined question can offer the criteria for what causes should be considered important and what others less important. An economic historian, because of the way his profession defines a problem, will put other causes forward for the outbreak of the First World War than a political historian."[29] Each historian who is looking for causal factors consciously or unconsciously makes use of a process of *weighing*, in which he attributes more weight to some factors than to others.

An example of a different way of weighing the influence of historical factors is the divergent explanations offered by Karl Marx and Max Weber for the development of capitalist society. For Marx it is the material "production factors" which determine the ideological, spiritual "superstructure." Weber inverts the process: it is not economic development which determines the ideology, but the ideology which determines the economic development. According to him it is the "ascetic" Protestant ethic which, with its economic rationalism, made capitalism possible. Weber criticizes what he calls "naive historical materialism, that such 'ideas' emerge as 'mirroring' or 'superstructure' of economic situations," and he points to the fact that "anyway without any doubt in Benjamin Franklin's country of birth (Massachusetts) the 'capitalist spirit' (in the sense we conceive of it) was already present *before* capitalist development...."[30] Both interpretations have their own force of persuasion, because they are formulated from a clear theory and this theory determines the choices.

EXPLAINING THE PAST FROM THE PRESENT

The difference between Marx and Weber lies in the weight they attribute to individual factors. According to the sociologist Vilfredo Pareto (1848–1923), "it is the weight of the facts that is important rather than their number; one single fact that is well observed and well defined has more value than many badly observed and badly defined facts."[31] Pareto continued: "Because direct knowledge of the facts is extremely rare, interpretations are necessary."[32] This is *a fortiori* true for historical facts. Ernst Cassirer has rightly pointed out that historical facts, unlike the facts of the physical sciences, cannot be observed directly. "But what is a historical fact?" he asks. "All factual truth implies theoretical truth. When we speak of facts, we do not simply refer to our immediate sense data. We are thinking of empirical, that is to say objective, facts. This objectivity is not given; it always implies an act and a complicated process of judgment."[33] There exists, moreover, a fundamental difference between the physical facts of the natural sciences and historical facts:

> "If a physicist is in doubt about the results of an experiment
> he can repeat and correct it. He finds his objects present at

every moment, ready to answer his questions. But with the historian the case is different. His facts belong to the past, and the past is gone forever. We cannot reconstruct it; we cannot waken it to a new life in a mere physical, objective sense. All we can do is to 'remember' it—give it a new ideal existence. Ideal reconstruction, not empirical observation, is the first step in historical knowledge. What we call a scientific fact is always the answer to a scientific question which we have formulated beforehand."[34]

The theories and interpretations which determine the individual historian's questions are the product of his own time and his own world, because "generally the unknown has to be explained from the known, and therefore the past is explained from the present rather than the present from the past, as from the beginnings of sociology most did and many are still doing."[35] Pareto emphasized that the past has to be explained from the present and not the other way around. In this he seems to be agreeing with Marx, who had already written: "The anatomy of man is the key to the anatomy of the monkey."[36]

This means that the evaluation of earlier epochs takes place from the present, and that the central thesis of historicism—that the key to understanding each epoch has to be sought in the *Zeitgeist* of that epoch—has to be rejected. The crucial role of historiography is not only analyzing and evaluating the past, but also understanding better one's own epoch. This is also emphasized by Karl Mannheim.

"As a matter of fact," he wrote, "no one has as yet really understood the present from the past who did not approach the past with the will to understand the present. The normal process is as follows: we comprehend past situations by means of analogous or contradictory forms which occur in our own contemporary world. This sense of actuality (in the best meaning of the word) which views life *in actu* and thereby gives actuality to the past, remains the *nervus rerum* of all historical and social knowledge."[37]

In the same vein Ernst Troeltsch (1865–1923) wrote: "Thus the understanding of the present is always the final goal of all history."[38] "Subjects which do not admit of such a relation to the present belong to the antiquarian...."[39] The historian stands with both feet on the ground of the present and analyzes and interprets the past from the present. Looking for causal relations, he applies a process of weighing, based on his philosophy of history, his value system, and his professional specialization. However, escaping from the present is not possible—even if he would wish so. The search for causal relations seeks to serve the understanding of the contemporary world in which the historian is living and working. E. H. Carr spoke in this context of the "dual and reciprocal function of history—to promote our understanding of the past in the light of the present and of the present in the light of the past."[40] The most important function, however, is to promote our understanding of the present in the light of the past. Because it is here that we can learn lessons from history, and the exploration of causal chains is therefore a challenging task for the historian.

NOTES

1   Thomas Carlyle developed these ideas in a series of lectures, delivered in London in 1840. This series was published in 1841 with the title *On Heroes, Hero-Worship, & the Heroic in History—Six Lectures* (London: James Fraser, 1841). The publication immediately became a bestseller. In these lectures he talked about not only statesmen, but also gods, prophets, poets, priests, and authors, although he attributed to statesmen a special place. The statesman (he did not mention women) was according to him "the Commander over Men, he to whose will our wills are to be subordinated, and loyally surrender themselves, and find their welfare in doing so, may be reckoned the most important of Great Men." (p. 316).

2   Jacob Burckhardt, "Das Individuum und das Allgemeine (Die historische Grösse)," in Jacob Burckhardt, *Weltgeschichtliche Betrachtungen* (Tübingen: Otto Reichl Verlag, 1949), p. 257.

3   Robert A. Nisbet, "History and Sociology," in Robert A. Nisbet, *Tradition and Revolt—Historical and Sociological Essays* (New York: Vintage Books, 1970), p. 91.

4   Ibid., p. 93.

5   Fernand Braudel, "Geschichte und Sozialwissenschaften—Die 'longue

durée'," in Hans-Ulrich Wehler (ed.), *Geschichte und Soziologie* (Cologne: Kiepenheuer & Witsch, 1976), p. 191.

6   Ibid.

7   The Dutch historian Henri Wesseling explains Braudel's interest in the *longue durée* by Braudel's childhood environment. "His preference for the almost immobile history of the long term…," he writes, "can be explained by his childhood in the French countryside. In the first decades of the twentieth century life there was not much different from that of hundred or even thousand years ago…." (H. L. Wesseling, "Fernand Braudel, historicus van de lange duur," in H. L. Wesseling, *Vele ideeën over Frankrijk—Opstellen over geschiedenis en cultuur* (Amsterdam: Uitgeverij Bert Bakker, 1988), pp. 294–95).

8   Fernand Braudel, *La Méditerranée et le monde méditerranéen à l'époque de Philippe II* (Paris: Armand Colin, 1979), Préface, p. 13.

9   Ibid., p. 14.

10   Ibid., p. 17.

11   On the difference between causality in the physical sciences and historical causality, see also Rolf Gruner, "Über einige Probleme der historischen Kausalrelation," in *Archiv für Philosophie,* Volume 10/1-2, Stuttgart 1960, pp. 107–13.

12   These were the words with which Marx characterized the coup d'état in 1851 in France, staged by Louis Napoléon Bonaparte, Napoleon's nephew, imitating his uncle's coup d'état of 1799. Cf. Karl Marx, "Der 18. Brumaire des Louis Bonaparte," in Karl Marx and Friedrich Engels, *Marx Engels Werke,* Volume 8 (Berlin: Dietz Verlag, 1960), p. 115.

13   Benedetto Croce, *Zur Theorie und Geschichte der Historiographie* (Tübingen: J. C. B. Mohr, 1915), p. 53.

14   Ibid.

15   Francis Fukuyama, *The Origins of Political Order—From Prehuman Times to the French Revolution* (London: Profile Books, 2012), p. 438.

16   Voltaire, "Chaîne des événements: Chain of events," in Voltaire, *Philosophical Diary,* edited and translated by Theodore Besterman (London and New York: Penguin, 2004), p. 111.

17   Heinrich Rickert, *Die Probleme der Geschichtsphilosophie – Eine Einführung,* op. cit., p. 59.

18   Ibid.

19   Georg Simmel, *Die Probleme der Geschichtsphilosophie—Eine erkenntnistheoretische Studie* (Leipzig: Verlag Duncker & Humblot, 1902), p. 126.

20   Ibid., p. 131.

21   These values need not *per se* be humanistic or democratic. A fascist historian can consider the modern epoch as a period of decline because in his view the "superior" white race will be replaced by "inferior races."

22 Heinrich Rickert, *Die Probleme der Geschichtsphilosophie,* op. cit., p. 130.

23 Cf. Leo Strauss, "Natural Right and the Historical Approach," in *The Review of Politics,* Volume XII, 1950, pp. 434–35: "Historicism asserts that all human thoughts or beliefs are historical, and hence deservedly destined to perish; but historicism itself is a human thought; hence historicism can only be of temporary validity, or it cannot be simply true ... As a matter of fact, historicism claims to have brought to light a truth which has come to stay, a truth valid for all thought, for all time.... Historicism thrives on the fact that it inconsistently exempts itself from its own verdict about all human thought."

24 Cf. Marcel Van Herpen, "Rousseau en de 'Sturm und Drang'—De vroegste receptie van Rousseau's cultuurkritiek in Duitsland," (Rousseau and the 'Storm and Stress'—The earliest reception of Rousseau's critique of culture in Germany), *De Gids,* 142, 1979, pp. 230–37. https://www.dbnl.org/tekst/_gid001197901_01/_gid001197901_01_0027.php

25 Johann Gottfried Herder, *Auch eine Philosophie der Geschichte zur Bildung der Menschheit,* with an afterword by H. G. Gadamer (Frankfurt am Main: Suhrkamp Verlag, 1967), pp. 44–45.

26 Johann Gottfried Herder, *Journal meiner Reise im Jahr 1769* (Stuttgart: Reclam, 1976), p. 30.

27 Georg G. Iggers, *Deutsche Geschichtswissenschaft—Eine Kritik der traditionellen Geschichtsauffassung von Herder bis zur Gegenwart* (Munich: Deutscher Taschenbuch Verlag, 1971), p. 53.

28 Friedrich Meinecke, "Über einige Probleme der historischen Kausalrelation," op. cit., pp. 111–12.

29 Ibid., p. 112.

30 Max Weber, "Die protestantische Ethik und der 'Geist' des Kapitalismus," in Max Weber, *Schriften—1894–1922,* selected by Dirk Kaesler (Stuttgart: Alfred Kröner Verlag, 2002), p. 166.

31 Vilfredo Pareto, *Trattato di sociologia generale,* First Volume (Milano: Edizioni di Comunità, 1981), § 538, p. 325: "Conta più il peso dei fatti che il loro numero; un solo fatto bene osservato e ben descritto ne vale moltissimi male osservati e male descritti."

32 Ibid., § 546, p. 335: "Appunto perché la conoscenza diretta dei fatti è molto rara, le interpretazioni sono indispensabili...."

33 Ernst Cassirer, *An Essay on Man—An Introduction to a Philosophy of Human Culture* (New Haven and London: Yale University Press, 1968), p. 174.

34 Ibid.

35 Vilfredo Pareto, *Trattato di sociologia generale,* op. cit., § 548, p. 336: "In generale l'ignoto si deve spiegare col noto, e perciò il passato si spiega col

presente, meglio che il presente col passato, como hanno fatto i più, al principio della Sociologia, e molti seguitano pure a fare."

36 Karl Marx, "Grundrisse. Einleitung zur Kritik der politischen Ökonomie," *Marx Engels Werke,* Volume 13, (Berlin: Dietz Verlag, 1974), p. 636.

37 Karl Mannheim, *Man and Society in an Age of Reconstruction—Studies in Modern Social Structure* (London and Henley: Routledge & Kegan Paul, 1980), pp. 188–89.

38 Ernst Troeltsch, *Protestantism and Progress—A Historical Study of the Relation of Protestantism to the Modern World* (Boston: Beacon Press, 1958), p. 3.

39 Ibid., p. 2.

40 E. H. Carr, *What is History?* With a new introduction by Richard J. Evans (Houndmills, Basingstoke: Palgrave Macmillan, 2001), pp. 101–02.

CHAPTER 6
CAN ONE LEARN LESSONS
FROM HISTORY? THREE CASES

If one wants to take responsibility for the present generation, it is necessary that one learns the lessons from history to avoid pitfalls and to emulate promising models. Can one learn lessons from history? We have seen that over the years historians, philosophers, and sociologists have given different answers to this question. Hegel did not believe that history contained lessons for posterity, but other thinkers were less apodictical and did not exclude this *in principle*. In fact, it is dependent on a series of conditions.

1   The first, and most important, of these is that one considers history as an *open* process in which nothing is preordained.
2   Historiography, as a science that describes, orders, and analyzes historical facts and processes, should strive for the maximum possible truth and objectivity. This presupposes that it has to be free from government influence.
3   One should not consider history as a collection of unique, unrelated facts, without any coherence.
4   One accepts the existence of historical causalities.
5   These causalities have not the same importance. They have different weights. The historian explores those causalities which have the greatest heuristic value—based on his philosophy of history, his value system, and his professional interest.
6   Exploring and discovering causalities is not exclusively the work of professional historians. Sociologists and other social scientists can also make major contributions. The different professions can complement each other. Historians will be more interested in the unicity

of a historical phenomenon; sociologists and political scientists will rather be interested in recurring patterns and historical parallels. The latter are important if one wants "to learn from history."

One should note that the need to learn from history will not be the same in all historical periods. In a society in which everything goes smoothly, a society in which one is living in peace, which is prosperous, and where this prosperity is equally shared, a society in which a climate of optimism reigns and one is looking with confidence to the future, the need to learn "lessons" from the past will be felt in a lesser degree. However, this will be different when a society is in crisis and optimism gives way to pessimism and fear of the future. At such moments the past, which shortly before was still in a state of *benign neglect* and as a study object left to the professional historians, suddenly attracts broad attention again for two reasons. First, in such a crisis situation there emerges a tendency to idealize the past and to present it as a "golden age." Second, there is another, opposite tendency, namely, to analyze crisis periods in the past to see how our ancestors reacted to these. In the latter case the question is: do there exist parallels with the present situation? And if so, what kind of parallels? This is the point at which one starts looking for eventual "lessons": situations and strategies which must be avoided, or creative solutions which one could possibly imitate or improve on. Examples of such crisis situations are revolutions, wars, and pandemics. These offer, therefore, excellent examples to explore in the present context. In this chapter we will have first a look at the phenomenon of revolution. Did revolutions lead to the study of historical parallels? And if so, did one learn lessons from it? We will take a closer look at the different peace settlements after the First and Second World War, and see how the first functioned as a lesson for the second.

DO PARALLELS BETWEEN REVOLUTIONS EXIST?

Revolutions occurred in different periods. Although there were already political upheavals in ancient Athens as well as in ancient Rome, these rebellions must be distinguished from modern revolutions. While in Antiquity popular upheavals were a question of political power struggles, in modern revolutions much more is at stake; often the revolutionaries intend to make a fundamental break with the past and create a completely new civilization. The French Revolution is a case in point. The revolutionaries even tried to "reorder time": they abolished the Christian calendar and introduced a new one, which started on September 22, 1793 (the "Year I"), the day on which the First Republic was proclaimed. The new calendar was coupled with a rigorous introduction of decimalization—another invention of the revolution. Months consisted of three decades and a week had ten days. One year later the system was further refined: now the days too were decimalized, consisting of ten hours each. Each hour consisted of hundred minutes and each minute of hundred seconds. The months got equally new names. These were derived from nature, such as Brumaire (the "fog month"), Nivôse (the "snow month"), Pluviôse (the "rain month"), or Ventôse (the "wind month"). The French revolutionaries didn't strive for a change only of political power: they wanted a complete reordering of society. The will to bring about a complete break with the past is characteristic of modern revolutions.

> "As a general characteristic one could say that 'revolution' is a new beginning, [which is] coupled with the most fundamental break with the past: break with its political and juridical order as political revolution, break with the spiritual matters and value systems as spiritual and cultural revolution, revolution of the worldview, of science and other aspects of culture."[1]

This new character of the revolution is related to the advent of a new, modern view of the world. History is no longer conceived as a cyclical process, as in Antiquity, or as a Christian history of salvation in which everything happens according to a pre-established divine plan. This modern view of the world "presupposes not only knowledge about the possibility of changing the world, but also an evaluation of the new and revolutionizing which earlier epochs as such didn't know ..."[2] Modern revolutionaries don't want to accept the world as they have found it. For them the world becomes a "project" in the literal sense of the word: a projection into the future of the ideal society they dream of. They want not only to interpret the world, but—as Marx famously formulated in his eleventh Thesis on Feuerbach—also to change it, and they had complete confidence that they were up to the task.

For this reason, modern revolutions are radical and fundamental events. They are most of the time not only political, but also social earthquakes, and the aftershocks can often still be felt many decades later. They determine the character of their time and also have major geopolitical consequences. Even generations later they can lead to emotional debates between proponents and adversaries. Seismologists can calculate the risk of an earthquake taking place, but they cannot exactly predict the moment. The same is true for revolutions. Like earthquakes, revolutions erupt spontaneously, often on the occasion of an unexpected and unforeseen minor event. Another aspect is that revolutions influence each other. The French revolutionaries of 1789 were inspired by the success of the American Revolution. Marx, in his turn, considered the French Revolution as a model for the proletarian revolution he wished to bring about. The French July Revolution of 1830 led to revolutions in Belgium and Poland, while the French February Revolution of 1848 was followed by a whole series of what Heinrich Winkler would call *Folgerevolutionen* (follow-up revolutions), "which, taken together, formed one overarching revolution—the first and last 'great European revolution....'"[3]

CRANE BRINTON AND THE ANATOMY OF REVOLUTION

Does there exist, between these different revolutions, similarities that are more specific than the simple fact of a change in power? This is a question which many historians, sociologists, and political analysts have dealt with. One of them is the American historian Crane Brinton who, in his book *The Anatomy of Revolution* (1938), compares four revolutions: the revolution of Cromwell in seventeenth-century England, the American Revolution, the French Revolution, and the Russian October Revolution. Brinton rejects the idea that each revolution is unique and that for this reason revolutions could not be compared with each other. "Most of us," he writes, "would assume that on the rough level of common sense some kind of uniformities can be discerned in history. But at least among many professional historians there is a tendency to deny that these uniformities are real and important...."[4] Brinton disagrees fundamentally with this position, and writes that "the doctrine of the absolute uniqueness of events in history seems nonsense."[5] In his book he tries to refute the skeptics.

His method is to divide the revolutionary process into different phases which these revolutions could be seen to share. All revolutions are preceded by growing dissatisfaction amongst the population, which expresses its dissatisfaction increasingly loudly. The eruption of the crisis happens with one or more events, which later become mythical moments in the collective memory. In France this was the occupation of the Bastille on July 14, 1789. In the Russian October Revolution, it was the storming of the Czar's Winter Palace on October 25, 1917. If the revolution is to be successful, then a conflict will ensue between moderate and extremist revolutionaries. Because the latter are more disciplined and better organized, they are, most of the time, able to seize power. This leads to a period in which the extremists rule. The extremists are ascetic ideologues, who are prepared to do anything to realize their ideal. Their fanaticism leads to a period of terror in which real and supposed enemies of the revolution are eliminated. This period of terror can be observed in three of the four revolutions analyzed by Brinton (the American Revolution is an exception).[6] Robespierre, the leader of the French Terror period, who with few qualms sent his adversaries to the guillotine, "had convinced himself that his enemies were scarcely men at all...."[7] The period of terror, however, comes to an end and is followed by a phase of *convalescence*. In France the beginning of this phase can be identified precisely. It is the day of Robespierre's fall: July 27, 1794— or the 9th Thermidor of the year II of the new revolutionary calendar. "Thermidor" has become the general name of the phase in the revolutionary process in which the terror period comes to an end and society enters a calmer period.[8] However, this does not mean that this leads to the introduction of a functioning democracy. On the contrary. "Politically, the most striking uniformity to be noted in the period of convalescence is the ultimate establishment of a 'tyrant' in something like the old Greek sense of the word, an unconstitutional ruler brought to power by revolution. This uniformity has been frequently noted: Cromwell,

Bonaparte, Stalin, all seem to confirm it."[9] This process is logical, continues Brinton, because "after a revolution has undergone the crisis and the accompanying centralization of power, some strong leader must handle that centralized power when the mad religious energy of the crisis period has burned itself out. Dictatorships and revolutions are inevitably closely associated...."[10]

Does this mean that revolutions are *per se* negative events? No, because revolutions also bring important achievements. One of these achievements is the centralization of state power, mentioned above, which leads to an increased government efficiency.

> "This achievement of governmental efficiency is really the most striking uniformity we can note in estimating the political changes effected by our revolutions. With suitable allowances for local differences, for accidents, and for the inevitable residue of the unique with which all history and sociology must deal, England, America, and Russia also emerged from their revolutions with more efficient and more centralized governments."[11]

Although these achievements may be recognized and valued by later generations, they may not be directly obvious to contemporaries for whom the revolution often stands for a period of blind violence and a bloody reign of terror.

CASE #1: KLEMENS VON METTERNICH AND THE FRENCH REVOLUTION

In the nineteenth century, the French Revolution became the single most important historical event from which one could and should learn lessons. What those lessons were depended on the worldview (and often also the class position) of the person who tried to learn them. Conservatives considered this revolution as the work of the devil. They pointed to the chaos, the terror, the dictatorship, and the revolutionary wars which led to Napoleon's imperialistic military campaigns. Joseph de Maistre (1753–1821), for instance, spoke in his book *Considerations on*

France (1797) about "an entirely criminal revolution."[12] According to him, "never has the Divinity revealed itself so clearly in any human event. If it employs the most vile instruments, it is to regenerate by punishment."[13] For the conservative monarchist De Maistre, the French Revolution was a punishment imposed by God. Liberals, on the other hand, although they condemned the excesses of the revolution, supported its ideals, such as the equality of all citizens, universal human rights, democracy, republicanism, popular sovereignty, the end of censorship, and the abolition of slavery. However, it was not the liberals, but mainly conservative monarchists who, in 1815 at the Congress of Vienna, built a new international order which was intended to "learn the lesson from the French Revolution" and avoid a repetition of these events in France and Europe.

The great architect of this new European order was Prince Klemens von Metternich (1773– 1859), Minister of Foreign Affairs and later Chancellor of the Hapsburg Empire. In his memoirs he described how, as a young man, he reacted to the revolution: "The French Revolution was beginning. From that moment I was its close observer, and subsequently became its adversary; and so I have ever remained, without having been once drawn into its whirlpool."[14] And he continued: "I felt that the Revolution would be the adversary I should have to fight, and therefore I set myself to study the enemy and know my way about this camp."[15] At school he was supported in this by his history teacher Nicolas Vogt, about whom he writes: "Often have I recalled the saying with which he concluded a discussion between us on the subject of historical criticism: 'Your intellect and your heart are on the right road; persevere therein also in practical life, the lessons of History will guide you.'" [16]

His teacher encouraged him to let himself be guided by the lessons of history. Metternich took this advice to heart. He considered it his life's mission to fight revolutions and to build an international order which was not based on the egoistic imperialism of one country, but on the shared values and interests of the community of nations. During the Congress of Vienna in 1815 he was the most important architect of this new international order. The new European equilibrium was based on two alliances: the Quadruple Alliance of England, Prussia, Austria, and Russia, and the Holy Alliance of Prussia, Austria, and Russia. While the first had the task of maintaining geopolitical stability, the second was founded to maintain the internal stability within the countries.

> "For Metternich, the ultimate cause of war was revolution, and in a convoluted set of mental gymnastics he was able to convince himself, the Tsar, and others that any revolution, anywhere in Europe, was a threat to the 1814–1815 settlements. The task of the governors [the great powers, MHVH], therefore, was to root out revolutionary conspiracies and to intervene—collectively, if possible, but unilaterally if necessary—to quell any disturbances."[17]

The Holy Alliance could rightly be called an "antirevolutionary" alliance. Its goal was to defend the internal (conservative) status quo and the *droit divin* of the monarchs in the participating countries and the rest of Europe against the democratic demands of the liberals. Henry Kissinger, a great admirer of Metternich, praised him for his organization of this "European Concert."[18] "After the Congress of Vienna," he wrote, "Europe experienced the longest period of peace it had ever known. No war at all took place among the Great Powers for forty years, and after the Crimean War of 1854, no general war for another sixty."[19] As one of the reasons for this success, Kissinger mentions the newly created balance of power in Europe. "But the most important reason," he continues, "was that the Continental countries were knit together by a sense of shared values."[20] These "shared values" were the "lessons" Metternich and his colleagues had learned from the French Revolution, and these lessons were that revolutionary movements everywhere in Europe had to be nipped in the bud and that defeated France had to be treated with due consideration and respect. Henry Kissinger was not the only one who gave a positive assessment of Metternich's policy. Other historians wrote approvingly:

> "As major international settlements go, that of Vienna was a good one, in many respects more successful than its two predecessors—Westphalia (1648) and Utrecht (1713)—and the Versailles settlement of 1919–1920. There was to be no war involving

several powers until the rather second-rate Crimean conflict of the 1850s, and no major war embroiling the whole of Europe until a century after 1815. Seldom have victors treated a defeated aggressor with the wisdom and generosity displayed in 1815."[21]

CASE #2: WHAT LESSONS DID THE LIBERALS LEARN?

But apart from the conservatives there was another, second group, which had learned its own "lessons" from the French Revolution: the liberals who wanted to realize the democratic and republican ideals of the Revolution while avoiding its excesses. Particularly in France the influence of this group remained strong—even after the Restoration of 1814. The dissatisfaction of the liberals grew when King Charles X, who came to the throne in 1824 after the death of his brother Louis XVIII, implemented increasingly authoritarian policies, neglecting the will of the parliamentary majority. This led in July 1830 to a new revolution. During the *Trois glorieuses*—the "three glorious days" from July 27 through 29—bloody fights took place on the barricades. The town hall, Notre Dame, and the Louvre were occupied, while soldiers of the Paris garrison defected to the rebels. The king abdicated and a moderate liberal government was formed, which was immediately confronted with radical demands to abolish the monarchy and proclaim a republic. The question was whether the revolutionary dynamic, mentioned by Brinton, would repeat itself. Would the extremists take over the power of the moderates? However, the revolutionary government had clearly learned its lesson. "The moderates around Thiers wanted to avoid at any cost a radicalization of the revolution as was the case after 1789 and, therefore, arranged the immediate enthronement of the Duke of Orléans."[22] François Guizot (1787–1874), who became Minister of Education in the new government and would later become Prime Minister, had first-hand knowledge of the Terror period. As a six-year-old boy he had lost his father, who was beheaded in Nîmes. The moderates, wanting to avoid a radicalization of the revolution, chose a change of dynasty to take the wind out of the sails of the radicals. The new monarch, Louis Philippe, Duke of Orléans, was a smart choice: having fought in 1792 in the revolutionary armies he was also acceptable to the radicals. This change of dynasty, although it proved to be a clever move, was not sufficient to completely quell revolutionary Jacobinism. "The Jacobin episode manifests itself again in the years 1831–1834...."[23] "The four years which follow the July days are characterized by street fights and sporadic riots which were suppressed by the army...."[24]

Despite this resistance the moderate French liberals succeeded in avoiding a radicalization. They seemed to have learned their lesson. The same is true in the Netherlands for the Dutch King William II (1792–1849). When, in February 1848 a revolution again broke out in Paris, he was confronted with the demands of the liberal opposition in parliament which wanted the introduction of a parliamentary democracy. William II had personally experienced the consequences of revolutions. He had participated in the Battle of Waterloo on June 18, 1815, during which he was wounded in the shoulder and had distinguished himself by his courage.[25] Some years later, in 1818, at the age of 26, he appealed to European monarchs in an essay, titled *Essai sur le siècle, dans lequel je vis* (Essay on the century in which I live), to allow more freedom in order to avoid a *bouleversement* (revolution).[26] He would himself soon be confronted by a revolution when his father, King William I, sent him to the Southern Netherlands (today's Belgium) as commander of the Dutch army to quell the Belgian revolution. Despite the military successes during the Ten Days' Campaign (August 2–12, 1831), the Dutch government had no choice other than to consent to Belgian independence, which was supported by the great powers. Even in 1839, one year before he ascended the throne, William II did not hide his liberal sympathies. "He had sympathy for liberalism. As vice chairman of the Council of the State he proposed with others in 1839 to introduce ministerial responsibility. That did not then happen."[27] However, after having become king in 1840 he became more conservative. In 1848, nevertheless, the alarm bells were ringing. This time the French revolutionaries had succeeded in abolishing the monarchy and introducing a republic. "William II, who in recent years had adopted a more authoritarian position, feared that the Netherlands, too, might soon be engulfed in revolution. He thus transformed himself from a 'conservative to a liberal in one night,' as William himself described it."[28] William II, who feared a revolution, avoided a conflict with the liberal opposition by giving in to their demands and agreeing to a change in the constitution, which would make the government accountable to parliament. Thomas Beaufils calls William II therefore a "pragmatic and prudent monarch, with a very sensitive ear for the shock waves of History."[29] That William II had "a very sensitive ear for the shock waves of History" could be stated differently: namely that William II had clearly learned his lessons from history. The same European wave of revolutions which would transform him overnight from a conservative into a liberal, put an end to the career of Metternich who, as a consequence of the revolution, had to resign.

Metternich and Willem II are two personalities, both in essence conservative, but with different characters and different careers, who learned—each in his own way—his "lesson" from history. Which of the two was right? And who was the most successful? This is difficult to say, because—at a certain moment of history—both were right and both, each in his own way, were successful. Henry Kissinger is right that Metternich's "Concert of Europe" was a great diplomatic achievement. And it is completely understandable that Metternich wanted to introduce that system after Napoleon's defeat and the excesses of the French Revolution. However, Metternich had not understood that the French Revolution was not only characterized by the violence of its Terror period or Napoleon's imperialist wars. He was blind to the universal message of the French Revolution, its message of freedom and equality. He simply did not *want* to understand this message. He opted for a purely repressive policy against liberal and nationalist movements, and in the long term this policy was not sustainable because it went against the spirit of its time. William II, who in 1830–1831 had still hoped (in vain) that the Holy Alliance would intervene and help the Dutch government to suppress the Belgian Revolution, had in 1848 understood that repressive policies no longer worked. William's "liberal conversion" fitted within a historical trend and helped the Netherlands to avoid a deep political crisis.

CASE # 3: GERMANY'S REINTEGRATION INTO THE INTERNATIONAL COMMUNITY AFTER 1945

It is particularly in dramatic situations that lessons can be learned. Another example is what happened in the aftermath of the First World War, when

Germany had to recognize full liability in the "war guilt" clause of the Treaty of Versailles. The allied countries imposed huge reparations on Germany. "Though the Germans accepted the treaty in the formal sense of agreeing to sign it, none of them took the signature seriously. The treaty seemed to them wicked, unfair, dictation, a slave treaty. All Germans intended to repudiate the treaty at some time in the future, if it did not first fall to pieces of its own absurdity."[30] The payment of the reparations became a permanent bone of contention between Germany and the allied countries. It was one of the drivers of a renewed animosity, which two decades later led to the Second World War. The historian A. J. P. Taylor observed that "there was no such reconciliation as there had been after the Great War a century previously, when the Allies made out that they had been fighting only Napoleon, not France."[31] It was thanks to Metternich's prudent and conciliatory diplomacy that after the Napoleonic wars France was accepted as a full-fledged partner in the "Concert of Nations." However, after the First World War Germany became an international outcast, which entered into a secret military cooperation with another international outcast, the Soviet Union.[32] One century after the Congress of Vienna, the lessons of Metternich's diplomacy seemed to be forgotten—due to a short historical memory. George Kennan, former U. S. Ambassador to the Soviet Union, asked therefore "whether World War II was not perhaps implicit in the outcome of World War I," adding that this didn't mean "absolving the Western statesmen of the twenties and thirties of all responsibility for the second war and to regarding them exclusively as the actors in a tragedy beyond their making or repair."[33] And he continued: "Over the long term (and two decades is a respectable length of time) there are always some choices at their disposal. I think it fair to say that World War I ... significantly narrowed the choices of Western statesmen in the postwar period; but it did not eliminate those choices entirely."[34] What were these choices? "First, we could have tried to give greater understanding, support and encouragement to the moderate forces in the Weimar Republic. And if that did not succeed in preventing the rise of naziism (sic), then we could have taken a stiffer and more resolute attitude against Hitler's earlier encroachments and provocations."[35]

When the allied countries won the Second World War, they did not repeat the mistakes made after the First World War. This time they had learned their lesson: Germany was accepted as a full partner in the newly established European and transatlantic structures, such as the European Coal and Steel Community (the forerunner of the European Union),[36] and NATO. George Kennan, who was closely involved in the negotiations about the post-World War II order, wrote in his memoirs:

> "Was European unification really necessary for economic reasons as a precondition for European recovery, as had been commonly supposed in Washington? The answer was generally "No".... But unification *was* needed to provide a framework in which the German problem could find a satisfactory solution ... the idea of a renewed fragmentation of Germany was unrealistic; to leave Germany to continue to realize her national ideals and aspirations within the sovereign-national framework would almost inevitably lead to a repetition of the general sequence of developments that had followed the Versailles settlement; only some sort of European federation could provide for Germany a place in the European community that would be comfortable and safe for everyone concerned."[37]

The integration of Germany into the new European and transatlantic order was a great success—and could be compared with the integration of post-Napoleonic France into Metternich's Concert of Nations. Apparently, sometimes lessons *can* be learned and *are* learned. However, we should remain aware that "learning lessons from history" is not an easy task. It is, therefore, good to take Reinhart Koselleck's warning to heart, who wrote: "Who wants to learn lessons from the history of Prussia, would be wise to remember the old dictum: You can prove anything from history. *Historia docet:* there are as many histories as there are interests. Or, formulated differently: one finds what one is looking for. It is obvious that a lesson one is looking for quickly influences the interpretation of the supposedly real history, or is distorting it. Who wants to learn lessons from history, quickly falls into the trap of a history colored by wishful thinking, which interprets the supposed reality with indignation or approval."[38] There exists still another trap: that is that one can *unlearn* the lessons from history, as we will see in the next chapter.

NOTES

1   Karl Griewank, *Der neuzeitliche Revolutionsbegriff—Entstehung und Geschichte* (Frankfurt am Main: Suhrkamp Verlag, 1973), p. 20.

2   Ibid., p. 22.

3   Heinrich August Winkler, *Geschichte des Westens—Von den Anfängen in der Antike bis zum 20. Jahrhundert* (Munich: C. H. Beck, 2010), p. 570.

4   Crane Brinton, *The Anatomy of Revolution* (New York: Vintage Books, 1965), pp. 18–19.

5   Ibid., p. 19.

6   The American Revolution was, unlike the other three, a territorial-national revolution. It lacked the characteristic of being a religiously tainted civil war shared by the three other revolutions, which there led to terror.

7   Crane Brinton, *The Anatomy of Revolution* (New York: Vintage Books, 1965), op. cit., p. 158.

8   Ibid., p. 207.

9   This doesn't mean that there is always only one terror period in a revolution. Brinton gives the example of the October Revolution which led first to the "Red Terror" of "War Communism" (1918–1921), and later to Stalin's terrorism (in the period 1936–1939). (See Crane Brinton, op. cit., p. 189.)

10 Ibid., p. 208.

11 Ibid., pp. 239–40.

12 Joseph de Maistre, "Considerations on France," in Joseph de Maistre, *The Works of Joseph de Maistre,* with a new foreword by Robert Nisbet (New York: Schocken Books, 1971), p. 49.

13 Ibid., p. 50.

14 Klemens von Metternich, *Memoirs of Prince Metternich 1773–1815,* Book I. Materials for the History of my Public Life 1773–1815, edited by Prince Richard Metternich (New York: Charles Scribner's Sons, 1880), p. 5. Digitalized text available at https://babel.hathitrust.org/cgi/pt?id=coo1.ark:/13960/t9183wc1n;view=1up;seq=49

15 Ibid., p. 10.

16 Ibid., p. 11.

17 K. J. Holsti, "Governance without Government: Polyarchy in Nineteenth-Century European International Politics," in James N. Rosenau and Ernst-Otto Czempiel (eds.), *Governance without Government: Order and Change in World Politics* (Cambridge and New York: Cambridge University Press, 1998), p. 37.

18 To Henry Kissinger has been ascribed the ambition to follow in Metternich's footsteps. On this ambition wrote Peter Berger: "All too often he has been compared to Metternich. Whatever may be the usefulness of this

comparison, it is important to remember that Metternich was eminently *successful.* The design of international order he created at the Congress of Vienna lasted for almost exactly one century—which, in terms of human history, must be reckoned as almost incredible success. Kissinger's restless efforts to keep together the disintegrating fabric of an international order in which American power is a key element seem unlikely to achieve comparable success." (Peter L. Berger, "The Greening of American Foreign Policy," in Peter L. Berger, *Facing Up to Modernity—Excursions in Society, Politics, and Religion* (Harmondsworth and New York: Penguin Books, 1979), p. 139.)

19 Henry Kissinger, *Diplomacy* (New York and London: Simon & Schuster, 1994), p. 79. Elsewhere Kissinger wrote: "For Metternich, the national interest of Austria was a metaphor for the overall interest of Europe—how to hold together many races and peoples and languages in a structure once respectful of diversity and of a common heritage, faith, and custom. In that perspective, Austria's historic role was to vindicate the pluralism and, hence, the peace of Europe." (Henry Kissinger, *World Order—Reflections on the Character of Nations and the Course of History* (London and New York: Penguin, 2014), p. 75.)

20 Henry Kissinger, *Diplomacy,* op. cit., p. 79.

21 Crane Brinton, John B. Christopher, and Robert Lee Wolff, *A History of Civilization—1715 to the Present* (Englewood Cliffs, New Jersey: Prentice-Hall, 1971), p. 719. Karl Polanyi wrote in the same vein: "The nineteenth century produced a phenomenon unheard of in the annals of Western civilization, namely, a hundred years' peace—1815–1914. Apart from the Crimean War—a more or less colonial event—England, France, Prussia, Austria, Italy, and Russia were engaged in war among each other for altogether only eighteen months. A computation of comparable figures for the two preceding centuries gives an average of sixty to seventy years of major wars in each. But even the fiercest of nineteenth century conflagrations, the Franco-Prussian War of 1870–1871, ended after less than a year's duration.... This triumph of pragmatic pacifism was certainly not the result of an absence of grave causes for conflict." (Karl Polanyi, *The Great Transformation—The Political and Economic Origins of Our Time,* with an Introduction by R. M. MacIver (Boston: Beacon Press, 1957), p. 5.)

22 Heinrich August Winkler, *Geschichte des Westens—Von den Anfängen in der Antike bis zum 20. Jahrhundert,* op. cit., p. 511.

23 François Furet, *La Révolution en débat* (Paris: Gallimard, 1999), p. 38.

24 Ibid., pp. 37–38.

25 See J. C. H. Blom and E. Lamberts, *History of the Low Countries* (New York and Oxford: Berghahn Books, 2006), p. 307.

26 Cf. Joris Abeling, *Teloorgang en wederopstanding van de Nederlandse monarchie (1848–1898)* (Amsterdam: Prometheus, 1996), p. 18.
27 Geertje Dekkers, "Koning Willem II voelde zich niet thuis in Nederland," *Historisch Nieuwsblad,* 4/2012. https://www.historischnieuwsblad.nl/nl/artikel/28788/koning-willem-ii-voelde-zich-niet-thuis-in-nederland.html
28 J. C. H. Blom and E. Lamberts, *History of the Low Countries,* op. cit., p. 400.
29 Thomas Beaufils, *Histoire des Pays-Bas – Des origines à nos jours* (Paris: Éditions Tallandier, 2018), p. 213.
30 A. J. P. Taylor, *The First World War* (London and New York: Penguin Books, 1966), p. 270.
31 Ibid., p. 264.
32 On this secret military cooperation between Germany and the Soviet Union, see Condoleezza Rice, "The Making of Soviet Strategy," in Peter Paret (ed.), *Makers of Modern Strategy—From Machiavelli to the Nuclear Age* (Princeton, N.J.: Princeton University Press, 1986), p. 666: "This marriage of convenience existed since the Treaty of Rapallo in 1922. The Germans needed a place to rearm out of view of the signatories to the Treaty of Versailles and the Soviets needed foreign military assistance. The collaboration helped the Soviets through joint production of military equipment and through German instructors sent to the Soviet Union who taught tactics and training."
33 George F. Kennan, *American Diplomacy 1900–1950* (Chicago: The University of Chicago Press, 1951), p. 69.
34 Ibid.
35 Ibid., pp. 69–70.
36 However, we should not forget that the European Coal and Steel Community, the forerunner of the present EU, had a double function: integrating Germany in a new, peaceful, international post-war structure, as well as placing its coal and steel production—the basis of a war industry—under a supranational authority.
37 George F. Kennan, *Memoirs 1925–1950* (New York: Pantheon Books, 1967), p. 452.
38 Reinhart Koselleck, "Lernen aus der Geschichte Preußens," in Reinhart Koselleck, *Vom Sinn und Unsinn der Geschichte – Aufsätze und Vorträge aus vier Jahrzehnten"* (Berlin: Suhrkamp Verlag, 2014), p. 152.

CHAPTER 7

OUR SHORT HISTORICAL MEMORY: THE THREE-GENERATION TRAP

In the same way that one can learn lessons from history, one can also *unlearn* lessons, when some generations later not only the causes of conflicts and historical dramas are forgotten or neglected, but even the reasons why some institutions were built. This same process seemed to be happening when the Trump administration attacked the European and transatlantic structures the US and its allies had put in place after the Second World War, and which had preserved peace for about seventy years. "If one were devising a formula to drive Europe and Germany back to some new version of their past, one could hardly do a better job than what U.S. President Donald Trump is doing now," wrote Robert Kagan. "Overtly hostile to the EU, the Trump administration is encouraging the renationalization of Europe...."[1] A lack of a sense of history, as well as an apparently deficient knowledge of history, are impediments to learning lessons from history. But this is not the only example. One can also observe an *unwillingness* to learn lessons as, for instance, is the case in Putin's Russia, where Stalin has been rehabilitated and statues are erected in his honor, notwithstanding the fact that his regime was characterized by mass murder and genocide. According to estimates, "the Soviets committed a democide of almost 62 million people, over 7 million of them foreigners. This staggering total is beyond belief."[2] The Russian government has never opened a serious investigation into Stalin's crimes, and it was therefore no surprise that it followed in his footsteps when it started wars of aggression against Georgia and Ukraine. The same is true of China, where the portrait of Mao is still on the banknotes despite his murderous legacy.

LEARNING LESSONS FROM HISTORY: BUT HOW?

What can we conclude from this? We may conclude that, indeed, we can sometimes learn lessons from history. These lessons concern particularly dramatic events, such as revolutions, wars, and crises, which have a deep impact on contemporaries. However, that said, we must add a number of qualifications. In the first place is there the fact that these "lessons" will not be the same for everyone. We saw that Metternich and King William II, although living in the same epoch, learned different lessons from the revolutions of their time.

Second, there is the question of the *effectiveness* of the lessons. When political leaders learn lessons, the impact will be greater than when it is the average citizen who learns his lesson—although we should not forget that in a democratic society politicians need the support of the electorate to realize their goals. But even the effectiveness of political leaders who learn "lessons" will often be limited. Was Metternich successful in his efforts to avoid a repetition of the French Revolution? Not completely, because in 1830 a new revolution broke out in France, and it was thanks to, among others, the moderate liberals that the extremists were unable to seize power. There is no doubt that the wave of European revolutions of 1848 which would finally put an end to his political career was experienced by Metternich as a personal defeat. However, although liberals did not like him, Metternich deserves praise for having played a major role in organizing an international system which could guarantee peace and stability on the European continent for about one century after the upheavals of the Napoleonic period. William II, on the other hand, who decided in 1848 to give in to liberal demands, equally deserves praise. Dutch history books agree that his reign was an important step in the development of a parliamentary democracy in the Netherlands.

Third, we should also take into account that there can exist an overt or covert *unwillingness* to learn lessons—even if there exists a possibility. This is, for instance, the case when a government neglects the crimes of its predecessors. Post-communist Russia is a case in point. It has never come to terms with the purges and crimes of Stalin's regime, implicitly delivering the message that in Russia the powerful are never held accountable for their crimes and that history can repeat itself.[3] The French sociologist Maurice Halbwachs (1877--945) has pointed to the fact that not only politicians tend to forget and neglect unpleasant events of the past, but that this unwillingness to confront the past is also present in the general population:

> "Today people are concerned about the immediate or far away future," wrote Halbwachs. "We may anticipate much good luck, but also much bad luck from the future: both the good luck and the bad luck are undefined. People from the past ... may have once expressed good or bad intentions in relation to us, but now we expect nothing from them: they evoke in us neither uncertainty, rivalry, nor envy. We cannot love them nor can we detest them. In short, the most painful aspects of yesterday's society are forgotten because constraints are felt only so long as they are effective and because, by definition, a past constraint has ceased to be effective."[4]

THE ROLE OF GENERATIONS AND THE IMPORTANCE OF "VISCERAL EXPERIENCE"

There is still another factor which we should take into account. This is the fact that most people have a relatively *short historical memory*. This is not only true for their personal memory, but also for their collective memory. This short memory is a result of what I would like to call "the three-generation trap." Historical events—even dramatic historical events—have a tendency to fade away in the collective memory. Generally speaking, this collective memory will remain vivid for no longer than three generations: these include the generation which experienced the events, the generation of their children, and—in a lesser extent—the generation of their grandchildren. Paul Ricoeur spoke in this context about the necessity of

> "... widening the circle of close relations by opening it in the direction of a past, which, even while belonging to those of our elders who are still living, places us in communication with the experiences of a generation other than our own. The

notion of generation that is the key here offers the twofold sense of contemporaneousness of the 'same' generation to which belong beings of different ages, and the succession of generations, in the sense of the replacement of one generation by another."[5]

Different generations live for some time together. During this period the first generation transmits its experience directly to the second generation, which is raised and educated with the stories and narratives of their parents. The third generation of the grandchildren will still be exposed to the narratives of their parents and grandparents, so that this transmission will continue. The generation of the grandchildren is often interested in experiences of their grandparents which their parents would rather like to forget.[6] But in the fourth generation this vivid memory will begin to fade away and definitively become "history"—which means that events no longer have an impact on our lives here and now. It is a common experience that as soon as the last witnesses have disappeared, the ebb and flow of time takes over with the emergence of new imperatives, and the idea emerges "that these things are no longer possible today." The traces of historical dramas tend to be slowly washed away and with it the need to learn lessons. In the best case, dramatic events of the past will become an occasion for official commemorations. This "short-termism" does not only take the form of historical amnesia, but it can also equally take the form of a neglect of the future. According to two German authors, such a neglect would be a characteristic of individualistic cultures. They write that "due to the dominance of individualistic views and experiences, the future horizons of people living in individualistic cultures are more or less restricted to the life span of individuals. These life spans extend to only a bit more than a few years or, at best, decades. Wider horizons are only opening if there are supra-individual perspectives, for instance by taking into consideration the life chances of future generations or of the population as a whole."[7]

It is not difficult to find examples of this "short-termism" and collective amnesia. When in 2020 the world was suddenly confronted with the global Covid-19 pandemic, the first reaction was one of disbelief. How could this happen in the modern world? One had completely

forgotten that only one century earlier—the lifetime of *four* generations—an estimated twenty to fifty million people had died in the Spanish flu pandemic. While every year all over the world "Great War"
commemorations are taking place, the 1918 flu, which had a death toll
of more than twice that of the Great War, had apparently faded in our
collective memory. One can clearly trace this amnesia, for instance, in
a book on globalization published in 1999. In this book the authors present a schedule for "key global flows and networks" in four historical periods, respectively the pre-modern, early modern, modern, and
contemporary eras. As one of these global flows they mention "plagues
and pandemics" for the premodern era and "epidemiological flows" for
the early modern era.[8] Then it stops: pandemics and epidemics are no
longer mentioned for both the modern and contemporary era as if, by a
sudden miracle, pandemics would have completely disappeared from
the surface of the earth—despite the global Spanish flu pandemic of
1918–1920. One should also not forget that the Spanish flu was only the
latest global pandemic. In the first half of the nineteenth century there
were two deadly cholera pandemics which both originated in British
India. The first cholera pandemic lasted seven years, from 1817 to 1824,
and the second eleven years, from 1826 to 1837. They were followed
by more waves later in the century. According to Charles Rosenberg,
"Cholera was the classic epidemic disease of the nineteenth century, as
plague had been of the fourteenth."[9] While the first cholera pandemic
reached the coast of the Mediterranean before receding, the second
cholera pandemic spread further around the globe, hitting the heartlands
of Europe and the United States.

> "Russian troops carried the disease into Poland in the winter
> of 1831. By June of that year, it had arrived in Hungary, Aus-
> tria, and Germany. By April of 1832, cholera reached Paris.
> The approach of the cholera pandemic toward Europe in the
> early 1830s was greeted with extraordinary public anxiety,
> dread, and concern in all the major cities."[10]

In Britain, in 1831 and 1832, 32,000 people died of this disease.[11]
People died everywhere, and famous people didn't escape. It is telling

that the German philosopher Hegel is thought to have died from cholera in November 1831. In 1832 there were in the city of Paris alone 19,000 victims.[12] The total number for (metropolitan) France was 100,000.[13] To put these numbers in perspective: in 1832 the population of France was only a bit more than 32 million, which is about one-half of today's population.[14] The pandemic also arrived in North America, where "New York was probably the most thoroughly scourged among the states."[15] As regards pandemics, the modern world seemed to be subject to a disturbing memory loss and collective amnesia—at least until the recent Covid-19 pandemic served as a rude wake-up call. The result was a massive, worldwide unpreparedness when the Covid-19 pandemic broke out. No lessons had been learned, apart from some Asian countries which in recent years had already been confronted with pandemics.

Another example? Take the war of aggression against Ukraine started by Putin's regime on February 24, 2022. People were shocked. "They didn't expect this to happen." Why not? There had already been writing on the wall, such as the 2008 war against Georgia and the invasion of Ukraine in 2014 which led to the annexation of the Crimea. Even these flagrant violations of international law were soon forgotten and became part of the "new normal." French President Emmanuel Macron criticized NATO, the backbone of the Western security system, calling it "brain dead." War on the European continent, so went the prevailing opinion, had become "unthinkable." Unthinkable? The wars in the former Yugoslavia ended in 2001. This was just twenty years ago, the lifetime of *one* generation!

Another example of the "three-generation trap" is the vanishing nuclear taboo.

> "Part of the issue," wrote *The Economist,* "may simply be one of time and forgetting. Save for Queen Elizabeth II … there is no one anywhere near the corridors of power who remembers, as an adult, hearing the news from Hiroshima and Nagasaki. All but the most precocious of the children who picked up on their parents' dread at the time of the Cuban missile crisis are in their late 60s. The Cold War shadows in which the nuclear taboo grew up, which only started to

disperse after Reagan and Mikhail Gorbachev agreed that 'a nuclear war cannot be won and must never be fought,' have been gone for 30 years."[16]

It is this relatively short historical memory which is one of the reasons why history repeats itself. Of course, education and the media can play an important role in keeping these memories alive,[17] but nothing is more effective than the visceral experience of contemporaries which is transmitted to their offspring. It is with these qualifications in mind that we can answer the question: "Can we learn from history?" in the affirmative. History is not an autonomous process which takes place above our heads; it consists of a multitude of cumulative human choices. These choices lead to positive or negative results (or mixed forms of both). One can therefore agree with Reinhart Koselleck, who wrote that one cannot expect a direct application of the lessons of the past. "However," he continued, "for this reason one should not neglect the lessons from our past. There exists a knowledge which can be based scientifically on how one ruined opportunities in the past or seized [these] and used them to our advantage."[18]

NOTES

1   Robert Kagan, "The New German Question—What Happens When Europe Comes Apart?" *Foreign Affairs*, Volume 98, No. 3, May/June 2019, p. 119.
2   R. J. Rummel, *Death by Government* (New Brunswick and London: Transaction Publishers, 2004), p. 81.
3   "Every spring," writes Nikita Petrov, "buses covered in portraits of Joseph Stalin appear on the streets of Russian cities.... With each passing year, the dictator gets more handsome and more glamorous." "The resurgence in public appreciation for the Soviet regime became possible in large part because Russia has never put its communist past on trial.... More than six decades since Stalin's death, there has been no official reckoning with this lawlessness." (Nikita Petrov, "Don't Speak, Memory—How Russia Represses Its Past," *Foreign Affairs*, Volume 97, No. 1, January/February 2018.)
4   Maurice Halbwachs, *On Collective Memory,* Edited, Translated, and with an Introduction by Lewis A. Coser (Chicago and London: The University of Chicago Press, 1992), p. 51.

5   Paul Ricoeur, *Memory, History, Forgetting* (Chicago: The University of Chicago Press, 2006), pp. 394–95.

6   Aarons and Berger write, for instance, that "Post-Holocaust generations are mostly guided by stories told by parents and grandparents, cautionary talks with which they might navigate an historically detailed, emotionally explosive past." (Victoria Aarons and Alan L. Berger, *Third-Generation Holocaust Representation: Trauma, History, and Memory* (Evanston, Ill., Northwestern University Press, 2017), p. 22.) The Dutch author Natascha van Weezel, who is a representative of this third generation, described in her book *De derde generatie—Kleinkinderen van de Holocaust* (The Third Generation—Grandchildren of the Holocaust) (Amsterdam: Uitgeverij Balans, 2015), the visceral feeling, experienced by victims of the Holocaust and the next generations. She cites her father, the journalist Max van Weezel, a representative of the second generation, who remarks: "If it had happened differently and one of my parents had been rounded up, I simply would not have been born." (p. 138) He added: "I grew up with: now it is sunny, but when is the storm coming? You are always worried about the future, your whole life." (p. 147)

7   Meinhard Miegel and Stefanie Wahl, *Das Ende des Individualismus—Die Kultur des Westens zerstört sich selbst* (Munich and Landsberg am Lech: Verlag Bonn Aktuell, 1993), p. 65.

8   David Held, Anthony McGrew, David Goldblatt, and Jonathan Perraton, *Global Transformations— Politics, Economics and Culture* (Stanford, Cal.: Stanford University Press, 1999), p. 432.

9   Charles Rosenberg, *The Cholera Years: The United States in 1832, 1849, and 1866* (Chicago and London: The University of Chicago Press, 1987), p. 1.

10   G. William Beardslee, "The 1832 Cholera Epidemic in New York State—19th Century Responses to *Cholerae Vibrio* (Part 1)," *The Early America Review,* 3 (2), 2000. Available at https://www.varsitytutors.com/earlyamerica/early-america-review/volume-4/the-1832-cholera-epidemic

11   "Cholera in Sunderland," *UK Parliament* (no date). https://www.parliament.uk/about/living-heritage/transformingsociety/towncountry/towns/tyne-and-wear-case-study/introduction/cholera-in-sunderland/

12   Molly Guinness, "The deadly epidemic that helped shape today's Paris," *RFI,* November 18, 2010. https://www.rfi.fr/en/visiting-france/20101118-1832-epidemic-helped-shape-todays-paris

13   Maurice Samuels, "Conspiracy Theories, Class Tension, Political Intrigue: Lessons From France's Mishandling of a 19th Century Cholera Outbreak," *Time,* May 15, 2020. https://time.com/5837393/paris-cholera-lessons/

14   "Mouvement de la population de la France depuis 1800 jusqu'en 1869," *Journal de la Société Statistique de Paris,* Volume 12-13 (1871–1872), pp. 221–24. http://www.numdam.org/article/JSFS_1871-1872__12-13__221_0.pdf

15 Charles Rosenberg, *The Cholera Years: The United States in 1832, 1849, and 1866,* op. cit., p. 36.

16 "Thinking the unthinkable," *The Economist,* June 4–10, 2022.

17 An interesting educational approach is the project "Open History" ("Offene Geschichte"), developed by the German Federal Center for Political Education (Bundeszentrale für politische Bildung), in which high school students are confronted with information on major historical crisis situations, such as the Crusades, the Black Death, the end of World War II, Chernobyl, etc. They are then asked to write a paper—not with the aim of finding some unique "historical truth," but trying to answer questions such as: "How did it happen?" "How did people react to the crisis?" "What resources were available?" "What had changed?" The initiators of the project stress that they are working with open historical situations. (See Rainer Lupschina, Mia Schepe, Theresa Kühnert, "Von der Geschichte für die Zukunft lernen," *Bundeszentrale für politische Bildung,* June 20, 2022. https://www.bpb.de/lernen/digitale-bildung/werkstatt/509423/von-der-geschichte-fuer-die-zukunft-lernen/?pk_campaign=nl2022-06-22&pk_kwd=509423).

18 Reinhart Koselleck, "Lernen aus der Geschichte Preußens," in Reinhart Koselleck, *Vom Sinn und Unsinn der Geschichte,* op. cit., p. 173.

PART III

HOW OUR VISION OF THE FUTURE
INFLUENCES OUR SENSE OF
RESPONSIBILITY FOR
FUTURE GENERATIONS

CHAPTER 8

THE OPTIMISM OF THE ENLIGHTENMENT PHILOSOPHERS

Our responsibility for future generations—generations which will live hundreds and even thousands of years from now—is a rather new phenomenon. It is a product of the technological progress mankind has made in the last century and the growing awareness that this technological progress can have major long-term consequences. Another factor which enabled this new responsibility was the emergence of a new philosophy of history. Existing philosophies of history were mainly of two types: the first characterized by an unlimited historical optimism, the second by an equally unlimited pessimism. Both philosophies of history were one-sided and conveyed the idea of helplessness in the face of fate, the idea of being at the mercy of quasi-autonomous "historical forces" which have their own dynamic. In this part we will have a closer look at these theories and see how they were replaced by a more realistic assessment of positive and negative tendencies in history and man's role in it. It was this new, realistic assessment which made this new responsibility for future generations possible.

LINEAR PHILOSOPHIES OF PROGRESS: TURGOT, CONDORCET, AND CONSTANT

An example of a philosophy of unlimited optimism is the eighteenth-century Enlightenment's philosophy of linear progress, in which the world is supposedly making its way to an ever greater perfection. A representative of this concept is the French philosopher Anne Robert Turgot (1727–1781). In a speech at the Sorbonne in Paris, he looked to the future and developed a bold perspective. In the future, he told his audience, one can expect a reversion to neither barbarism nor stagnation, but continuous progress which, as such, is unstoppable, because mankind possessed unlimited possibility for perfecting himself. "Once in quiet times, then in turbulent times, now in prosperity, then in adversity, the total mass of the human race is continually making progress, although slowly, toward a greater perfection."[1] Turgot didn't know periods of regression. According to him progress is unstoppable: it occurs always and everywhere, and therefore will continue into the future, which still bears great promise in her womb. Turgot didn't think that there are limits to man's capacity to become more perfect. Even man's irrationality could, in his opinion, be overcome in principle. Therefore, not only progress in the arts and the sciences, but also a moral progress could be expected. At the end of his speech Turgot expressed the hope "that the people continue to take steps forward in the development of the truth! Even more, that they can continue to become better and happier!"[2] In fact, this is for him not a wish, but a forecast for the future in which he himself has no doubt.

Turgot's optimism was shared by his younger contemporary Nicolas de Condorcet (1743–1794), whom Turgot had befriended. Like Turgot, Condorcet had an indestructible faith in the power of man's reason. This faith was so great that it survived even the darkest period of the French Revolution, when the guillotines were working day and night and the Jacobin Terror was claiming thousands of victims. It is telling that at the very moment that he had to hide to save his life, Condorcet wrote from his hideout his *Sketch of a historical table of the progress of the human mind,* a work in which he wanted to show

"... that nature has placed no limits on the perfection of human capabilities; that the possibilities for man to become more perfect are unlimited: that progress of this possibility for self perfection, independently of the will of those who would want to stop it, has no other limit than the lifetime of the globe on which nature has placed us. Of course this process of progress can go quickly or less quickly, but it must be continuous and never go backward as long as the earth maintains its place in the system of the universe and the general laws of this system don't cause a general revolution, nor changes which would no longer permit the human race to keep and deploy the same powers and to find the same resources."[3]

Humanity, making continuous scientific, technical, and economic progress, will amass ever more knowledge, extend its control over nature, and enjoy greater prosperity. Like Turgot, Condorcet does not limit progress to these fields. According to him, mankind will also perfect itself politically and morally. There will come a point, he predicts, "at which the sun on earth will shine only over free peoples who have no other master than their reason; at which the tyrants and the slaves, the priests and their foolish or hyprocrite instruments will exist only in history books or on the stage."[4] War also will become a rare phenomenon, because "the most enlightened peoples ... will slowly learn to consider war as ... the greatest of all crimes."[5] He predicts also that "all causes which ... perpetuate national feelings of hatred will slowly disappear."[6] Condorcet was confident in forecasting this moral progress with certainty, because "people cannot acquire knowledge ... as concerns moral principles ... without making progress also in practical morals...."[7] All this shows clearly, according to him, "that we are approaching the epoch of one of the great revolutions of the human species," and "the present situation of enlightenment guarantees that it will be happy."[8] Condorcet not only expected of the future further developments in science, technology, and the economy, but also the realization of the ideals of the Enlightenment, such as freedom, equality, and brotherhood. Convinced of the power of reason, he predicted that these ideals will be realized with an immanent necessity. Man can only hasten this process or slow it down, but he cannot change it: *nolens volens* humanity is heading towards a future epoch of peace, freedom, happiness, and harmony.

A third author who thought along the lines of Turgot and Condorcet is Benjamin Constant (1767–1830). He formulated as his goal "to investigate whether there exists in man a tendency to perfect himself, what is the cause of this tendency, what is its nature, if it has limits or if it is unlimited, [and] finally what obstacles slow down the effects or thwart them."[9] He answered the first question in the positive because, he wrote,

"Man has obtained more instruments to work on the objects outside him and to subject them to his will than was the case earlier on."[10] "Those who don't recognize this march forward," he continued, "suppose that mankind is condemned to move continuously in a circle, and, in an eternal alternation, always from ignorance to enlightenment and from enlightenment to ignorance, from a primitive situation to civilization and from civilization to a primitive situation again."[11] Constant's belief in human progress was solid as a rock. Therefore, he concluded: "It is certain that the majority of mankind through regular and continuous progress is making gains daily in happiness and especially in enlightenment. It is constantly moving forward with a quicker or slower pace. When it seems to be going backwards for a while it is for the immediate removal of the powerless obstacle which it will soon overcome."[12]

Philosophies of progress remained popular in the second half of the nineteenth century. In his novel *Les Misérables* Victor Hugo presents it as follows: "Progress is the way of life of man. Man's life in general is called Progress; the collective step of mankind is called progress. Progress marches; it makes man's great journey on earth towards heaven and the gods."[13]

Philosophies of progress were not restricted to France. The German philosopher Johann Gottlieb Fichte (1762–1814) was no less convinced that history had a systematic, immanent development and that mankind was necessarily moving forward to an ever greater perfection.

> "The life of the human race does not depend on blind fate,"
> he wrote, "neither does it, as superficial people often remark,
> remain everywhere the same, so that it always has been as it
> is now, and always will remain so: but it goes hand in hand
> with and moves forward according to a fixed plan, that nec-
> essarily *has* to be reached, and therefore *will* be reached."[14]

However, not all Enlightenment philosophers were adepts of this philosophy of linear progress. An exception, for instance, was Voltaire. "Voltaire was too intelligent to exaggerate the idea of progress. He believed in moderate progress, which was interrupted by periods of decline and is subjected to chance as long as reason did not rule completely.

Through this sober view he distinguished himself from Condorcet and his enthusiast expectations; it distinguishes him also from the Christian hope of a final salvation."[15]

DIALECTICAL PHILOSOPHIES OF PROGRESS: HEGEL AND MARX

For the philosophers of progress, one doesn't need to worry about the fate of future generations, because they are supposed to be better off than those that live before them. A similar idea can be found in the representatives of a dialectical philosophy of history. However, these don't describe history as a process of linear progression, but as one which not only contains periods of crisis, but even *needs* these crises to be able to further develop itself. History is presented as a sequence of periods that negate each other. After a positive epoch there would follow a negative epoch and after that negative epoch there follows—on a higher level—again a positive epoch, etc. The German philosopher Hegel is the most well-known exponent of this theory. Different from most French Enlightenment philosophers, Hegel gave the historical process a metaphysical foundation. Through this metaphysical foundation the historical process became a fortress of security, because it was *a priori* certain that history would move in a positive direction. The final subject of history was no longer fallible man, but infallible god (whom Hegel transformed into an abstract spiritual principle, called *Geist* or *Vernunft*). The omnipotence of this *Geist* (Spirit) guaranteed that it would reach its goal, while its unlimited goodness guaranteed that this goal was a positive goal. Hegel's dialectical philosophy of history was a stroke of genius, because it made it possible to integrate effortless contemporary crisis phenomena into a philosophy of progress. If the positive outcome of history was certain, then crisis phenomena also would finally serve this positive goal. It was only because of our poor knowledge that it was impossible for us to understand why Providence deemed these crises necessary.

Before Hegel, a similar idea was already present in the German writer and philosopher Gotthold Ephraim Lessing (1729–1781). In his book *Die Erziehung des Menschengeschlechts* (The Education of the Human Race) he exclaimed:

"Go ahead imperceptibly, eternal Providence! But let me not lose my faith in you because of this imperceptibility. Let me not lose all faith in you, even when your steps seem to me to be going backward! It is not true that the shortest line is always the best."[16]

For Lessing, just as for Hegel, history was part of a metaphysical development, according to the adage "Man proposes, God disposes." Hegel considered history as the movement of a "divine Spirit" which used the human passions to realize his plan. Human history consisted of "an endless mass of volitions, interests, and acts" and these, he said, "are the instruments and means of the *Weltgeist* [World Spirit] to reach his goal."[17]

Karl Marx (1818–1883) adopted not only Hegel's dialectic, but also the historical determinism of his master. However, in his case it was not the divine Spirit, but the dynamic of economic development which would determine, with iron necessity, the course of history. This development happened, equally, through a process of dialectical negation: feudalism was negated by capitalism, and capitalism would be negated by the future communist society. If one agrees with Marx that "the historical movement can only go in one direction, namely that of communism,"[18] then there is no place to worry about the fate of future generations. They are lucky generations who will have the privilege of living in a communist paradise. Marx's historical determinism became a kind of religious belief in the former Soviet Union. In 1976, in a period in which one already had severe doubts about the sustainability of the communist economy, a Russian historian could still write that "the historical experience of the twentieth century has irrefutably shown that the major social meaning of the epoch is defined by the transition from a capitalist to a socialist mode of production." [19]

NOTES

1   Turgot, "Tableau philosophique des progrès successifs de l'esprit humain," in *Œuvres*, Tome I (Paris: Éditions Schelle, 1913), Reprint, Glashütter im Taunus, 1972, pp. 215–16.

2   Ibid., p. 235.
3   Condorcet, *Esquisse d'un tableau historique des progrès de l'esprit humain* (Paris: Éditions sociales, 1971), p. 77.
4   Ibid., p. 259.
5   Ibid., p. 275.
6   Ibid., p. 276.
7   Ibid., p. 273.
8   Ibid., p. 86.
9   Benjamin Constant, "De la perfectibilité de l'espèce humaine," in Benjamin Constant, *Écrits politiques* (Paris: Éditions Gallimard, 1997), p. 702.
10 Ibid., p. 711.
11 Ibid., pp. 711–12.
12 Ibid., pp. 715–16.
13 Quoted in Pierre-André Taguieff, *Du progrès* (Paris: Librio, 2001), p. 7.
14 Johann Gottlieb Fichte, *Die Grundzüge des gegenwärtigen Zeitalters* (Hamburg: Felix Meiner Verlag, 1956), p. 20. (Emphasis in original, MHVH.)
15 Karl Löwith, *Weltgeschichte und Heilsgeschehen—Die theologischen Voraussetzungen der Geschichtsphilosophie* (Stuttgart/Berlin: Kohlhammer Verlag, 1967), p. 105. According to Friedrich Meinecke, "Voltaire was not capable of the full optimism and belief in the future of the later philosophers of Enlightenment, because he was still influenced by the end of the 17th century, [and] its sober sense of reality." (Friedrich Meinecke, *Die Entstehung des Historismus* (Munich: R. Oldenbourg Verlag, 1965), p. 98.)
16 Gotthold Lessing, "Die Erziehung des Menschengeschlechts," in *Lessings Werke,* edited by G. Witkowski, Volume 7 (Leipzig and Vienna: Meyers Klassiker Ausgaben, no year), p. 449.
17 G. W. F. Hegel, "Vorlesungen über die Philosophie der Geschichte," *Werke,* Volume 12, op. cit., p. 40.
18 Marcel Van Herpen, *Marx en de mensenrechten—Politiek en ethiek van Rousseau tot Marx* (Weesp: Het Wereldvenster, 1983), p. 125.
19 L. V. Skvortsov, *Istoriya i Anti-Istoriya – K kritike metodologii burzhuaznoy filosofii istorii* (Moscow: Politizdat, 1976), p. 122.

CHAPTER 9

PROPHETS OF DOOM:
FRIEDRICH NIETZSCHE
AND OSWALD SPENGLER

A quite different category of philosophers is the "philosophers of doom." Different from the philosophers of progress, they view history as a process of decline. At first sight this could make them more concerned about the fate of future generations. However, this hardly seems to be the case. A representative of this category is Oswald Spengler (1880–1936), who, in 1918, had great success with his book *Der Untergang des Abendlandes* (The Decline of the West). The book was written before the First World War but published only after the war. It immediately became a national bestseller in the defeated and humiliated post-war Germany where pessimistic feelings prevailed. His book fit the national mood extremely well. As becomes clear from the title of the book, Spengler did not share the optimism of his predecessors. On the contrary, he rejected the idea that one could observe in history a linear development toward an ever greater perfection. Instead, he developed a cyclical model that was inspired by organic nature. Like living creatures which were born, grew up, and finally died, history consisted of different cultures which, according to him, in a cycle of about one thousand years had a similar development of rise, prosperity, and decline. Spengler distinguished eight cultures, of which seven would have completed this cycle.[1] The last remaining culture was the *Abendländische,* the Western culture. This culture, which had emerged around the year 900, would, according to him, have reached the final phase of its decline around the year 1900.

Like the philosophers of progress, Spengler had no doubts about the *necessary* character of his philosophy of history. This becomes clear in the opening sentence of the Introduction to his book, where he writes: "In this book for the first time an attempt is made to predict history. It is about following the fate of a culture, the only one which finds itself today on our planet in the phase of completion, namely the West Euro-pean-American, in its as yet unfinished stages."[2] Spengler believed he had found the philosopher's stone and was able to forecast the future with his theory of the different stages. Is it possible, he asked, "to dis-cover the stages which must be gone through and in a sequence which doesn't admit any exceptions? Do the basic concepts of all organic life: birth, youth, old age, lifespan, have a strict meaning in this field that no one yet has discovered? In short, are there general biographic prototypes which are the basis of all historical events?"[3] His answer to these ques-tions was an unambiguous: yes.

Spengler claimed to have discovered the general laws of history which described the organic cycle of rise, prosperity, and decline. Be-cause the heyday of Western culture had peaked, he could find signs of decline everywhere: in decadent Western democracy, in women's eman-cipation, in the growing irreligiosity, or in the decline in fertility. How-ever, Spengler's theory of history was less univocal than the title of his book suggested, because the decline of old civilizations was accompa-nied by the emergence of new ones. Spengler considered, for instance, the First World War as a war between the old, declining Western powers and the newcomer Germany, in which he did not hesitate to compare this war with the Punic Wars between Rome and Carthage (264–146 BCE), in which he attributed the role of Rome to Germany and the role of Carthage to Britain.[4] For Spengler, Britain was an empire in decline and he was therefore heavily disappointed with Germany's defeat in World War I. Spengler was a reactionary antidemocrat, who abhorred the young democracy of the Weimar Republic.[5] He was convinced of his prophetic powers and had no self-doubt. "I can see further than all others," he wrote.[6] And, indeed, one should admit that he wasn't wrong when he wrote, "We possibly are already standing close to the Second World War...."[7]

THE INFLUENCE OF NIETZSCHE'S
THEORY OF "ETERNAL RETURN"

Spengler's philosophy of history was inspired by the ideas of Friedrich Nietzsche (1844–1900). Nietzsche criticized "historical man" who, like the philosophers of the Enlightenment, had put all his hope in the future.

> "We want to call them historical men," he wrote, "looking to the past encourages them on the way to the future, spurs on their courage to endure life even longer, stimulates the hope that good things are yet to come, that happiness lies beyond the mountain towards which they are heading.... They don't realize how unhistorically they are thinking and acting, despite all their history...."[8]

Elsewhere he wrote that "a happy era is not possible because people only want it as a wish, but they don't want it as a reality.... It is man's fate to experience *happy moments*—each life has these—but not happy eras."[9] Nietzsche compared "historical man" with "superhistorical man, who does not see salvation in the historical process, for whom, rather, the world is at any moment ready and has reached its end."[10] And he exclaimed: "What can ten new years teach us that we couldn't learn in the last ten years!"[11] For Spengler as for Nietzsche, history is not a future-oriented process, but a cyclical repetition in which nothing fundamentally new happens. Nietzsche developed this theory later in his book *Also sprach Zarathustra* (Thus Spoke Zarathustra). He called Zarathustra, the hero of this book, the *Lehrer der ewigen Wiederkunft* (The Teacher of the Eternal Return).[12] "Everything is going, everything is returning," he wrote, "the wheel of existence is eternally rolling. Everything dies, everything flourishes, the year of being is eternally moving. Everything breaks, everything is put back together, the same house of being is eternally under construction."[13] Nietzsche's cyclical philosophy of history was influenced by the models of classical Antiquity as, for instance, the Roman poet Horace (65–8 BCE), who wrote: *Multa renascentur quae iam cecidere, cadentque quae nunc sunt in honore....* (Many things that fell will be born again, and will fall that are honored now....)[14]

Nietzsche's and Spengler's theories were based on speculation rather than on serious historical research. Thomas Mann spoke about Spengler's "death prophecies" and explained: "When I perceived that the hand this man reached out towards the yearnings and wishes of the human being was actually just the old, natural Satanic claw, then I averted my own face from so much inhuman hate and put the book out of my sight, lest I find myself admiring so harmful and deadly a work."[15] Walter Laqueur called it "a guide for disturbed people"[16] and Eric Weitz wrote that the book "reads like the work of an erudite crank, perhaps even an idiot savant."[17] But even he had to admit that "… *The Decline of the West* clearly captured something of the mood in Germany and beyond after World War I. Its prevailing pessimistic tone coupled with grandiose visions of rebirth and revival; the mix of psychology and history; and its expansive ambition … to predict the future as well—resonated with the sense of despair and the longings that many Germans felt."[18]

Spengler is the prophet of a period of deep crisis. The First World War was a turning point in German history. The German sociologist Georg Simmel summarized this feeling of crisis in a speech he made in Strasbourg in November 1914—four months after the beginning of the war. Simmel said that

> "The Germany in which we became what we are, has disappeared like a dream that is over, and that, however present events may finish, we will experience our future in another Germany. No one will positively try to figure out how the form and contents of this [Germany] will come to look; but maybe, because we don't exactly know the 'how,' but only the 'that,' we are all the more dominated by this essentially vague idea: another Germany will emerge from the war than entered it."[19]

Simmel continued: "When no one can predict today what this other Germany will look like, but only that it will look different, then this knowledge of not-knowing is exactly a first sign that we have arrived at a turning point in time."[20] And he concluded: "That is also why we all feel so strongly that we are experiencing *history,* that is to say, something unique; all comparisons with events from the past contain something that doesn't fit."[21] Simmel's description of Germany's crisis situation completely fit with the definition of a crisis given by Reinhart Koselleck, who wrote: "It is part of the essence of a crisis that a decision has to be taken, but that [this decision] has not yet be taken. And it is also a part of the crisis that it remains open what kind of decision will be taken."[22]

Philosophies of history don't fall from the sky. They are fed by the historian's own experiences and the expectations he has of the future, based on these experiences. For these experiences the development of the economic situation is often decisive. The French historian Fernand Braudel, for instance, established a clear relationship between the philosophies of history which emerge in a certain epoch and the economic development in the same period.

> "Economic life," he wrote, "never ceases to fluctuate, at intervals sometimes long and sometimes short. Good times and bad times succeed each other, and societies and civilizations feel their effects, especially when the upturn or downturn is prolonged. The pessimism and disquiet that were widespread in the late fifteenth century ... reflected a marked recession in the economy of the West. European Romanticism, likewise, coincided with a long economic recession between 1817 and 1852. The expansion in the mid-eighteenth century (from 1733 onwards) saw some setbacks (for instance on the eve of the French Revolution); but in general at that time economic growth placed the intellectual development of the Enlightenment in a context of material well-being, active trade, expanding industry, and growing population."[23]

Both the almost limitless optimism of the Enlightenment philosophers, as the pessimism of the Romantics, now becomes understandable. Philosophers and historians tend to extrapolate the experiences from their own epoch and their own generation and to project these onto the future. We saw how the optimism of the philosophers of the Enlightenment stood in the way of a critical reflection on their own time. Progress was thought to be preordained and even phases of regression were not considered to be negative because they were thought, finally, to serve progress. However, this was totally different for historians who lived in another period, like Oswald Spengler, who preached doom and decline. Their negative valuation of their own, contemporary societies brought them to idealize models from the past, which were countermodels to the ideals of the Enlightenment.[24] The emphasis in these was no longer on rationalism, liberalism, egalitarianism, individualism, critical thinking, and democracy, but on respect for tradition, religion, and the established powers, attributing a positive role to authority, mysticism, and irrational emotions.

CULTURE PESSIMISM AS A POLITICAL DANGER

The German-American historian Fritz Stern (1926–2016) has pointed out how this pessimism, which refers to mythical models from the past, can develop into a major political danger. "The nostalgia for a perfect world—blessed by God—needs a radical rejection of science and liberal openness…," he wrote.[25] In Weimar Germany in particular the representatives of this "conservative revolution" had a disastrous influence. Their ideas "were an undercurrent … which became visible only in moments of crisis. But they influenced the rejection of modern society by 'German idealists' and their resentment against the failures of 'Western' ideals and institutions, through which democracy in Germany was severely damaged."[26] A representative of this "conservative revolution" in the Weimar period was Arthur Moeller van den Bruck, who, in 1923, published a book titled *Das dritte Reich* (The Third Reich), a title which would later be used by the Nazis. In this book he announced the advent of a third German Reich, which would be a combination of two earlier German empires: the Holy Roman Empire and Bismarck's German Empire. Van den Bruck's distinction between "old" nations, such as France and England, which would be in a process of decline, and "young" nations, such as America, Russia, and Germany, which would be emerging nations, was clearly inspired by Spengler's theory.

Theories of doom were not, however, a typically German phenomenon, although it was there that they had the most catastrophic consequences.

They were also to be found in France. The most well-known French author is Georges Sorel (1847–1922), who, in his book *Les illusions du progrès* (The Illusions of Progress), criticized the optimism of the Enlightenment philosophers. Sorel didn't see progress in the world around him, only decline. In his view, the clearest symptom of this decline was the advance of democracy—a political model, which was mistakenly presented by the philosophers of progress as the "advance of humanity toward the light."[27] However, for him democracy was by no means a progressive achievement. "Democracy leads to confusion in the mind," he wrote, "because it stops many intelligent people seeing things as they are, because it is served by advocates skilled in the art of making questions complicated through the use of catchy language, a supple sophistry, [and] an enormous amount of scientific theory."[28]

These examples show clearly that a philosophy of history is not politically neutral but, on the contrary, determines and colors our political vision. In *Mein Kampf* Hitler described, for instance, how at an early stage the lessons of his history teacher, Dr. Leopold Pötsch, at his secondary school were influencing definitively his world vision and his political ideas. This teacher, he wrote,

> "... was, through his brilliant presentation particularly, capable of not only fascinating us, but really enthralling us. Still today I remember with a certain emotion the grey-haired man, who in the heat of the debate sometimes let us forget reality and conjured us away back to past times and transformed dry historical memory through the haze of the millennia into a living reality. We sat there, often with great enthusiasm, sometimes even moved to tears. The joy was still greater when this teacher used the present to explain what happened in the past, [or] drew consequences from the past for the present."[29]

"Our modest national fanatism (sic)," Hitler continued, "became for him an instrument for our education."[30] He concluded, "Indeed, I was already becoming, although as far as he was concerned unwillingly, a young revolutionary."[31] There is little known about this teacher Pötsch.

However, one thing is certain: this German-speaking Austrian was a nationalist, who experienced the loss of the hegemony of the German-speaking Austrians in the Hapsburg double monarchy as cultural decline and a political threat. Considering the influence this teacher had on the young Hitler, begs the question of whether the history of the twentieth century would have taken a different direction if Hitler had a different history teacher.

TRANSFORMING DIFFUSE ANXIETY INTO CONCRETE FEAR

Hitler's national socialists shared Spengler's vision that modern society with its parliamentary democracy and individualism was an aberration and that, led by the Führer, one should return to a society in which virility, hierarchy, authority, discipline, and national unity were the supreme values. Philosophies of decline, coupled with theories of national "rebirth," are the hard core of fascist ideologies.[32] This is one of the reasons why different historians warn against these philosophies of doom. The Dutch historian Pieter Geyl said in an interview, "It is our duty not to believe in decline. Defeatism is the worst enemy."[33] He added, "That is not a very scientific remark, but I say this out of conviction. That is everyone's right … defeatism … is against reasonableness and it is in reasonableness that I see the great reliance."[34] The same conviction is expressed in a different way by Pierre Rosanvallon, according to whom one "should couple the pessimism of intelligence with the optimism of the will"[35] and by David Riesman, who pleads for "reasonable despair."[36] Another interesting approach is offered by Herfried and Marina Münkler, who distinguished between *Angst* (anxiety) and *Furcht* (fear). "Anxiety," they write, "is a feeling of helplessness, which one cannot escape. It comes from inside…. Fear, on the contrary, is a reaction to identified dangers and threats, against which one should prepare and protect oneself."[37] They write that "the transformation of anxiety into fear is one of the major tasks of politics."[38]

An example of a politician who put this adage into practice is the American president Franklin Delano Roosevelt, a man who was confronted with the disastrous consequences of the stock market crash in 1929 and the ensuing economic crisis. Roosevelt had no magic formula to solve the crisis. However, he was conscious of the fact that he could not return to earlier models of society, but that new solutions had to be found for new problems. His economic policy was one of *trial and error,* and in this process he was not afraid to go into unchartered territory. Roosevelt's "pessimism of the intelligence" made him realize that his task was almost hopeless. But his "optimism of the will" gave him the courage and the faith that he could bring this task to a successful end. "Thus Roosevelt," wrote Isaiah Berlin, "stands out principally by his astonishing appetite for life and by his apparently complete freedom from fear of the future; as a man who welcomed the future eagerly as such, and conveyed the feeling that whatever the times might bring, all would be grist to his mill...."[39] That we can mold the future was also the firm belief of Roosevelt's wife Eleanor, who said, "The future is literally in our hands to mold as we like." She added, "But we cannot wait until tomorrow. Tomorrow is now."[40]

Our conclusion is that optimistic theories of progress and philosophies of doom both have their limitations. The first have an inborn tendency to have too rosy a view of the future and to pay insufficient attention not only to real problems, but also to the eventual negative consequences of developments which are in themselves positive. In fact, the philosophers of progress are the secular heirs of the Christian philosophy of history in which the history of mankind is part of a metaphysical process of divine salvation. In this metaphysical narrative the human race can be confronted with all kinds of problems, however, finally everything ends well in the divine order. It is this faith in a divine Providence which brought the philosopher Leibniz to his formula that we live "in the best of all possible worlds," an idea that was criticized by Voltaire in his famous persiflage *Candide ou l'Optimisme.* The philosophers of doom don't share this blind faith in historical progress. On the contrary, they tend to see their own epoch as a period of decline in a cyclical historical process, which leads them to idealize earlier stages and to reject modern political and social achievements. It is this historical pessimism in particular which often leads to reactionary political attitudes, and which is also an essential part of fascist ideologies which preach a "national rebirth." The most important defect which both theories share is that they consider history to be a deterministic process in which progress, and respectively decline, can be predicted with certainty. Both Turgot and Spengler offer, each in his own way, deterministic and closed historical systems.

It is telling that both totalitarian systems of the twentieth century—German National Socialism and Stalinist Soviet Communism—projected themselves into the future without showing any special concern for the fate of future generations. Hitler's Reich, which proudly called itself the Thousand-Year Reich, projected itself no less than a millennium into the future. This German Empire was supposed to represent a new civilization in Spengler's calendar and—like the other civilizations in Spengler's book—to stand on the threshold of completing a cycle of one thousand years. However, the cycle lasted only twelve years, during which the living generation was sacrificed on the battlefield. Stalin's Soviet Union projected itself equally into the future. Relying on Marx's dialectical theory of history the Soviets predicted that a socialist paradise would be realized with iron certainty. In this historicist view there was equally no place for a special concern for future generations because later generations were considered to be the beneficiaries of the sacrifices of their forebears. It is rather through historians and political scientists who distance themselves from historicist ideas of history that a concern for the fate of future generations can develop. They no longer consider history as preordained—be it as a process of necessary progress on the one hand or a process of necessary decline on the other. David Riesman's "reasonable despair," Pierre Rosanvallon's conviction that one "should couple the pessimism of the intelligence with the optimism of the will," or the appeal of the Münklers to focus on fear instead of on *Angst,* show the way. Although they don't hide their pessimism and despair, they view history as a fundamentally *open* process in which the future is neither given or preordained, nor ruled by iron laws, but is a product of human action. It is this fact which opens up the way for developing a responsibility for future generations.

NOTES

1   These were the Egyptian, Babylonian, Indian, Chinese, Greek-Roman, Arabic, and Mexican cultures.

2   Oswald Spengler, *Der Untergang des Abendlandes,* Band 1, Reprint of the original (Altenmünster: Spengler Jazzybee Verlag Jürgen Beck, no year), p. 4.

3   Ibid.

4   Herfried and Marina Münkler, *Abschied vom Abstieg – Eine Agenda für Deutschland* (Berlin: Rowohlt, 2019), p. 121.

5   Although he was attracted by Italian Fascism, Spengler was not a National Socialist. He met Hitler in June 1933, but distanced himself from the Führer. In his book *Jahre der Entscheidung* (Years of Decision), published in the same month that he met Hitler, he praised Bismarck and Mussolini. The latter was for him a *Herrenmensch,* a modern Caesar. "Mussolini," he wrote, "is above all a statesman, ice-cold and sceptical, realist, diplomat." (Oswald Spengler, *Jahre der Entscheidung: Deutschland und die weltgeschichtliche Entwicklung,* edited by Frank Lisson (Graz: Ares Verlag, 2007), p. 150.)

6   Oswald Spengler, *Jahre der Entscheidung: Deutschland und die weltgeschichtliche Entwicklung,* op. cit., p. 34.

7   Ibid., p. 35.

8   Friedrich Nietzsche, "Vom Nutzen und Nachteil der Historie für das Leben," (Unzeitgemässe Betrachtungen, Zweites Stück), in Friedrich Nietzsche, *Werke,* Volume I (Munich: Carl Hanser Verlag, 1977), p. 217.

9   Friedrich Nietzsche, "Menschliches, Allzumenschliches—Ein Buch für freie Geister," Volume I, in Friedrich Nietzsche, *Werke,* Volume I, op. cit., p. 678.

10 Friedrich Nietzsche, "Vom Nutzen und Nachteil der Historie für das Leben," (Unzeitgemässe Betrachtungen, Zweites Stück), in Friedrich Nietzsche, *Werke,* Volume I, op. cit., p. 217.

11 Ibid.

12 Friedrich Nietzsche, "Also sprach Zarathustra," in Friedrich Nietzsche, *Werke,* Volume II (Munich: Carl Hanser Verlag, 1977), p. 466.

13 Ibid., p. 463.

14 C. O. Brink, *Horace on Poetry,* Volume 1, The Ars Poetica (Cambridge: Cambridge University Press, 1963), p. 58.

15 Thomas Mann, "The German Republic," in Anton Kaes, Martin Jay, and Edward Dimendberg (eds), *The Weimar Republic Sourcebook* (Berkeley and London: University of California Press, 1994), p. 109.

16 Walter Laqueur, *Weimar—Die Kultur der Republik* (Frankfurt am Main and Berlin: Ullstein, 1977), p. 119.

17 Eric D. Weitz, *Weimar Germany—Promise and Tragedy* (Princeton and Oxford: Princeton University Press, 2007) p. 335.

18 Ibid.

19 Georg Simmel, "Deutschlands innere Wandlung—Rede, gehalten in

Straßburg, November 1914," in Georg Simmel, *Gesamtausgabe,* Volume 16 (Frankfurt am Main: Suhrkamp Verlag, 1999), p. 13.

20 Ibid., p. 16.

21 Ibid.

22 Reinhart Koselleck, *Kritik und Krise—Eine Studie zur Pathogenese der bürgerlichen Welt,* op. cit., p. 105.

23 Fernand Braudel, *A History of Civilizations* (New York and London: Penguin Books, 1995), pp. 19–20. In the same way the rise of fascism is linked to the economic development of society, as Karl Polyani explains. "In reality," he writes, "the part played by fascism was determined by one factor: the condition of the market system. During the period 1917–23 governments occasionally sought fascist help to restore law and order: no more was needed to set the market system going. Fascism remained undeveloped. In the period 1924–29, when the restoration of the market system seemed ensured, fascism faded out as a political force altogether. After 1930 market economy was in a general crisis. Within a few years fascism was a world power." (Karl Polanyi, *The Great Transformation—The Political and Economic Origins of Our Time,* with a Foreword by Robert M. MacIver, op. cit., p. 242.)

24 An early critic of a cyclical philosophy of history and its "golden age"nostalgia was the German philosopher Johann Gottlieb Fichte, who wrote that "the Golden Age is in every respect ... a deadly limitation ... history ... does not evolve according to the hidden and whimsical rules of a circle dance, but real, actual man makes history himself, not repeating what was already there, but creating something completely new in time. Therefore, he doesn't expect a mere repetition...." (Johann Gottlieb Fichte, "Reden and die deutsche Nation," in *Fichtes Werke*, Volume VII (Berlin: Walter de Gruyter & Co., 1971), p. 368.)

25 Fritz Stern, *Kulturpessimismus als politische Gefahr—Eine Analyse nationaler Ideologie in Deutschland* (Stuttgart: Klett-Cotta, 2018), p. XVII.

26 Ibid., p. 4.

27 Georges Sorel, *Les illusions du progrès* (Paris: Marcel Rivière, 1927), p. 265.

28 Ibid., p. 10.

29 Adolf Hitler, *Mein Kampf* (Munich: Verlag Franz Eher Nachfolger, 1933), p. 12.

30 Ibid., pp. 12–13.

31 Ibid., p. 13.

32 Roger Griffin makes this the essence of a fascist ideology. According to him fascism is "a palingenetic form of populist ultra-nationalism." (Roger Griffin, *The Nature of Fascism* (London: Routledge, 1993), chapter 1.) This definition emphasizes the presence of an ultra-nationalist ideology in which

ideas of rebirth (Greek: "palingenesis") are expressed. Ideas of national rebirth were present in Mussolini, who wanted to reconstitute the Roman
empire, as well as in Hitler, whose Third Reich was considered a reincar-
nation of two earlier German empires: the Holy Roman Empire and Bismarck's German Empire.

33   "Interview van Bibeb met Geyl" in Pieter Geyl, *Verzamelde opstellen, 1*
     (Utrecht and Antwerp: Het Spectrum, 1978), p. 28.

34   Ibid.

35   Pierre Rosanvallon, *Pour une histoire conceptuelle du politique* (Paris: Édi-
     tions du Seuil, 2003), p. 47.

36   According to David Riesman, "Measured despair of our society, expressed
     publicly, can serve to warn us against catastrophe and to arouse us from
     somnolence; extravagant despair, however, can lead some to withdraw
     from political and cultural action while others feel justified in acts of de-
     structiveness and fail to grasp the potentials for nonviolent change that do
     exist." (Riesman, David, *The Lonely Crowd – A Study of the Changing
     American Character,* with Nathan Glazer and Reuel Denney (New Haven
     and London: Yale University Press, 1978), p. xiii.)

37   Herfried and Marina Münkler, *Abschied vom Abstieg—Eine Agenda für
     Deutschland,* op. cit., p. 89.

38   Ibid.

39   Isaiah Berlin, "Winston Churchill in 1940," in Isaiah Berlin, *The Proper
     Study of Mankind—An Anthology of Essays* (New York: Farrar, Straus and
     Giroux, 1997), p. 615. In the same vein John Kenneth Galbraith wrote:
     "All of the great leaders have had one characteristic in common: it was the
     willingness to confront unequivocally the major anxiety of their people in
     their time. In 1933, the Great Depression was the great and pervading
     source of anxiety.... Roosevelt, in his Inaugural Address and in the legis-
     lation of the first hundred days, left no one in doubt. All his energies would
     be committed to the economic miseries of the time. The people's concern
     was his concern. What could be done, he would do. There would be no
     pretense." (John Kenneth Galbraith, *The Age of Uncertainty* (London:
     British Broadcasting Corporation, 1977), pp. 330–32.)

40   "Anna Eleanor Roosevelt," *Our White House,* no date. https://ourwhite-
     house.org/anna-eleanor-roosevelt/

CHAPTER 10
CAN HISTORICAL OPTIMISM SURVIVE
AFTER THE HOLOCAUST?

Both historical optimism and historical pessimism have their limitations when they interpret history as a deterministic process of which the development is known in advance. However, a healthy dose of optimism is necessary if one wants to face the future with confidence. This doesn't mean that one should have blind faith in the "historical process" or a mythical *World Spirit* which will automatically solve all the problems. It *does* mean that without this basic confidence one loses one's hold on the historical process, even if this hold is per definition limited and restricted. This means that one should keep the idea of "progress" in mind. Not as a certainty, even less as some kind of an intrinsic "goal" of history, but rather as a Kantian moral imperative: an appeal to mankind to promote the common good, including that of future generations, implied in the word "progress."

However, at the same time as this appeal is being made, new problems emerge. In the first place one could ask the question: what exactly is this "progress" which promotes the common good? Don't new inventions and modes of production lead to winners and losers, the losers asking what common good is served by this highly praised progress? Of course, one can argue, in the spirit of Benjamin Constant and Jeremy Bentham, that the goal is "the greatest happiness for the greatest number," discounting the dissatisfaction of a minority against the supposed happiness of the majority. However, even then there remains the question of how to measure happiness. It is, therefore, not surprising that the word "progress" was, after its original victory march in the eighteenth century, increasingly criticized. Nietzsche, Spengler, and Sorel were only early exponents of this new pessimism, which quickly spread after the First World War.

THE OPTIMISM OF JOHN MAYNARD KEYNES

One of those who fought this pessimist mood was John Maynard Keynes, who wrote in 1930:

"We are suffering just now from a bad attack of economic pessimism. It is common to hear people say that the epoch of enormous economic progress which characterised the nineteenth century is over; that the rapid improvement in the standard of life is now going to slow down—at any rate in Great Britain; that a decline in prosperity is more likely than an improvement in the decade which lies ahead of us."[1]

The pessimism to which Keynes referred is completely understandable. He wrote these words one year after the New York stock market crash, which was the start of the Great Depression. However, Keynes didn't let himself be influenced by this general mood of moroseness. "I believe that this is a wildly mistaken interpretation of what is happening to us," he wrote.[2] "We are suffering, not from the rheumatics of old age, but from the growing pains of over-rapid changes, from the painfulness of readjustment between one economic period and another."[3] Keynes accused his contemporaries of letting themselves be blinded by the visible phenomena on the surface instead of looking at the deeper trends underneath.

"The prevailing world depression, the enormous anomaly of unemployment in a world full of wants, the disastrous mistakes we have made, blind us to what is going on under the surface—to the true interpretation of the trend of things. For I predict that both of the two opposed errors of pessimism which now make so much noise in the world will be proved wrong in our own time—the pessimism of the revolutionaries who think that things are so bad that nothing can save us but violent change, and the pessimism of the reactionaries who consider the balance of our economic and social life so precarious that we must risk no experiments."[4]

In the end history proved Keynes right, helped by the new economic insights that Keynes himself developed. Keynes was no eighteenth-century philosopher of progress. He did not count on "history" to solve the problems with its supposed innate "iron laws." Keynes was a rationalist, who argued from the premise that in principle, for each problem there exists a rational solution. His optimism was not based on a deterministic philosophy of history, but on a faith in the capabilities of the human intellect and the human will. Another thinker who warned against "extravagant despair" was David Riesman, who wrote:

> "Measured despair of our society, expressed publicly, can serve to warn us against catastrophe and to arouse us from somnolence; extravagant despair, however, can lead some to withdraw from political and cultural action while others feel justified in acts of destructiveness and fail to grasp the potentials for nonviolent change that do exist."[5]

THE DIALECTIC OF ENLIGHTENMENT: ADORNO AND HORKHEIMER AND THEIR DOUBTS ABOUT PROGRESS

But can one keep faith in progress, against one's own belief and, even more so against one's own experience? This was the question for Max Horkheimer (1895–1973) and Theodor Adorno (1903–1969), two German sociologists and leading figures of the famous *Frankfurt School.* Both had Jewish roots and fled Germany when the Nazis came to power. They migrated to America, where they wrote together the *Dialektik der Aufklärung* (The Dialectic of Enlightenment), which was published in 1944. The authors were in a singular position. Both believed in the power of reason, in the power of critical thinking, and they shared Keynes's conviction that the future—a better future—was possible. However, both authors argued in the book that the idea of linear progress, as propagated by the Enlightenment philosophers, did not fit with reality. This didn't mean that they relinquished the ideals of the Enlightenment. On the contrary:

> "We don't have any doubt...," they wrote, "that freedom in society cannot be separated from enlightened thinking. However, we believe with the same clarity that this thinking, and

less the concrete historical forms, the institutions of society
in which it is realized, already contains the seed of the regression which today is happening everywhere. If Enlightenment does not reflect on this regression it will be doomed.
By leaving the destructive side of progress to its enemies,
[critical] thinking, having become blind and pragmatic, loses
its critical character and therefore also its relationship to
truth."[6]

Like Hegel and Marx, Adorno and Horkheimer point to the dialectical development of the historical process. But—unlike Hegel and
Marx—they didn't consider this dialectic as a necessary process, but
rather as an undesirable development. Their message was that societal
progress has negative side effects, and when one is blind to these and
doesn't try to avoid these effects or remove them, political adversaries—
and especially reactionaries—will take advantage of this opportunity. It
was particularly the huge growth of productive forces, which in prosperous America had led to a culture of mass consumption and unequal
economic power, which captured their attention. "The growth of economic productivity, which on the one hand creates the conditions for a
more just world, on the other hand gives the technical apparatus and the
social groups who control it a disproportionate supremacy over the rest
of the population. The individual completely disappears against the economic powers."[7] Their conclusion was that "in these circumstances the
goods of happiness themselves become elements of unhappiness."[8]

THE GROWING CRITICISM
OF THE CONCEPT OF "PROGRESS"

When even sociologists of the Frankfurt School, proud heirs of the Enlightenment who believe in the ultimate victory of reason, express their
doubts about progress, it is not surprising that after 1945—despite
Keynes's important contribution to the solution of the crisis, and despite
the allied victory in the Second World War—the concept of "progress"
was increasingly criticized. In 1960, Nobel Prize Laureate Friedrich Hayek
made in his book *The Constitution of Liberty* the following observation:

"Writers nowadays who value their reputation among the more sophisticated hardly dare to mention progress without including the word in quotation marks. The implicit confidence in the beneficence of progress that during the last two centuries marked the advanced thinker has come to be regarded as the sign of a shallow mind. Though the great mass of people in most parts of the world still rest their hopes on continued progress, it is common among intellectuals to question whether there is such a thing, or at least whether progress is desirable."[9]

Hayek wrote these words in 1960 and not, like Keynes, in 1930—in the middle of a deep economic crisis. In 1960 the economies of Europe and the United States were booming, in Germany the *Wirtschaftswunder* (economic miracle) was bringing unknown prosperity, the French were celebrating their *Trente Glorieuses* (thirty glorious years)*,* and the Americans were preparing to make the first manned moon landing. If one couldn't talk about progress in this period, when could one? Was it because in this era one became aware that "progress" was an ambiguous concept, open to different interpretations, and maybe even a two-edged sword—in keeping with Adorno's and Horkheimer's analysis? Because the same economic and technological progress which had led to a level of prosperity for the great masses in the West, which had never been reached before, and had enabled a bold project such as the first manned moon landing, had also led to the invention of nuclear weapons, a totally new category of weapons of mass destruction which, for the first time in history, could completely wipe out human life on the planet.

Progress resembled less and less the linear rising to greater perfection, such as was described by Turgot, Condorcet, and Constant. In its place came another picture: that of mankind who made progress in one field but paid for it with increasing problems and catastrophes in other fields. Additionally, there was the fact that progress was exclusively measured in terms of technological progress or growth of the Gross Domestic Product. "With respect to the advanced countries of the West," wrote Hayek, "it is sometimes contended that progress is too fast or too exclusively material. These two aspects are probably closely connected.

Times of very rapid material progress have rarely been periods of great efflorescence of the arts, and both the greatest appreciation and the finest products of artistic and intellectual endeavor have often appeared when material progress has slackened."[10]

Hayek differentiates here between material progress and cultural progress. These do not necessarily go together, as he rightly argues, but can even move in opposite directions. This is the case, for instance, when citizens of a prosperous society increasingly pursue stupid, dull, and boring activities. It is the specter which Tocqueville depicts at the end of the second part of his study on democracy in America, where he warns against the advent of a "soft despotism": "I see an innumerable mass of the same people, resembling each other," he wrote, "who are continually busy procuring for themselves small and vulgar pleasures with which to fill their minds."[11]

Another author who criticizes the belief in progress is Christopher Lasch, who opens his book *The True and Only Heaven—Progress and Its Critics* with the following sentence:

> "This inquiry began with a deceptively simple question. How does it happen that serious people continue to believe in progress, in the face of massive evidence that might have been expected to refute the idea of progress once and for all? The attempt to explain this anomaly—the persistence of a belief in progress in a century full of calamities—led me back to the eighteenth century...."[12]

Lasch writes that instead of the word "progress" he prefers the word "hopefulness." This, because

> "It serves us better, in steering troubled waters ahead, than a belief in progress. Not that it prevents us from expecting the worst. The worst is always what the hopeful are prepared for.... Believers in progress, on the other hand, though they like to think of themselves as the party of hope, actually have little need of hope, since they have history on their side. But

their lack of it incapacitates them for intelligent action. Improvidence, a blind faith that things will somehow work out for the best, furnishes a poor substitute for the disposition to see things through even when they don't."[13]

JOHAN HUIZINGA ON "CULTURE BENEFITS" AND "CULTURE LOSSES"

These modern authors rightly criticized the concept of "progress," because it is less univocal and positive than the Enlightenment philosophers thought it was. The Dutch historian Johan Huizinga (1872–1945) also wrote about the concepts of "progress" and "decline." In the Introduction to his book *Geschonden Wereld* (Damaged World), written in 1943 during the German occupation of the Netherlands and published posthumously after the liberation in 1945, he wrote: "It is sufficiently clear that this most bitter of all centuries, which, in unparalleled agony, is nearing its midcentury, carries, as an epoch, the hallmark of an advancing decline of civilization, which could end in catastrophic destruction."[14] One can understand that Huizinga, who wrote these words during the war, describes his own time as an epoch characterized by "an advancing decline of civilization." However, the subtitle of his book: "The Chance of Restoration for Our Civilization," has an optimistic tone—not because of a new-found certainty that progress is imminent, but rather as an expression of hope. The subject of his book is not to lament, but to explore a way forward. When one wants to restore the civilization, the question is how one defines "civilization." This is less easy than it seems at first sight. Huizinga turns himself against global typifications—such as those made by Spengler[15]—in which whole cultures rise and fall. The process is, according to him, much more complex. He refers to his famous study *The Waning of the Middle Ages*. "I have myself tried to see a large part of the late Middle Ages under the aspect of the decline and death of a culture, but you don't always pronounce such general historical judgments when you evoke for a moment the picturesque images of all those special things that you find pleasing in this period or that period. It is the images of rise and fall which are always unstable and insufficient."[16] He proposes, therefore, "to say goodbye to the subject of rise and fall of culture, which adds next to nothing to an understanding of the civilization process."[17] Huizinga prefers to speak about "culture benefits" and "culture losses" and he discerns a "surprising difference" between these two. "It consists of this, that culture benefit takes place as it were before our eyes, in detail, in the form of real events, while culture losses are always characterized by slow changes of circumstances, visible only for calm and deliberate historical judgment and always then only characterized as a loss if for the observer it means a reduction in his spiritual wealth."[18] It is striking that Huizinga defines "culture benefits" as "spiritual wealth." According to him economic and scientific-technological progress cannot per se be qualified as "culture benefits." "Alas," he writes, "we know that the highest forms of scientific development can be accompanied by the worst barbarism."[19] "Culture loss" is for him a "general weakening of judgment, a decrease in critical need, the relinquishing of the knowledge ideal and the decline of moral norms."[20]

Huizinga wrote this in 1943 in a country that was occupied by the Nazis, and he knew what he was talking about. The Second World War brought huge destruction and immense human suffering. But the war also led to new inventions: the British invented the radar, the Germans invented the V-1 and the V-2 and were the first to be capable of constructing modern missiles, while the ultra-secret Manhattan Project in the U.S.A. led to the production of the first atomic bombs which in August 1945 would be dropped on Hiroshima and Nagasaki. The Greek philosopher Heraclitus had already written: "Πόλεμος πάντων πατήρ ἐστιν" (war is the father of all things). But was this technological progress during the Second World War a "culture benefit" in Huizinga's sense? Purely technologically yes, because it meant greater control over nature. But this "benefit" was made within the general context of "culture loss," characterized by a decline of moral norms. However, despite the regression he observed around him Huizinga insisted on giving his book the subtitle, "The Chance of Restoration for Our Civilization." His message was that the historian should not give in to his feelings of despair. It was his duty to keep the hope of future "culture benefits" alive.

HANNAH ARENDT AND RAYMOND ARON: HISTORY REMAINS AN OPEN PROCESS

The same prudent navigation between blind optimism and equally blind pessimism can be found in two authors who personally had every reason to embrace a pessimistic philosophy of history: Hannah Arendt and Raymond Aron. In her book *The Origins of Totalitarianism,* published in 1951, shortly after the Second World War, Hannah Arendt wrote: "This book has been written against a background of both reckless optimism and reckless despair. It holds that Progress and Doom are two sides of the same medal; that both are articles of superstition, not of faith."[21] In the same vein Raymond Aron wrote in 1943:

> "It has become trivial today to attack naive optimism, the certain expectation of an event that corresponds with our wishes. For the same reason it would be necessary to attack the opposite attitude, the fearful and resigned anticipation of the catastrophe which [before it happens] is characterized as unavoidable. One usually talks about wishful thinking, one does not recognize so easily fearful thinking."[22]

It is striking that both Raymond Aron (1905–1983) and Hannah Arendt (1906–1975) came to this conclusion: both had to leave their fatherland due to their Jewish family background. During the war, Raymond Aron stayed in London and Hannah Arendt fled to America. Even the terror of Hitler's regime was insufficient reason for them to give in to historical fatalism. For them human history remained an open process. A century earlier the same thought had already been expressed by a kindred spirit, the liberal Alexis de Tocqueville. Concern about what the future may bring is legitimate, said Tocqueville, but the question is what we do with this concern. "Let us have a healthy fear of the future that makes us vigilant and makes us fight, and not the passive and weak panic that demoralizes and makes us nervous."[23] Another author who stressed that history is principally an open process in which there is room neither for unbridled optimism, nor for a passive fatalism is the Italian philosopher and political scientist Norberto Bobbio (1909–2004).

"Indeed, what has happened in this century," he wrote, "is neither the end, nor the interruption of progress, but the end of the confident belief, initially of the Enlightenment and later of positivism, that technological and scientific progress would go hand in hand, would in a certain way be interconnected, and, particularly, that the light of knowledge would not only dispel the darkness of ignorance, but also improve the behavior, [and] elevate man to a more conscious and lasting morality."[24]

The Holocaust was one of the factors that made an end to the—almost religious—belief in progress. But these authors rightly stressed that one should not make the mistake of embracing the opposite view. History is a process in which nothing is preordained in advance. The vision of an open future is also important for another reason: it permits us to assess in a realistic way the implications and consequences of human action for future generations.

NOTES

1   John Maynard Keynes, "Economic Possibilities for our Grandchildren (1930)," in John Maynard Keynes, *Essays in Persuasion* (London: Macmillan and Co., 1931), p. 358.
2   Ibid.
3   Ibid.
4   Ibid.
5   David Riesman, *The Lonely Crowd—A Study of the Changing American Character,* with Nathan Glazer and Reuel Denney (New Haven and London: Yale University Press, 1978), p. xiii.
6   Max Horkheimer and Theodor W. Adorno, *Dialektik der Aufklärung* (Frankfurt am Main: S. Fischer Verlag, 1969), p. 3.
7   Ibid., p. 4.
8   Ibid.
9   Friedrich Hayek, "The Common Sense of Progress," in F. A. Hayek, *The Constitution of Liberty* (London and Henley: Routledge & Kegan Paul, 1976), p. 39.
10 Ibid., p. 49.
11 Alexis de Tocqueville, *De la démocratie en Amérique,* Volume 2 (Paris: Garnier Flammarion, 1981), p. 385.

12   Christopher Lasch, *The True and Only Heaven—Progress and Its Critics* (New York and London: Norton & Company, 1991), p. 13.

13   Ibid., p. 81.

14   Johan Huizinga, *Geschonden wereld—Een beschouwing over de kansen op herstel van onze beschaving* (Haarlem: H. D. Tjeenk Willink & Zoon N. V., 1945), p. 1.

15   "The admiring applause," writes Huizinga, "which Spengler received abundantly in the beginning, was certainly not based on the essential idea of his book, the image of cultures as mythical entities, gifted with a life of their own, which develops in a sequence from youth to old age. This idea is, as far as I know, accepted by no-one anywhere, or even taken seriously." (p. 20)

16   Ibid., p. 66.

17   Ibid., p. 79. Pieter Geyl agrees with Huizinga. "We talk easily—I've done it myself and will certainly do it again—of a golden age, or an age of decline. If one studies the golden age in depth one will find signs of decay, of weakness or misery at least as awful as those that frighten us today. Conversely there is no period of decline in history that doesn't have some refreshing traits of trial or of freshly coming into bloom. Measuring one group of factors against the other, the historian cannot [do it] with absolute certainty." Pieter Geyl, "Ongeluksprofeten," in Pieter Geyl, *Historicus in de tijd* (Utrecht: Uitgeversmaatschappij De Haan N.V., 1954), p. 108.

18   Johan Huizinga, *Geschonden wereld—Een beschouwing over de kansen op herstel van onze beschaving,* op. cit., p. 81.

19   Ibid., p. 82.

20   Ibid., p. 83.

21   Hannah Arendt, *The Origins of Totalitarianism,* Preface to the First Edition (New York and London: Harcourt Brace Jovanovich, 1973), p. vii.

22   Raymond Aron, "Du pessimisme historique" in Raymond Aron, *Penser la liberté, penser la démocratie* (Paris: Gallimard, 2005), p. 331.

23   Alexis de Tocqueville, *De la démocratie en Amérique,* Volume 2, op. cit., p. 397.

24   Norberto Bobbio, *Teoria generale della politica* (Turin: Einaudi Editore, 1999), pp. 634–635.

CHAPTER 11
THE ROLE OF GENERATIONS
AND THEIR DIFFERENT MOODS

Waves of historical optimism and pessimism develop in parallel with the experience of the generations which are living in different periods. One of the first social scientists who analyzed the role of generations was Karl Mannheim (1893–1947). In a famous article, published in 1928, he emphasized that "the generation problem is a serious and important problem."[1] A "generation" was defined by him as an age cohort, born and living at the same time. The number of birth years of a generation is variable. It usually spans a 16-year to 25-year range. Mannheim emphasized that a generation was not an organized group. "The unity of a generation," he wrote, "is not a social relationship which aims to form a concrete group, but a 'loose association' (*bloße Zusammenhang*)."[2] Having been born in the same time period is a necessary condition to constitute a generation, but it is, as such, not a sufficient condition. There are two additional conditions: firsty, one should share the same experiences, and, second, one should react in a similar way to these experiences. As regards the first: the same age cohort, living in 1945 in China and in the U.S., does not form a generation because the experiences of these groups are too different. The most important characteristic of a generation is the fact that they experience the same events in their formative years, when they are adolescents or young adults. Although older generations go through the same experiences, they will be less affected. "It is decisive for the formation of the mind," wrote Mannheim, "what kind of experiences enter the mind as "first impressions," "youth experiences," and what experiences are added [later] as a second or third layer."[3]

In the United States one usually distinguishes six generations since the beginning of the twentieth century, and one ascribes to each generation certain characteristics. The first generation, called the "G.I. Generation," consists of those born in the period 1901–1924. This generation lived through the Great Depression and fought in the Second World War. They are described by William Strauss and Neil Howe as "good," "constructive," "rationalist," and displaying "friendliness, optimism, and community spirit."[4] "The G.I.s have been the confident and rational problem-solvers of twentieth-century America," they wrote, "the ones who knew how to get things done—first as victorious soldiers … later as builders of rockets and highways, lastly as aging Presidents in the era of democracy's economic triumph over communism."[5] The G.I. Generation was followed by the "Silent Generation," born in the period 1925–1945. This generation was considered more cautious and "quiet" than the previous one. The "Silent Generation" was followed by the "Baby Boom" generation, born in the period 1946–1964.[6] This generation was considered more turbulent, a reason why it was also called the "Protest Generation" or "1968 Generation."[7] The "Baby Boom Generation" was followed by "Generation X," born in the period 1965–1980, and this generation was followed by "Generation Y," also called the "Millennials"—those born between 1981 and 1996. Finally, at the end of the century, from about 1997, began to arrive "Generation Z", which encompasses those born between 1997 and 2012.

We have to bear in mind, however, that these different generations are, as such, not "entities"—readily available in society, only waiting to be "discovered." They are rather social constructs, created by pollsters, journalists, marketing experts, and—finally—social scientists. A central question is: where does a generation begin and where does it end? Michael Dimock of the Pew Research Center explains the difficulties in determining the generational cutoff points:

> "Pew Research Center has been studying the Millennial generation for more than a decade," he writes. "But by 2018, it became clear to us that it was time to determine a cutoff point between Millennials and the next generation. Turning 38 this year, the oldest Millennials are well into adulthood, and they first entered adulthood before today's youngest adults were born. In order to keep the Millennial generation analytically

meaningful, and to begin looking at what might be unique
about the next cohort, Pew Research Center decided a year
ago to use 1996 as the last birth year for Millennials for our
future work. Anyone born between 1981 and 1996 (ages 23
to 38 in 2019) is considered a Millennial, and anyone born
from 1997 onward is part of a new generation."[8]

Why did one choose the name Generation Z for this new generation
and why was the cutoff point set in 1997? Dimeck explains: "We hesi-
tated at first to give them a name—Generation Z, the iGeneration and
Homelanders were some early candidates.... But over the past year, Gen
Z has taken hold in popular culture and journalism."[9] Dimeck admits
that "generational cutoff points aren't an exact science," adding that
"they should be viewed primarily as tools," but he insists that "their
boundaries are not arbitrary."[10] However, in a certain way of course they
are. Someone born in 1990 does not necessarily share all the characteristics ascribed to millennials. Globally, however, the generation concept
is considered to capture something of the "mood" of a certain age cohort.
The "G.I. Generation," for instance, is supposed to be constructive and
rationalist, the "Protest Generation" of the baby boomers is supposed to
be rebellious, anti-conformist, post-materialist, and anti-authoritarian.
For instance, on the baby boomers, Albert O. Hirschman wrote:

> "An important ingredient of the 'spirit of 1968' was a sudden
> and overwhelming concern with public issues—of war and
> peace, of greater equality, of participation in decision-mak-
> ing. This concern arose after a long period of individual eco-
> nomic improvement and apparent full dedication thereto on
> the part of large masses of people in all of the countries where
> these 'puzzling' outbreaks occurred."[11]

It is a well-known fact that older generations often tend to blame
younger generations for their supposed neglect of traditions and loose
morals. However, this blame game can also be played the other way round
when a younger generation is blaming a preceding generation for its woes.
When, in 2019, during a debate on climate change in the parliament of

New Zealand, Chlöe Swarbrick (25 years old), a young deputy of the Green Party, was interrupted by an older colleague, she answered "OK, boomer." This little phrase went viral on the social media. It immediately "became a global phenomenon, attributing to the generation of the baby boomers unflattering ideas and attitudes (conservatism, inaction, ecological skepticism)."[12] Helen Andrews, a millennial, published in 2021 a book, titled *Boomers—The Men and Women who Promised Freedom and Delivered Disaster,* which can be read as a scathing indictment of the baby boomers.

> "Every generation is dealt its own challenge," she wrote, "and handles them as well as it can. The boomers were dealt an uncommonly *good* hand, which makes it truly incredible that they should have screwed up so badly. They inherited prosperity, social cohesion, and functioning institutions. They passed on debt, inequality, moribund churches, and a broken democracy."[13]

She could have added that the baby boom generation produced the baby boom President Donald Trump. The divide between the younger and older generations manifested itself also in 2021 at the COP26 climate conference in Glasgow. "A march … was led by young climate activists," wrote *The New York Times,* "some barely old enough to vote in their countries. They accused the world leaders of wasting what little time remains to safeguard their future."[14] And the paper added: "The two sides have vastly divergent views of what the summit should achieve. Indeed, they seem to have different notions of time."[15]

The specific history of a country can also play a role in these generational blame games. Germany, for instance, is a case in point. According to Mark Roseman, "German history offers fascinating ground on which to analyse generational identities and generation conflict."[16] In Germany it was particularly the Nazi past that haunted the country. "So many parents, be it as functionaries in the regime, as former supporters of the National Socialists, as soldiers on the Eastern Front, or whatever, had some facet of their past which they were unhappy to talk about openly."[17] The coming of age of a new generation, born after the

Second World War, made it possible to openly discuss the crimes of the Nazi regime: "Since the 1960s the children of the war generation and post-war generation, distancing themselves critically and morally from their own parents, promoted the confession of guilt for the national-socialist crimes."[18] The supposed active or passive support of the older German generation for the Nazi regime made the '68 Protest Generation's criticism of the preceding generation in this country much more vehement than elsewhere.

OPTIMISM AND PESSIMISM
OF THE DIFFERENT GENERATIONS

Generations are considered to have their own, specific "generation properties" and their own "psychological mood"—they mirror their *Zeitgeist*. Collective experiences of a generation during their formative years influence their moral values, the way they think, the way they socialize, and how they view the future. How the optimism or pessimism of a generation is influenced by its shared youth experience is described by Karl Mannheim.

> "It is well known," he argued, "that the lives and writings of eighteenth-century thinkers and politicians show a remarkable optimism and belief in progress. This attitude can either be explained by tracing the causes of this optimism to events in their private lives, or by making a historical study of the psychological tendencies of the age, groping in the past for the first traces of this confident belief in progress. But neither method is really convincing as a final explanation of the universal mood which can only be explained by interpreting the optimism of individuals in terms of the common social situation. In the second half of the eighteenth century, France, as far as the intellectuals and the bourgeoisie were concerned, was in a very favourable position, owing to the development in economic processes and in the political sphere. Whole groups within these classes were given opportunities of rising in the social scale. The universal delight in progress, the

belief in action and reform, sprang from the common experience. This was the origin of the general inclination to take an optimistic view of history itself or to believe in such interpretations."[19]

Mannheim emphasized that the optimism of a generation could be explained by the situation of the society in which they lived. The same was equally true for the pessimism of other generations:

"The pessimistic tendency," he wrote, "so widespread in Germany after losing the [First World] War, has the same sociological significance, although confidence has been replaced by despair. This tendency is reflected in the popularity of Spengler's book *The Decline of the West* ... when we study the life of the mind and trace the development of moods, attitudes, and outlook, we are apt to forget that here too we only see a section of its collective history, and the individual's point of view, e.g. his private optimistic philosophy is very often only a single reaction in a uniform social and psychological development."[20]

We know today that the pessimism and desperation of the generation which grew up before the First World War and fought in the war had dire consequences.

"Many returning soldiers constituted Germany's lost generation," wrote Eric Weitz. "They never quite felt at home anywhere, were unable to seize the initiative and get their lives on course, and were plagued by the uncertainty of the future. But for others, politics had become the stuff of life. Everywhere in the winter of 1918–19, soldiers encountered meetings, demonstrations, and strikes.... The orderly German ... had become an unruly figure."[21]

In Germany and Italy this young generation was an easy prey for the emerging National Socialist and Fascist parties. In 1930, 68% of the members of the NSDAP were younger than 40 years.[22] Joseph Goebbels touted this attractiveness of the National Socialist Party for this generation and called it "the breakthrough of youth, young people who have experienced the hell fire of the World War and developed a political view which is different from what the liberal-democratic world considered to be possible."[23] In the same vein Mussolini praised the soldiers who fought in the trenches of the First World War. He called them a "trenchocracy." "The trenchocracy," he wrote, "is the aristocracy of the trenches. It is the aristocracy of tomorrow!"[24] Mussolini welcomed the "millions of demobilized soldiers." "This enormous mass," he wrote, "conscious of what it has achieved—is bound to cause shifts in the equilibrium of society."[25] Not only the members of these parties were young, but also the leaders. The average age of the leaders of Mussolini's Fascist Party was 32 years—much younger than the average age of the leaders of the other parties. (The average age of the leaders of the Italian Socialist Party was 45 years.)[26] Mussolini predicted that this new generation would shift the equilibrium of society. This is, indeed, what they did—with the known consequences.

The collective experiences of different generations—even of generations that immediately succeed each other—can be very distinct. It makes a difference if you are growing up during a prolonged period of economic growth and prosperity or during an economic crisis, not to mention the outbreak of war or a great culture shock. The optimism of the Baby Boom Protest Generation, for instance, which resembles the optimism that prevailed in the late eighteenth century, can be explained by the quasi-uninterrupted post-war boom which lasted for almost thirty years. This changed in the 1970s, when stagflation and two oil crises made an end to this boom period. The beginning of a new era was already announced in 1972, when the Club of Rome published its report *Limits to Growth,* in which the authors expressed their "overriding conviction that the major problems facing mankind are of such complexity and are so interrelated that traditional institutions and policies are no longer able to cope with them, nor even to come to grips with their full content."[27] They pointed to a complex of problems, such as: "poverty in the midst of plenty; degradation of the environment; loss of faith in institutions; uncontrolled urban spread; insecurity of employment; alienation of youth;

rejection of traditional values; and inflation and other monetary and economic disruptions."[28] The economic downturn had its impact on Generation X which succeeded the Baby Boom Generation. They were criticized for lacking the rebellious fervor of their predecessors and were labeled "the slacker generation." They lacked clear ideals and were aimless and disengaged.[29] Tellingly—due to the dire economic situation in which they grew up—this generation was also called the Lost Generation. You could, therefore, belong to a "lucky generation" or an "unlucky generation," or, as Herman Becker put it, you could belong to a generation of "Lucky Devils" or "Unlucky Dogs." The Lost Generation belonged clearly to the latter category.

> "The self-confidence of the Protest Generation," wrote Becker, "gave way to insecurity among young cohorts who were subsequently dubbed the Lost Generation, as many of its members became unemployed after leaving school and were given up for lost on the labour market. Nowadays they are referred to as Generation X."[30]

THE COVID-19 GENERATION: A NEW LOST GENERATION?

One may ask whether the Covid-19 pandemic, which hit the world in the years 2020–2022, followed by the war in Ukraine, created another Lost Generation. This is, indeed, a pressing question. Because is it realistic to expect that the pandemic, leading to the death of family members, to months of lockdown, remote learning, wearing masks, washing hands, social distancing, self-isolation, and the prohibition of touching or hugging other persons, will *not* have lasting consequences for the generation which experiences this in its formative years? Not to mention the economic consequences, because undoubtedly for many years to come we will be confronted with the economic fallout of this crisis. In the media one can already read about "Generation C"—a term which was originally invented by communication gurus to define a new "Consumer" or "Connected" generation.[31] But one decided that the "C" could equally stand for Covid, and this is what happened. It didn't take long before

Generation Z was rebaptized into "Generation Covid" or "Corona Generation."

In the fall of 2020 German TV channels were already speaking about the frustration of the "Corona Generation,"32 or "Forgotten Generation."33 The French TV channel France Culture broadcast a program titled "Covid Generation, Lost Generation," in which it was revealed that in France 29 percent of the age group 18–24 said they felt depressed and that young adults under 30 represented half of the country's poor population.34 In the United States the situation was no different. The historian David Perry wrote in the *Washington Post:* "My daughter is part of 'Generation Covid,' or Gen C. It's a generation that will not only be marked by the trauma of the disruption and death, but also by witnessing the total failures of adults to protect them and their world."35 He said that his daughter "talked about her last trip with her friends early in March, when their class went to a camp in Northern Minnesota. It's become a mythical Before Time, a pre-apocalyptic age."36 And he continued:

> "I worry that we may be overlooking the ways that all Gen C children old enough to remember will carry the trauma of this year into the rest of their lives, no matter how well they seem to be coping minute to minute. Mental health professionals and social workers are studying the issue, worried about high rates of clinginess, distraction, irritability, and fear among children."37

A UNICEF report, published during the crisis, spoke equally about a "Lost COVID Generation" and mentioned three threats to this age group: "direct consequences of the disease itself, interruption in essential services, and increasing poverty and inequality."38 The report also mentioned explicitly the "worries about the future" of this generation.39 A French magazine went so far as to announce a generation war in which— again—the baby boom generation was targeted. "Is Covid-19 inciting a generation war?" titled the magazine, pointing to the fact that "'ignored,' 'isolated,' and 'continually blamed' students and young working people no longer hesitate to speak out loud the resentment they feel against the older generation whom they accuse of mortgaging their future."[40] In the same vein, three authors argued in the paper *Le Monde* that it is the young "lockdown generation" which will pay for the boomers, because they are the ones who must reimburse the huge debts which are contracted to save the economy.[41] Covid-19 is not the only problem haunting the young generation. In an opinion article published in *the New York Times,* the Swedish climate activist Greta Thunberg and three colleagues pointed an accusing finger at the preceding generations, writing: "For children and young people, climate change is the single greatest threat to our futures. We are the ones who will have to clean up the mess you adults have made, and we are the ones who are more likely to suffer now."[42] In a survey conducted in France in February 2021, these feelings of resentment of the young generation were confirmed: 56 percent of the respondents were said to fear a generation conflict, a percentage that was even higher (60 percent) for the age group 18–34. Two-thirds (66 percent) of this age group were said to have suffered from a deterioration of their social relations with their family, friends, and colleagues, and 56 percent of this group said they were feeling depressed.[43]

THE COVID-19 GENERATION: THE FIRST GLOBAL GENERATION?

Generations are characterized by the fact that they share the same experiences when they grow up. The age group sharing these experiences can be smaller or larger, depending on the events and on the means of communication which are available. In the eighteenth and nineteenth centuries, a time when there were not yet modern communication media available, people tended to be influenced mainly by national events—which led to the creation of "national generations." This changed, however, in the twentieth century, when new inventions such as radio and TV made it possible not only to read about events abroad, but to hear eyewitness reports and to see dramatic events happen before one's eyes. The advent of the Internet and social media has only strengthened this trend. It has led to a new phenomenon: the formation of a *global* generation. In this sense the Covid-19 generation will be the first *global* generation for two reasons.[44] First, because the pandemic is a *global* event:

it will have a similar traumatic effect on the younger generation in countries as different as China and the US. Second, because the communication about the pandemic was not confined to national borders. The
Internet and social media have created a global interactive forum where
young people from different parts of the world interact and can exchange
their feelings and emotions.[45]

The question is how this new, global Covid-19 generation will react
to this dramatic period. Jürgen Habermas mentioned that "at this moment
an existential insecurity is spreading globally and simultaneously,
namely in the heads of the digitally connected individuals."[46] One may
expect Covid-19 to create a skeptical and pessimistic generation. Pessimism, as we have seen, is a negative force in history. Already before
the pandemic this generation had the reputation of being more anxious
than the preceding generation of the millennials. A poll conducted in
Britain in 2015 revealed that the members of this "smartphone generation," who are "permanently switched on, multi-screening and multi-
tasking," "feel profoundly anxious and distrustful."[47] "They feel the
world they inhabit is one of perpetual struggle—dystopian, unequal and
harsh." This generation "is coming of age in the shadow of economic
decline, job insecurity, increasing inequality and a lack of financial optimism … 79% worry about getting a job, while 72% worry about
debt—and not only student loans."[48] However, we should not forget that
crisis periods can also offer challenges and opportunities. German researchers emphasized, for instance, that "a part of the younger generation sees an opportunity in this crisis" and hope "that their ideas about
economy, politics and society will prevail in the period after the virus."[49]
In this context, an observation of the French paper *Le Monde* on the
Covid generation is also a reason for optimism, namely that

> "For the moment, this anger and this frustration … don't lead
> to a generalized pessimism. The majority of these young peo-
> ple say that they are optimistic about themselves if one asks
> them the question. If one had to resume this state of mind in
> one sentence it could be: 'The world is going bad, but as con-
> cerns me, I think I will make it.'"[50]

This optimism is shared by the Canadian sociologist Cécile Van de Velde who, after having observed that "a climate awareness was spreading among the young generation," added that "this discourse was characterized by [introducing] a new actor who had to be protected: the future generations. We find here a discourse which inverts the roles between children and adults, with young generations who very early accept their responsibility, against the adult generations who have been too reckless."[51] The Covid generation, being confronted at an early age with the devastating effects of a pandemic, could be more inclined than the preceding generations to develop a sense of responsibility for the destiny of future generations. This increased sense of responsibility of Generation Z is also emphasized by two American analysts, who wrote : "In the 2018 midterm elections and the 2020 presidential elections in the United States, members of Generation Z old enough to vote did so at significantly higher rates than either Generation X or Millennials did when they were the same age." "Gen Z ... also values protesting like Baby Boomers did decades before Gen Z took to the streets. These characteristics combine to suggest that Gen Z will be a powerful force for change for years to come."[52] A similar observation is made in *The New York Times,* where this group of teens is said to be "extremely politically aware and active around issues ranging from racial injustice in the wake of George Floyd's murder to climate change to L.G.B.T.Q. rights."[53] Maybe this is indeed the case, and in this sense, in the end the pandemic will have a silver lining.

NOTES

1   Karl Mannheim, "Das Problem der Generationen," *Kölner Vierteljahresheft für Soziologie,* 7 (1928), p. 168.
2   Ibid., p. 170.
3   Ibid., p. 181.
4   William Strauss and Neil Howe, *Generations—The History of America's Future, 1584 to 2069* (New York and London: Harper Perennial, 1991), p. 9.
5   Ibid., p. 28.
6   The US Census defines the baby boom generation as the age cohort born in the period 1946–1964. ("A Century of Population Change in the Age

and Sex Composition of the Nation," *US Census*, September 12, 2013.)
https://www.census.gov/dataviz/visualizations/055/

7 William Strauss and Neil Howe (*Generations—The History of America's Future, 1584 to 2069,* op. cit., p. 299) define the baby boom generation as those born between 1943 and 1960. This seems plausible if one considers that in a book on the Paris May Revolt of 1968—which is an iconic event for the Baby Boom Generation—the authors added a list with the names of the leaders of this movement: 18 of them are born in the period 1936–1942 and 9 in the period 1943–1945. Not one of them is born after 1945. (Hervé Hamon and Patrick Rotman, *Génération – 1. Les années de rêve* (Paris: Éditions du Seuil, 1987), pp. 603–07.)

8 Michael Dimock, "Defining generations: Where Millennials end and Generation Z begins," *Pew Research Center,* January 17, 2019. https://www.pewresearch.org/fact-tank/2019/01/17/where-millennials-end-and-generation-z-begins/ (Accessed January 13, 2021).

9 Ibid.

10 Ibid.

11 Albert O. Hirschman, *Shifting Involvements—Private Interest and Public Action* (Princeton, N.J.: Princeton University Press, 1982), p. 89.

12 Marion Dupont, "Boomeur," *Le Monde,* June 10, 2021.

13 Helen Andrews, *Boomers—The Men and Women who Promised Freedom and Delivered Disaster* (New York: Sentinel, 2021), pp. xiv–xv.

14 Somini Sengupta, "Generations are decades apart on fix for climate," *The New York Times,* November 8, 2021.

15 Ibid.

16 Mark Roseman, "Introduction: generation conflict and German history 1770–1968," in Mark Roseman (ed.), *Generations in Conflict—Youth revolt and generation formation in Germany 1770–1968* (Cambridge and New York: Cambridge University Press, 1995), p. 2.

17 Ibid., p. 42.

18 Liane Schäfer, "Wem gehört die Vergangenheit? Generationenbrüche im deutschen Erinnern," *Aus Politik und Zeitgeschichte* (70), 52–53, December 21, 2020, p. 40.

19 Karl Mannheim, *Man and Society in an Age of Reconstruction—Studies in Modern Social Structure,* op. cit., p. 25.

20 Ibid., pp. 25–26.

21 Eric D. Weitz, *Weimar Germany—Promise and Tragedy* (Princeton and Oxford: Princeton University Press, 2009), p. 23.

22 Pierre Milza, *Les fascismes* (Paris: Éditions du Seuil, 2001), p. 265.

23 Joseph Goebbels, "Der Faschismus und seine praktischen Ergebnisse," in Ernst Nolte (ed.), *Theorien über den Faschismus* (Cologne and Berlin: Kiepenheuer & Witsch, 1967), p. 315.

24 Benito Mussolini, "Trenchocracy," in Roger Griffin (ed.), *Fascism* (Oxford and New York: Oxford University Press, 1995), p. 28.

25 Ibid., p. 29.

26 Emilio Gentile, *Qu'est-ce que le fascisme? Histoire et interprétation* (Paris: Gallimard, 2004), p. 36.

27 Donella H. Meadows, Dennis L. Meadows, Jørgen Randers, and William W. Behrens III, *The Limits to Growth—A Report for the Club of Rome's Project on the Predicament of Mankind* (Washington, D.C.: Potomac Associates, 1972), pp. 9–10.

28 Ibid., p. 10.

29 Solitaire Townsend, "OK, Slacker. Can Gen X Save the World?" *Fortune,* January 7, 2020. https://www.forbes.com/sites/solitairetownsend/2020/01/07/ok-slacker-can-gen-x-save-the-world/?sh=3e4f70207399

30 Henk A. Becker, *Generations of Lucky Devils and Unlucky Dogs: Strategies for an assertive growing up, active ageing and intergenerational solidarity up to 2030* (Amsterdam: Rozenberg Publishers, 2012), p. 21.

31 "Introducing Gen C: The YouTube Generation," *Think with Google,* March 2013. Gen C is here defined as "not an age group, it's an attitude, a mindset."

32 Kirsten Girschick, "Frust bei der 'Generation Corona'," *Tagesschau,* October 18, 2020. https://www.tagesschau.de/inland/coronavirus-jugendliche-101.html

33 Adele Bunk, "Die vergessene Generation der Corona-Krise," *ZDF Heute,* September 17, 2020. https://www.zdf.de/nachrichten/panorama/coronavirus-jugend-kinder-folgen-100.html

34 "Génération Covid, génération perdue?" *France Culture,* November 28, 2020. https://www.franceculture.fr/emissions/le-temps-du-debat/generation-covid-generation-perdue

35 David Perry, "The pandemic is traumatic for kids like mine. I have no idea how to help," *The Washington Post,* December 17, 2020. https://www.washingtonpost.com/outlook/2020/12/17/generation-covid-kids-trauma-pandemic/

36 Ibid.

37 Ibid.

38 "Averting a lost COVID generation—A six-point plan to respond, recover and reimagine a post-pandemic world for every child," UNICEF, New York, *Brief,* November 2020. https://www.unicef.org/reports/averting-lost-generation-covid19-world-childrens-day-2020-brief

39 Ibid., p. 2.

40 "Merci Boomer! quand la 'génération Covid' en veut aux séniors," *La Depêche,* December 20, 2020. https://www.ladepeche.fr/2020/12/20/merci-boomer-quand-la-generation-covid-en-veut-aux-seniors-9269177.php

41 Emmanuel Blézès, Yama Darriet, Charles Mazé, "La génération confine-
    ment paiera pour les boomers," *Le Monde,* September 5, 2020.
    https://www.lemonde.fr/idees/article/2020/09/05/la-generation-confine-
    ment-paiera-pour-les-boomers_6051070_3232.html
42 Greta Thunberg, Adriana Calderón, Farzana Faruk Jhumu, and Eric Nju-
    guna, "Dear adults, you're failing us on climate," *The New York Times,* Au-
    gust 21–22, 2021.
43 Béatrice Jérôme, "Covid-19: le risque d'un choc des générations," *Le
    Monde,* February 19, 2021.
44 According to two authors, "the 1960s generation was the first global gen-
    eration." (June Edmund and Bryan S. Turner, "Global generations: social
    change in the twentieth century," *The British Journal of Sociology,* Volume
    56, Issue 4, November 25, 2005.) Although the 1960s Protest Generation
    was an international phenomenon, this generation remained mainly re-
    stricted to the Western world and could not yet be labeled "global." Calling
    it "global" would lump together heterogeneous groups, such as the Red
    Guards, who in 1966–1967 were mobilized by Mao Zedong to purge the
    Chinese Communist Party, with hippies attending the Woodstock festival,
    or students at Berkeley organizing a sit-in against the war in Vietnam.
45 One could argue that the Spanish flu pandemic, which hit the world from
    February 1918 until April 1920, was equally a global phenomenon. The
    pandemic infected one third of the world's population and killed about 50
    million people. It arrived in 1918, overlapping with the last year of the First
    World War and persisting afterwards. However, it did not create a global
    generation, because news about the pandemic was left underreported dur-
    ing the war, and—apart from the print media—international communica-
    tion was lacking.
46 Quoted in Markus Schwering, "Habermas über Corona: 'So viel Wissen
    über unser Nichtwissen gab es noch nie,'" *Frankfurter Rundschau,* April
    10, 2020.
47 Noreena Hertz, "Think millennials have it tough? For Generation K, life
    is even harsher," *The Guardian,* March 19, 2016. https://www.the-
    guardian.com/world/2016/mar/19/think-millennials-have-it-tough-for-gen-
    eration-k-life-is-even-harsher (Note that, for unknown reasons, the author
    prefers to call this generation "Generation K" instead of "Generation Z".)
48 Ibid.
49 Helga Pelizäus and Jana Heinz, "Stereotypisierungen von Jung und Alt in
    der Corona-Pandemie," *Aus Politik und Zeitgeschichte* (70), 52-53/2020,
    December 21, 2020, p. 15.
50 Jessica Gourdon, Léa Iribarnegaray, Éric Nunès, and Alice Raybaud, "Les
    18–25 ans, une génération meurtrie," *Le Monde,* June 3, 2021.

51 "La pandémie radicalise un sentiment d'impuissance et de colère," Interview of Marine Miller with Cécile Van de Velde, *Le Monde,* June 3, 2021.

52 Laurie L. Rice and Kenneth W. Moffett, "Generation Z – 'Lost' or Emerging Generation?" *Cicero Foundation Great Debate Paper,* No. 21/06, November 2021. https://www.cicerofoundation.org/wp-content/uploads/Rice_Moffett_Generation_Z.pdf

53 Jessica Grosse, "Gen Z is cynical. They've earned it," *The New York Times,* May 30, 2022.

CHAPTER 12

THE "COLLAPSOLOGISTS": SAVING THE FUTURE BY NOT HAVING KIDS

The growing concern about climate change can also have unexpected consequences. Recently a totally new category of philosophers of doom has emerged, the so-called "collapsologists" who paint the future in the darkest colors and don't recoil from predicting the total worldwide collapse of civilization. This group finds its inspiration in the book *Collapse* by the American author Jared Diamond, a geography professor at the University of California. In his book, published in 2005, Diamond defines *collapse* as a "drastic decrease in human population size and/or political/economic/social complexity, over a considerable area, for an extended time. The phenomenon of collapses is thus an extreme form of several milder types of decline, and it becomes arbitrary to decide how drastic the decline of a society must be before it qualifies to be labeled as a collapse."[1] Diamond gives some historical examples of civilizations which went through such a collapse, such as Easter Island, the Mayan culture, and the empire of the Khmers in Cambodia. He mentions five factors which would have played a role in this process: damage to the environment caused by the people, climate change, hostile neighbors, diminished support from friendly neighbors, and the answers which these societies formulate to their problems and their consequences.

The big question raised by Diamond in his book is whether what was possible in earlier epochs is also possible today. Diamond is very clear about that. He warns that regarding the problems of the environment,

"The only question is whether they [the world's environmental problems] will become resolved in pleasant ways of our own choice, or in unpleasant ways not of our own choice, such as warfare, genocide, starvation, disease, epidemics, and collapses of societies. While all of those grim phenomena have been endemic to humanity throughout our history, their frequency increases with environmental degradation, population pressure, and the resulting poverty and political instability."[2]

THE COLLAPSOLOGISTS AND THE ANNOUNCEMENT OF THE END OF THE WORLD

In particular the emphasis placed by Diamond on the problems of climate and environment and the message that it was five minutes before midnight hit a nerve in a wider audience. Soon groups emerged which wore the name "collapsologists" as a badge of honor. In Europe as well as in America, the influence of these groups is increasing. In 2019 the French paper *Le Monde* wrote an in-depth article about this new movement. "According to the 'collapsologists'," wrote the paper, "our civilization, based on fossil energy sources, will disappear in the 2030s, an idea which increasingly resonates in the general public."[3] In the Introduction to a book which became a bestseller in France, the authors immediately set the tone. "The idea that at this moment global catastrophes are taking place," they wrote, "is today more and more accepted, just like the idea that they will lead to a global collapse of the system."[4] This is followed by an enumeration of all kinds of catastrophic events. The authors write that "Fukushima, the successive waves of refugees in Europe, the terrorist attacks in Paris and Brussels, the disappearance of birds and insects, the Brexit referendum, and the election of Trump have undermined the peaceful image of continuity which reassured so many people."[5] The book was published before the Covid-19 crisis and the war in Ukraine, which would have offered additional arguments. However, the main subject for the collapsologists remains climate change. According to the authors, "the consequences of global warming have *as such* the power to cause worldwide massive and destructive catastrophes, which could lead to the end of civilization [and] even of the human species."[6] Other points which are emphasized are the exhaustion of energy sources and the massive population growth, which would lead to famines. As concerns the latter, the collapsologists seem to be following in the footsteps of Thomas Malthus (1766–1834) who, in his *Essay on the Principle of Population* (1798), argued that the population grew geometrically (1-2-4-8 etc.), while food production increased only arithmetically (1 – 2 – 3 – 4 etc.), which would lead to famines if the same pattern of population growth continued. In the same vein as Malthus, they warn that "global overpopulation, overconsumption by the rich, and insufficient technological choices have pushed our civilization down the path towards a collapse. Important and irreversible system shocks can very well take place tomorrow, and the deadline for a massive collapse seems closer than one usually assumes, around 2050 or 2100."[7]

The collapsologists don't restrict themselves to only climatological and demographical doom scenarios; they observe the symptoms of the imminent collapse everywhere around them. What they particularly fear is a *chain reaction,* in which one catastrophe necessarily leads to another, and so on, so that there will occur a cascade of successive calamities which cannot be dealt with individually. One model that is presented in their book is, for instance, a collapse of "five successive stages: financial, economic, political, social, and cultural."[8] What is at issue, they write, "is the interdependence of all 'problems' of the world. Everything becomes terribly systemic, that is to say unsolvable by individuals or [by] miraculous 'solutions,' and inaccessible for politics as it is understood at this moment."[9] The collapsologists, therefore, prefer not to speak about a "crisis" because, according to them, this word maintains "the hope that a return to a normal situation is possible."[10] This is clearly not the case, so they prefer to reserve for this the English word *predicament,* a concept, they write, "which better expresses the idea of a collapse. A *predicament* refers to an inextricable, irreversible, and complex situation for which there exist no solutions, only measures that have to be taken to adapt."[11]

"ENVIRONMENT MELANCHOLIA" AND "CLIMATE DEPRESSION" IN THE NETHERLANDS

In recent years this movement is gaining more followers worldwide. In the Netherlands, for instance, a meeting took place in February 2019 in the city of Utrecht. The title of the meeting was—tellingly—"Therapy for your climate depression." About two hundred people—mostly young women—participated in the meeting. A Dutch paper reported:

> "Ecophilosopher Evanne leads the reunion.... She speaks to the audience after having shown apocalyptic images of climate change: 'Close your eyes, and put both feet on the ground,' she says. 'What do you feel? What does it do to you?'"[12]

Apparently, a lot. One of the visitors, a 26-year-old female student, tells the reporters: "I am really looking for healing." Another female student says: "More than anything, I feel powerless." Other participants tell of having "a feeling of mourning," "panic," "obsession" or "apathy." René ten Bos, a philosopher who is the Dutch "'thinker of the fatherland," also contributes to the discussion and "gives a philosophically complex and rather pessimistic lecture. Climate change is according to him not even the worst problem for the planet and mankind. The wave of extinction amongst the animal species has already passed the crucial point, he says." "Even worse than global warming. Optimists are in fact unpleasant people."[13]

No one feels offended by the remark by the Dutch "thinker of the fatherland" that optimists are in fact unpleasant people. There are apparently not many optimists in the hall. At the end of the evening the moderator asks how many people have begun to think more positively. "Less than 10 per cent raise their hands."[14] According to the paper, the evening in Utrecht confirms research on what catastrophic forecasts do with the human psyche: "In the new field of research it deals with phenomena, such as 'pretraumatic stress,' 'environment melancholia,' 'climate depression.'"[15] As a matter of fact, collapsology, this new branch

of futurology, is not only interesting because of its content, but also because of what it does with its followers. In an opinion poll conducted in
October 2019 by the French pollster IFOP in France, the UK, Germany,
Italy, and the USA, most collapsologists were found in Italy (71%) and
France (65%). The results for the UK and USA were respectively 56%
and 52%, while Germany scored lowest with 39%. It is no surprise that
collapsologist ideas were particularly present in the electorate of right-
wing and left-wing populist parties. In Germany these ideas were supported by 57% of the AfD and 47% of Die Linke, in Italy by 74% of the
Lega, 71% of the Five Star Movement, and 73% of Berlusconi's Forza
Italia. France, with 76% of the adherents of La France Insoumise and
74% of the Rassemblement National supporting collapsologist ideas,
was called "the fatherland of collapsology."[16]

THE COLLAPSOLOGISTS
AS AN INITIATED AVANT-GARDE

How credible are these doom scenarios? Collapsologists are also asking
this question.

> "All predictions of a collapse of our societies, from the mil-
> lenaristic prophecies of the past to the contemporary fear of
> a nuclear winter," write Servigne and Stevens, "have until
> now failed—everyone can see a global collapse has not taken
> place. How can one be sure that we aren't making another
> mistake? That is easy, we can't. However, we can find some
> indications."[17]

These indications, that the collapsologist predictions will come true,
are, according to them, abundantly present. Therefore "collapse could
become our new normal situation, which would slowly lose its exceptional, catastrophic character."[18] If this is the case, should you not warn
the people? Yes, answer the authors, but one should take care, because
"if one ... announces a collapse too early, that is to say, at this point with
too weighty authority, for example via an official speech of a head of
state, then it is possible that it would cause a panic on the markets (or in

the population) and through anticipation one causes what one wanted to postpone."[19]

Collapsologists are conscious of the fact that they are an avant-garde in possession of a body of specific knowledge about the coming collapse, knowledge which they must share prudently with the rest of the population to prevent a panic. Collapsologists show all the characteristics of a religious sect, as defined by Max Weber, who wrote that members of a sect consider themselves to be a kind of semi-religious elite which, unlike the rest of the population, possesses its own, esoteric knowledge.[20] A sect is further characterized by ethical rigorism[21] which for collapsologists takes the form of relinquishing their dreams for the future. There is also a clear messianism present: members of the sect have the duty to spread the message, although this must be done in a cautious and prudent way. Another characteristic of a sect can also be observed: a certain martyrdom, the preparedness to suffer for one's conviction. All this becomes apparent in the way in which the two aforementioned authors present themselves:

> "Collapsology is not a neutral science which is disconnected from its subject of study," they write. "Collapsologists are directly involved in what they study. They can no longer remain neutral. They *shouldn't* remain so. Choosing such a path doesn't leave [someone] undamaged. The collapse theme is a poisonous theme which touches your innermost being. It is a huge shock that destroys dreams. During the years of research we are overwhelmed by anxiety attacks, rage, and deep sadness before feeling slowly a certain acceptance, and sometimes even hope and joy.... Indeed, when one starts to understand the possibility of a collapse and afterwards to believe in it, it means that one finally gives up the future which we had imagined. That means that one sees the hopes, dreams, and expectations which we have cherished from our earliest youth, or which we had for our children, cut off. To accept the possibility of a collapse means to accept that a future which was precious for us and comforted us, no matter how irrational, is dying."[22]

Collapsologists show the characteristics not only of a religious sect, but also of a recent religious *conversion*. This aspect puts pressure on relations with friends and family, who are not prepared to embrace the new message of doom. "We have had the unpleasant experience of a family member being angry with us," they write. "This is a well-known fact: to get rid of the bad message one prefers to kill the messenger, the Cassandras and the whistleblowers."[23] But it's not only family members who react negatively. "During our first public presentations we took care to show only facts and figures, to remain as objective as possible. Every time the audience's emotions surprised us. The clearer the facts, the stronger the emotions. We thought we were talking to the head, but we touched the heart: regularly sadness, tears, anxiety, resentment, or explosions of rage came up from the audience."[24]

Collapsologists don't promise their followers an easy life. This can also be clearly seen from the advice the authors give their readers.

> "If one wants to continue thinking about the collapse, trying to take action, giving sense to our lives, or simply getting up in the morning, then it is important not to go crazy. Crazy from the isolation, crazy from the sadness, crazy from the rage, crazy from thinking too much about it, or crazy from continuing our daily worries, while pretending to see nothing."[25]

The collapsologists are confronted by the task that "all or almost all has to be called into question, which is not only arduous, but can cut us off from an effectively stable and comforting environment ... there is a real risk of depression."[26] "We are confronted with a huge challenge," continue the authors. "To be interested in these subjects in their scientific or sociological form carries a certain risk for psychological health. The people who are personally involved in this question and who make it the central question of their life, are overloaded (and will remain so for a long period) psychologically, as well in their relations with the others as in their social and political engagement."[27]

It is telling that "climate anxiety" has become a modern psychological disorder. A French psychiatrist points to the fact that "because of their difficulty to project themselves into the future many are determined to never have children, or at least they consider this seriously. They are called 'Ginks' (Green Inclination, No Kids)."[28] The American Psychological Association's task force on climate change, in its 2009 report, included accounts of "eco-anxiety," whose symptoms include panic attacks, loss of appetite, and sleeplessness."[29] This pessimism, when it is taken too far, can have disastrous and even bizarre results. Jennifer Jacquet describes, for instance, a group which exists in the United States and is called The Voluntary Human Extinction Movement (VHEMT). This group "promotes a simple motto: "May we live long and die out." Members of the group equally renounce having children, because "phasing out the human race by voluntarily ceasing to breed will allow Earth's biosphere to return to good health."[30] One should not underestimate this trend. In the US "a 2020 Morning Consult poll found that a quarter of adults without children say climate change is part of the reason they didn't have children. A Morgan Stanley analysis found that the decision 'to not have children owing to fears over climate change is growing and impacting fertility rates quicker than any preceding trend in the field of fertility decline'."[31]

Collapsology seems to have become an integral part of the present pessimistic *Zeitgeist.* Its followers use each dramatic event to make their point. On April 15, 2019, when a fire destroyed the roof of the Notre Dame cathedral in Paris, the French historian Fanny Madeline, a collapsologist, wrote the following commentary in the paper *Le Monde:*

"Monday evening the image of the Notre Dame on fire appears as the unexpected, but evident manifestation of a collapse. This word, which is present in the Zeitgeist, which threatens us and projects us towards an unimaginable future, imposes itself to describe what is happening to one of the most iconic buildings of our history, while it hurts our memory and causes a crack in time through which the future bounces onto the past. Powerless in front of our screens, it is as though we are standing by [and seeing] what we don't want to see: the flames of Notre Dame, it is our world which is burning. That is the collapse, with a capital C, of biodiversity, the massive

extinction of the species, the end of Western liberal democracies.… Can we see in this tragedy anything else than the
frightening spectacle of a world which is collapsing?"[32]

Clearly the Covid-19 crisis which hit the world in 2020, and the war
in Ukraine in 2022, were only grist to the collapsologists' mill.

WHEN PROPHECY FAILS …

The collapsologists resemble a modern version of the millenarian movements of the past, which predicted the end of the world. In the 1950s the
American sociologist Leon Festinger and two colleagues published a
study titled *When Prophecy Fails—A Social and Psychological Study of
a Modern Group that Predicted the Destruction of the World.*[33] The authors explored how the followers of a visionary woman who predicted
the end of the world reacted when the expected end of the world did not
happen. The visionary, Dorothy Martin, a housewife from Chicago (in
the book referred to by the pseudonym Mrs. Keech), was said to have
received via automatic writing a message from extraterrestrials, telling
her that the end of the world was imminent and would happen on December 21, 1954. However, she and her followers, the message said,
would be saved because on December 20 they would be taken up by a
space ship that would bring them to another planet. In the days before
December 20 the followers waited nervously in the house of Mrs. Keech
for the arrival of the space ship. But then, suddenly, some hours before
the expected arrival, Mrs. Keech said she had received a message that
God had decided to save the world—due to the efforts of the group.
Thereupon the group, which so far had avoided publicity, contacted the
media to spread the good news.

Festinger's research was meant to test his theory of "cognitive dissonance." When the belief (the imminent end of the world) is not confirmed by the facts (the expected end doesn't take place), there is a case
of "cognitive dissonance." The normal reaction is to give up the (illu-
sionary) belief and to adapt to reality. But there are also other responses
possible. One of these is to change the date of the predicted phenomenon. This is a strategy which can be found in Christian apocalyptic

movements of the past. These believed, writes Reinhart Koselleck, "that with each unfulfilled prophecy the probability increases, with even greater certainty, that it will take place in the future. A past non-fulfillment assured an increasing chance of fulfillment. In this way failed prophecies also kept their right to future fulfillment increasing."[34] A third strategy is to ascribe the fact that a prophecy didn't materialize to the actions of the group of believers, who would have "saved" the world. After the failure of a prediction the followers organize a campaign to win new followers. If a large number of people embrace the message of the group, the cognitive dissonance of the original members will diminish, because they get support from the newcomers.[35] In Festinger's case study the group made use of the last strategy. The group pretended that its vigilance and its action had saved the world from its imminent end and, additionally, they recruited new followers who would increase the group and thereby strengthen their belief. As concerns the collapsologists, they give two dates for the expected global collapse: 2050 and 2100. Unlike Festinger's group they don't risk being exposed in the near future to a "falsification" of their prediction. These dates give them a broad and safe time margin.

HOW LIKELY ARE THESE DOOM SCENARIOS?

One might object that no one can guarantee that the collapsologists' doom scenarios are simply plucked out of the air. Who can be sure that they are not right? And isn't there a massive difference between Festinger's case—a small, select group which believed the most absurd predictions made by a housewife pretending to be a psychic—and the collapsologists' predictions which are based on existing actual trends? Indeed, predictions based on scientifically observed facts, such as global warming, are more realistic than predictions about a space ship with extraterrestrials which would pick up a group of chosen people one day before the end of the world. But despite this greater plausibility, there are still at least two reasons to approach the collapsologists' doom scenarios with the appropriate skepticism.

In the first place there is their *cascade theory.* The collapsologists' doom scenario of total collapse assumes a "waterfall" of disasters and catastrophes, in which one catastrophe automatically leads to another catastrophe, *ad infinitum*. David Wallace-Wells, an American collapsologist, predicts for instance "a climate system that will now go to war with us for many centuries, perhaps until it destroys us."[36] This author is also a proponent of the cascade theory. The way in which this happens, he writes, is via "a new kind of cascading violence, waterfalls and avalanches of devastation, the planet pummeled again and again, with increasing intensity and in ways that build on each other and undermine our ability to respond, uprooting much of the landscape we have taken for granted for centuries...."[37] It is a doom scenario in which everything is connected to everything, and one falling domino is enough to make all dominoes fall. Certainly, on a limited scale such a domino reaction can sometimes take place—for example a financial crisis which leads to an economic crisis or, for that matter, the Covid-19 pandemic which leads to an economic downturn. That said, it is extremely improbable that on a global scale such an all-embracing chain reaction will take place. Of course, there will be forest fires, inundations, heat waves, hurricanes, droughts, and other unpleasant natural phenomena. However, the expectation that all this will be compressed into one single, great, apocalyptic, all-devastating Armageddon, as collapsologists would have us believe, is extremely improbable.

There is still a second reason for their scenario being improbable. This is the fact that collapsologists have not sufficiently incorporated into their scenario the fact that man is gifted with reason and intelligence and has therefore a surprising capacity for adapting himself with great flexibility to changing circumstances. Man is, one could say, a preeminent *adaptive species.* And this ability to adapt himself leads not only to passive adaptation, but also to an *active* adaptation, interfering with his science and technology in nature to adapt to his need for survival. The Covid-19 crisis is a case in point. Never before has so much money been invested in vaccine research and never before have vaccines been developed and tested in such a short time. Examples of this adaptation can be found everywhere. When, for instance, on the night of January 31–February 1, 1953, in the Dutch provinces of Zeeland and South Holland a flood cost the lives of more than 1800 people, the Dutch government did not wait passively for the next disaster to happen, but launched the so called "Deltaplan," a project of huge, pharaonic storm surge barriers to prevent a future disaster. Such proactive adaptations are taking place all the time. Science and technology, after all, don't stand still. Under the pressure of climate change human inventiveness will only increase. The initiative to reduce the emission of greenhouse gasses by international agreements, such as the Paris Agreement of 2015, is only a first step. At the same time research is taking place in the field of geoengineering. This is active human interference in the climate in order to cool the earth. In a report of the British *Royal Society,* for instance, one can read that "geoengineering of the Earth's climate is very likely to be technically possible."[38] Concrete proposals have already been presented. One option consists of carbon dioxide removal techniques, whereby the CO_2 is actively removed from the atmosphere. "These technologies range from the old-fashioned practice of reforestation to high-tech machines that suck carbon out of the sky and store it underground."[39] According to experts from the Environmental Defense Fund, many of these technologies are "ready to be deployed at scale today, and they might make the difference between limiting warming to two degrees and failing to do so," and they assure us that "the transformative power of human ingenuity offers an endless source of hope."[40] Another option is solar radiation management, a procedure in which the absorption of solar heat by the earth is slowed down. This can be done in different ways: for example, by painting buildings white, by covering deserts with reflective material, by placing shields in space that reflect a small amount of solar energy, or by injecting aerosol into the stratosphere and thereby imitating the effects of volcanic eruptions. According to experts, injecting aerosol into the stratosphere would be a particularly promising option.[41] Of course, such geoengineering projects cannot replace the reduction in CO_2 emissions, but should rather be considered as supplementary tools. This is also understood by environmental organizations which originally were skeptical, fearing that geoengineering could have a negative impact on countries' commitment to achieving climate goals. A representative of the World Wildlife Fund, for example, wrote that "the WWF is cautiously supporting research into geo-engineering approaches to find out what is possible."[42] In 2022 a group at Harvard conducted an experiment called COPEX. The experiment involved "launching a balloon into the stratosphere, with the aim of releasing 2kg of material (probably calcium carbonate), and then measuring how it dissipates, reacts and scatters solar energy."[43] The Harvard group is aware of the risks. For this reason, it has established an independent advisory panel to consider the moral and political ramifications.

Geoengineering will certainly not be the panacea for climate change mitigation, but it could offer new, previously unavailable, or even not yet considered solutions. In a novel published in 1865, Jules Verne had people travelling to the moon. At the time it was very brave science fiction. In 1969—just one hundred and four years later—Jules Verne's visionary dream became reality. We should not overestimate human ingenuity, nor should we underestimate it. It is certainly true that the present generation is facing many profound, and even revolutionary changes—not only in the climate, but also in the economy, demographics, healthcare, and politics. Over the next thirty years the world's population could grow from over seven billion to ten billion. Digitalization, robotization, and artificial intelligence are developing into a whole new economy, while the West is losing its traditional hegemony in the world. What is new about this situation is that all these revolutionary changes are occurring at the same time, and it is certainly signalling the end of an era. All this can lead to an increased insecurity and, as the French historian Pierre Nora writes, can "nurture a premonition of the apocalypse."[44]

This fear of the future can also lead to nostalgic longing for an idealized past, for a society that was still "natural," "simple," "ecological," and not threatening. Zygmunt Bauman called such a utopia, projected into the past, tellingly a *retrotopia*. "'Retrotopias' are currently emerging," he wrote, "visions located in the lost/stolen/abandoned but undead past, instead of being tied to the not-yet, unborn—and so inexistent future...."[45] It is clear that such "retrotopias" are based on a romanticized past which, in reality, never existed. But these "retrotopias" are compensating for the apocalyptic feelings of our lives. Pierre Nora appealed to our common sense. "We also know...," he wrote, "that the end of *a* world is not the end of *the* world."[46] Common sense and level-headedness are, indeed, required. This doesn't mean that the collapsologists' feelings of apocalyptic panic should be replaced by a blind optimism about the future that leads to adopting a passive wait-and-see attitude based on a feeling that "it probably isn't as bad as that." One can agree with Otfried Höffe, who pleads for a *zukunftsfähige Haltung,* a "future-proof attitude" which consists of

> "Basic attitudes, moving between the two extremes of a fatalistic powerlessness and a technocratic illusion of omnipotence, and between foolish euphoria and destructive despair. The relatively emotion-free attitude, the level-headed curiosity about what the future will bring, leads to the preparedness to deconstruct a situation into its constituting parts and to assess the relationships between them, to check the facts, to draw conclusions and to discuss possibilities, as well as to design alternative scenarios, not least, where necessary, to obtain missing information."[47]

In short, we should analyze a situation with a cool head and tackle complex problems by reducing them to the constituting elements which can each be handled separately and have a bit more confidence in human reason.

NOTES

1 Jared Diamond, *Collapse—How Societies Choose to Fail or Succeed* (New York and London: Penguin, 2011), p. 3.
2 Ibid., p. 498.
3 Cécile Bouanchaud and Audrey Garric, "Le succès inattendu des théories de l'effondrement," *Le Monde,* February 6, 2019.
4 Pablo Servigne, Raphaël Stevens, Gauthier Chapelle, *Une autre fin du monde est possible – Vivre l'effondrement (et pas seulement y survivre)* (Paris: Éditions du Seuil, 2018), p. 15.
5 Ibid.
6 Pablo Servigne and Raphaël Stevens, *Comment tout peut s'effondrer – Petit manuel de collapsologie à l'usage des générations présentes* (Paris: Éditions du Seuil, 2015), p. 66.
7 Ibid., p. 249.
8 Ibid., p. 188.
9 Pablo Servigne, Raphaël Stevens, Gauthier Chapelle, *Une autre fin du*

monde est possible—Vivre l'effondrement (et pas seulement y survivre), op. cit., p. 29.

10 Pablo Servigne en Raphaël Stevens, *Comment tout peut s'effondrer—Petit manuel de collapsologie à l'usage des générations présentes,* op. cit., p. 180.

11 Ibid.

12 Wouter van Noort and Lars Zuidweg, "Ik moest laatst huilen om een paper van het klimaatpanel," *NRC,* February 16-17, 2019.

13 Ibid.

14 Ibid.

15 Ibid.

16 "La France: Patrie de la collapsologie?" *Fondation Jean Jaurès,* February 10, 2020. https://www.jean-jaures.org/publication/la-france-patrie-de-la-collapsologie/

17 Pablo Servigne and Raphaël Stevens, *Comment tout peut s'effondrer—Petit manuel de collapsologie à l'usage des générations présentes,* op. cit., p. 139.

18 Ibid., p. 144.

19 Ibid., p. 145.

20 Max Weber, "'Kirchen' und 'Sekten'," in Max Weber, *Schriften 1894–1922,* op. cit., p. 236.

21 Ibid., p. 237.

22 Pablo Servigne and Raphaël Stevens, *Comment tout peut s'effondrer—Petit manuel de collapsologie à l'usage des générations présentes,* op. cit., pp. 22–23.

23 Ibid., p. 23.

24 Ibid., p. 24.

25 Pablo Servigne, Raphaël Stevens, Gauthier Chapelle, *Une autre fin du monde est possible—Vivre l'effondrement (et pas seulement y survivre),* op. cit., p. 27.

26 Ibid., p. 30.

27 Ibid., p. 26.

28 Sandrine Cabut, "Le changement climatique peut engendrer un stress pré-traumatique" (Interview with the psychiatrist Antoine Pelissolo), *Le Monde,* October 27, 2021.

29 Jennifer Jacquet, *Is Shame Necessary? New Uses for an Old Tool* (London: Penguin Books, 2016), p. 45.

30 Ibid., p. 46.

31 Ezra Klein, "Climate change isn't a good reason to not have children, or hope," *The New York Times,* June 7, 2022.

32 Fanny Madeline, "Les flammes de Notre-Dame, c'est notre monde qui brûle," *Le Monde,* April 18, 2019.

33   Leon Festinger, Henry W. Riecken, Stanley Schachter, *When Prophecy Fails—A Social and Psychological Study of a Modern Group that Predicted the Destruction of the World* (New York: Harper & Row, 1964). First published in 1956.

34   Reinhart Koselleck, "Wiederholungsstrukturen in Sprache und Geschichte," in Reinhart Koselleck, *Vom Sinn und Unsinn der Geschichte—Aufsätze und Vorträge aus vier Jahrzehnten* (Berlin: Suhrkamp Verlag, 2010), p. 107.

35   Cf. Leon Festinger, Henry W. Riecken, Stanley Schachter, *When Prophecy Fails—A Social and Psychological Study of a Modern Group that Predicted the Destruction of the World,* op. cit., p. 212: "Most dramatic of all, of course, is the contrast in the behavior of the group as they awaited the coming of the spacemen before the major disconfirmation and afterward. On December 17 and 21, they shielded themselves completely from outsiders, and the innermost circle alone watched for saucers in the privacy of Mrs. Keech's back yard or living room. On December 24 they not only informed the press, but invited the public to their Christmas carol vigil in the street in front of the Keech home. There is no doubt that, after disconfirmation, the members of the group made themselves far more available to outsiders, and thus to potential converts."

36   David Wallace-Wells, *The Uninhabitable Earth: Life After Warming* (New York: Tim Duggan Books, 2019), p. 20.

37   Ibid., p. 21.

38   "Geoengineering the climate—Science, governance and uncertainty," *RS Policy Document 10/09,* The Royal Society, London, 2009. https://royalsociety.org/~/media/royal_society_content/policy/publications/2009/8693.pdf

39   Fred Krupp, Nathaniel Keohane, Eric Pooley, "Less Than Zero—Can Carbon-Removal Technologies Curb Climate Change?" in *Foreign Affairs,* Volume 98, No. 2, March/April 2019, p. 143.

40   Ibid., p. 152.

41   Peter J. Irvine, David W. Keith, and John Moore, "Brief communication: Understanding solar geoengineering's potential to limit sea level rise requires attention from cryosphere experts," *The Cryosphere,* 12, 2501-2513, 2018.

42   Jon Taylor, "Geo-engineering—useful tool for tackling climate change, or dangerous distraction?" *WWF UK Blog,* September 6, 2012.

43   "What next? Solar geoengineering," *The World Ahead 2022* (published by *The Economist),* November 1, 2021.

44   Pierre Nora, "La fin d'un monde n'est pas la fin du monde," *Le Monde,* March 12, 2019.

45   Zygmunt Bauman, *Retrotopia* (Cambridge: Polity Press, 2017), p. 5.

46 Pierre Nora, "La fin d'un monde n'est pas la fin du monde," op. cit. (My italics, MHVH).

47 Otfried Höffe, *Ist die Demokratie zukunftsfähig?* (Munich: C.H. Beck, 2009), p. 33.

PART IV

OUR RESPONSIBILITY
FOR FUTURE GENERATIONS

CHAPTER 13

THE MODERN RISK SOCIETY AND OUR INCREASED RESPONSIBILITY FOR FUTURE GENERATIONS

More than the preceding generations, the "Covid-generation" feels a responsibility for future generations. This responsibility for future generations is a new phenomenon and is related to a growing awareness that man and not some metaphysical power is the creator of history. If we consider history as a preordained, teleological process—led by God, Providence, a Hegelian *Geist*, or an abstract principle such as *Progress*—some alien power seems to be directing history, instrumentalizing human passions, interests, and activities for the realization of its own, more or less metaphysical "goal." In such a system human responsibility for future generations is restricted and the only way to anticipate the future is through the prophecies of holy men: divine messengers who pretend to have direct access to the secret plans of the Supreme Being, or—as in the case of Hegel—philosophers who think that they are clever enough to decrypt the plans of the *Geist*. Knowledge of the future is here mainly a question of *revelation*—dependent on the willingness of the Supreme Being to have his goals disclosed.

However, it is different when history is conceived as a purely human undertaking in which there exists no divine, all-embracing teleological goal, which is realized behind the people's backs. The only teleology is a *human* teleology, the plans and projects for the future made by humans. For the rest, history remains a causal process and it is this causality which leads to trends and developments which can eventually be extrapolated and make it possible for historians and social scientists to make more or less precise predictions—including predictions on the consequences of certain political developments or the introduction of new technologies. Extrapolating negative trends can lead to probabilistic future scenarios which then become a stimulus for action to avoid these trends from materializing.

A MODERN "RISK SOCIETY"?

In 2003 the Organization for Economic Cooperation and Development (OECD) published a report, titled *Emerging Systemic Risks in the 21st Century: An Agenda for Action,* in which the authors warned that

> "Globalisation in all its dimensions—economic, technological, cultural, environmental—is growing apace and increasing interdependence, making it all the easier for dangerous pathogens, pollutants, and technical failures to spread. Equally important, the frontiers of scientific discovery and technological innovation are expanding at breathtaking speeds, confronting society with unknown (indeed, unknowable) impacts, and therefore immensely difficult choices."[1]

It is interesting that in a period in which globalization was still widely praised as a motor of the neoliberal economic order, the OECD pointed at the risks of this development and also asked attention for the potential downside of scientific discovery and technological innovation. "Risk" was the new magic word. And risks changed: "One hundred years ago, there was no risk of nuclear disaster; 50 years ago, there was no risk of computer viruses, let alone cybercrime; and 10 years ago, you could not be killed by a 'drone.' As our world changes as a result of new technologies, the risks we face also change."[2] The German sociologist Ulrich Beck called a society in which the present is no longer determined by the past, but by a growing preoccupation with the future, a "risk society."

> "A risk society," he wrote, "means: the past loses its determining influence on the present. In its place comes the future, so something that does not exist, [something] that is constructed, fictional, informs what we are experiencing and

doing today. When we talk about risks, we argue about something that is *not* the case, but that *could* happen, when not *now* immediately one changes course."[3]

Very imaginatively, Beck called risks "negative pictures of utopias."[4] The concept of risk has its origin in sixteenth- and seventeenth-century navigation, when European adventurers began to explore unknown and uncharted continents.[5] Although Beck coined the concept of a "risk society," he was not the first who drew attention to this problem. In her book *The Human Condition,* published in 1958, Hannah Arendt had already pointed to the risks related to the increased power of the physical sciences which, according to her, were "sciences of potentially irreversible irremediable "processes of no return" …"[6] She warned that in modern society one had acquired the power "to start new unprecedented processes whose outcome remains uncertain and unpredictable whether they are let loose in the human or the natural realm."[7]

Due to modern technology risks have, indeed, increased exponentially. Risks are the unintended negative consequences of human action. A well-known example is the invention of nuclear weapons. In his book *Nuclear Ethics,* published in 1988, Joseph S. Nye Jr. asks the question: "What are the risks of nuclear war?" And he answers:

"That is a critical question, but unfortunately there is no fully satisfactory answer. In recent years public opinion polls have shown anything from one-third to one-half of the American public saying they expect nuclear war with the Soviet Union within the next decade. In contrast, my informal polling of a few score nuclear specialists over the past few years has produced a modal answer of expectations of nuclear war between the United States and the Soviet Union in the next decade of about one chance in one hundred."[8]

It is telling that in 1988 "one-third to one-half" of the American public expected in the next decade a nuclear war with (what then still was) the Soviet Union—different from specialists who estimated the risk no higher than about one percent. One can therefore overestimate, as well as underestimate risks. The American public clearly overestimated the risk. Does this mean that the public should unconditionally trust the experts? Far from it. "Experts are rather a part of the problem than the solution," wrote Gerd Gigerenzer, himself a risk expert. "Many experts have themselves problems to understand risks." He added that "bitter experience teaches us that the advice of experts can be dangerous."[9]

Let us take another example: the peaceful use of nuclear energy. Nuclear energy offers a relatively cheap and clean energy. But this peaceful use of nuclear energy is also not without risks. One risk is the possibility of a terrorist attack from the air on a nuclear plant in a 9/11 scenario, in which a hijacked plane crashes into the plant and makes a split in the concrete shell releasing radiation, making a large part of the surroundings uninhabitable and killing thousands, possibly even tens of thousands of people. Another problem is the storage of nuclear waste. This is stored in isolated underground salt domes, granite layers, or clay layers, which should prevent the ground water from being radioactively contaminated. But because the degradation of nuclear waste takes many thousands, and even hundreds of thousands of years, future generations are confronted with the risk that geological instability might jeopardize their drinking water resources.[10]

FUKUSHIMA AS A *BLACK SWAN*

To illustrate the problem of risk, Nassim Nicholas Taleb used the concept of *black swans*. These "black swans" are "large-scale unpredictable and irregular events of massive consequence."[11] According to Taleb, history consists for the most part of such *black swan events*. With hindsight these extraordinary events become normal, he argues, because "Black Swans hijack our brains, making us feel we 'sort of' or 'almost' predicted them, because they are retrospectively explainable."[12] This means that "our minds are in the business of turning history into something smooth and linear, which makes us underestimate randomness."[(1)] Taleb points here to an important problem, namely man's tendency not only to minimalize risk *before* the events, but also *after* the events. The future seems to be less threatening because the risks which humanity ran in the past are known, making these risks understandable and explainable with hindsight, enabling us to "find a place for them" in a linear, almost logical historiography.[14] Apart from this psychological tendency to underestimate risks, there is yet another problem, namely that "we cannot calculate risks and probabilities of shocks and rare events, no matter how sophisticated we get."[15]

An example is the disaster with the Daiichi nuclear plant in Fukushima, Japan, on March 11, 2011. The nuclear plant was built in a region which was prone to earthquakes and tsunamis. According to a report by the Carnegie Endowment for International Peace, "insufficient attention was paid to evidence of large tsunamis inundating the region surrounding the plant about once every thousand years."[16] This was the reason why "the Fukushima Daiichi Nuclear Power Station was not designed to withstand a tsunami even half the size of the one that ultimately struck the Japanese coast in March 2011."[17] Many human errors were made. But the most important error, pointed out by the authors of the report, was that "many believed that a severe accident was simply impossible."[18] We see here how two factors—man's psychological tendency to underestimate risks and the difficulty in estimating these risks realistically—can lead to catastrophes.

Another tendency mentioned by Taleb can be observed: taking disasters from the past—even the recent past, such as the case of Fukushima—and later giving it a place in the "normal course of history." This becomes clear, for example, from an interview with Gregory Jaczko which took place eight years after the disaster. Jaczko was president of the American Nuclear Regulatory Commission from 2009 to 2012. On the question of whether America, which has about one hundred nuclear plants, has learned any lessons from the Fukushima disaster, he replied: "That is for me a very great disappointment: a part of the people in the industry have minimalized the problem, assuring that it was a Japanese problem which would not happen in the United States. However, the technology used in Japan is inspired by the American technology. It is a mistake to minimalize the disaster of Fukushima. We should have learned the lessons from it."[19] All this is a reason for some authors moving away from probabilistic scenarios, which per definition cannot be trusted, and replacing them with "worst-case scenarios" or *possibilistic* scenarios, which take into account situations in which almost all what can go wrong *does* go wrong. "In this approach, things that never happened before are possible. Indeed, they happen all the time."[20]

WORST–CASE SCENARIOS

But can we exclude all risks, even when we make use of these *worst-case* scenarios? What should one think, for instance, about the following event, described by Lee Clarke in his book *Worst Cases:*

> "On June 30, 1908, about 7:00 in the morning a meteorite (most likely—scientists still aren't sure) exploded some three to five miles over Siberia, near the Tunguska River. The object was probably 150 to 250 feet in diameter. Trees within a nine-mile radius were incinerated; those within twenty-five miles were flattened. The Tunguska Event, as astronomers call it, was fifteen times as powerful as the nuclear weapon that destroyed Hiroshima. Shock waves from Tunguska circled the globe twice. If an object of similar size exploded five miles over Manhattan millions of people would be incinerated. Survivors would say it was the worst disaster that ever happened."[21]

This does, indeed, appear to be an extraordinary event—something which happens once in a thousand years if not more. But is this so? On February 15, 2013—that means just over one hundred years later—a meteorite again exploded in Russia with a diameter of 20 meters and weighing more than the Eiffel Tower. The meteorite fell near the town of Chelyabinsk and caused a huge shockwave which had a force of about 450 kiloton TNT, thirty times the force of the nuclear bomb dropped on Hiroshima. Thanks to the fact that, again, the meteorite exploded in a sparsely populated region, there were "only" 1500 people wounded. Once again one might ask: imagine that this meteorite had fallen not in an almost empty region, but on New York, Moscow, or another megalopolis? In a report of the American National Academy of Sciences one can read that "for impactor diameters exceeding about 2 to 3 kilometers, worldwide damage is possible, thus affecting all of humanity and its entire living space."[22]

The meteorite which fell 66 million years ago in Mexico and led to the extinction of 75 percent of all animal species—including the dinosaurs—had a diameter of 10 kilometers. This risk, therefore, which is described by the report as "low probability, high-consequence," should clearly be taken seriously. Modern technology has made it possible for this risk to be reduced. At the University of Hawaii, for instance, a telescope was built which is used to watch the night sky in order to detect small asteroids which have escaped attention, making it possible for the authorities, in the case of an alarm, to warn and evacuate the population. Thanks to modern missile technology, it is even no longer necessary to sit and wait passively. There exist different methods for deflecting objects which are flying towards the earth. This may be done by destroying the asteroid with a nuclear weapon—which is one of the options studied by NEOShield-2, a project of the European Union.[23] Other options are the use of a "kinetic impactor," a heavy object which pushes the asteroid out of its trajectory, or the method of bringing a missile close to the object, and, by its gravity, changing the course of the asteroid.[24] These projects are no longer science fiction. On November 30, 2021, NASA launched the Double Asteroid Redirection Test Mission (DART) from a U.S. Space Force base in California. A 1,200-pound, refrigerator-size spacecraft orbited the sun on September 26, 2022, to slam into a small asteroid, named Dimorphos, at 15,000 miles per hour. The impact of the collision was more than expected. "We conducted humanity's first planetary defense test," said Bill Nelson, the administrator of NASA, "and we showed the world that NASA is serious as a defender of this planet."[25]

OUR INCREASED RESPONSIBILITY
FOR FUTURE GENERATIONS

Our increased interest in the future cannot only be explained by the longer causality chains and the increased risks related to the unintended consequences of human action, but also because of the availability of new technical opportunities for preventing natural disasters which are *not* caused by man—like the risk of meteorites. This has led to a new kind of moral responsibility for the future well-being and survival of mankind, as well as for the continued existence of animal and plant life.

The fact that causality chains have become longer is also clear from the climate problem. The generations who lived in the twentieth century have exploited natural energy sources without thinking much about the consequences. The awareness that CO_2 emissions were changing the climate developed only recently. Concrete steps to stop this process, announced at international climate conferences like the yearly COP conferences,[26] are not implemented by some countries and not sufficiently by others. The problem is that it will not be the generations which caused the problem that will suffer from its consequences, but mainly future generations.[27] According to Anthony Giddens, "The notion of risk becomes central in a society which is taking leave of the past, of traditional ways of doing things, and which is opening itself up to a problematic future."[28] He speaks in this context about "the colonization of the future."[29] However, it is just this "colonization of the future" which should be avoided. A colonial attitude implies that one exploits the resources of the earth without considering the interests of the colonized peoples which, in this case, aren't the "indigenous" peoples of conquered, overseas territories, but the "indigenous" peoples who live in the future, who happen to be our descendants.[30]

The question, therefore, is whether human ethics has adapted itself sufficiently to this new situation. Are we sufficiently conscious of the responsibility imposed by our increased ability to intervene in nature? According to Friedrich Hayek, "Only a confessed immoralist could indeed defend measures of policy on the grounds that 'in the long run we are all dead.' For the only groups to have spread and developed are those among whom it became customary to try to provide for children and later descendants whom one might never see."[31] But one need not to be immoral to neglect the interests of future generations. Hannah Arendt points to the problem of eventual unintended negative consequences:

"They have known that he who acts never quite knows what he is doing, that he always becomes 'guilty' of consequences he never intended or even foresaw, that no matter how disastrous and unexpected the consequences of his deed he can never undo it, that the process he starts is never consummated unequivocally in one single deed or event, and that its very meaning never discloses itself to the actor but only to the backward glance of the historian who himself does not act."[32]

Here, Hannah Arendt is talking about guilt. But is "guilt" here the right word? Guilt implies the transgression of a norm.[33] But is a scientist who, with the best intentions, introduces a new product or a new method, "guilty" because of unforeseen effects which appear much later? A more appropriate word to use is *responsibility*.[34] "Guilt" concerns only an individual's deeds in the past (which cannot be undone); responsibility, on the contrary, concerns also the consequences of his deeds in the future. Responsibility is related to concepts such as "prudence," "caution," "thoughtfulness," and "patience." A person who is cautious develops different scenarios in which he considers all eventual consequences of his actions, and will only take action if he can exclude major negative consequences—or if the positive consequences exceed by far the negative consequences (and these negative consequences are evenly spread among the population and do not harm one segment of the population in particular).

IMMANUEL KANT ON LATER GENERATIONS: "LUCKY DEVILS"

It is striking how our vision of the future has changed since 1784, when Kant wrote his essay "Idea for a Universal History with a Cosmopolitan Purpose." In this essay Kant considered the later generations not as potential victims, but as "lucky devils"—they were for him the beneficiaries of the endeavors and hard work of the preceding generations. Kant observed

"that the earlier generations seem to perform their laborious tasks only for the sake of the later ones, so as to prepare for them a further stage from which they can rise still higher the structure intended by nature; and secondly, that only the later generations will in fact have the good fortune to inhabit the building on which a whole series of their forefathers (admittedly, without any conscious intention) had worked without themselves being able to share in the happiness they were preparing."[35]

In the Enlightenment theory of linear progress there was no place for responsibility for the later generations because these were considered to be more prosperous and happier than the preceding generations. The category of risk could be developed only when it became clear that technological progress had also important downsides.

One of the first to have developed such an ethics of responsibility was the sociologist Max Weber. In his article *Politik als Beruf* (Politics as a Vocation) from 1919 he formulated this not as a general ethics, but as an ethics for a special group of people—politicians—because they had the power to decide on war and peace and therefore determined more than anyone else the future of their country. Weber criticized a Kantian *Gesinnungsethik,* a moral theory which only looks at the good intentions behind the deeds and not at the consequences, and he spoke about a "Verantwortung für die Zukunft" (responsibility for the future). "The believer in an ethic of responsibility...," he wrote, "doesn't feel in a position to pass on to others the consequences of his own actions, insofar he could foresee these."[36]

Hans Jonas has expanded the scope of this ethic of responsibility, not restricting it—as Weber did—to a select group of politicians, but making it a general ethical principle, valid for everyone. In his view, in traditional ethics human beings focus on their *shared present.* "The [traditional] ethical universe," he writes, "consists of contemporaries and its future horizon is restricted to their expected lifetime."[37] However, is such a limited ethic which restricts its guiding rules to living contemporaries still adequate in the advanced technological world in which we live? His answer is in the negative.

> "As concerns technology," he writes, "ethics has to do with actions ... which have an unprecedented causal reach into the future, accompanied by a prior knowledge which also exceeds, although incomplete, all that existed before. Add to this the sheer size of the later effects and also their irreversibility. All this places responsibility at the center of ethics, with time and space horizons which correspond with those of the actions."[38]

The greater and more far-reaching responsibility of the present generation is a consequence of its increased knowledge and power. "Both were in the past so limited that as concerns the future one had to leave most of it to chance and the continuity of the natural order...."[39] This is no longer the case. Our increased interest in the future is also linked to this new ethic of responsibility: our future has become increasingly constructible. With this increased makeability the risks also have increased, and together with it our collective responsibility. This new moral responsibility, which tries to avoid causing damage, is different from "old fashioned," juridical responsibility, which comes *post factum, after* the damage has been caused. Juridical responsibility is a strictly *personal* responsibility for a transgression which took place in the past. It is the basis for the attribution of guilt. "Guilt," writes Hannah Arendt, "unlike responsibility, always singles out; it is strictly personal. It refers to an act, not to intentions or potentialities."[40] Our responsibility for future generations, on the contrary, is a *collective* responsibility—admittedly with different gradations for different groups: politicians, scientists, and captains of industry bearing the brunt of this responsibility—but in principle no one is excluded, which is also why the populace at large should have a voice when far-reaching decisions are being taken.

An important question is, *how far* into the future does our responsibility reach for future generations? The answer of Paul Ricoeur is clear. He argues "that one needs a new imperative which imposes us to act in such a way that there are still humans after us."[41] This means there is in principle *no* exact time limit. Of course, in practice it will not always be easy to determine the risks. There is the problem of unintended negative collateral effects of innovations. Ricoeur mentions two opposite attitudes concerning these risks which should be avoided:

> "A short-term vision restricting the responsibility to predictable and controllable effects, and a long-term vision of an unlimited responsibility. The complete negligence of collateral effects of the action would make it unscrupulous, but an unlimited responsibility would make action impossible."[42]

And he concludes: "Between the flight for responsibility of

the consequences and the inflation of an endless responsibility one should find a middle ground...."[43]

To organize this collective responsibility, Otfried Höffe proposed a clear strategy for the decision-making procedure of far-reaching technologically innovative processes.

"... In the first place," he writes, "we need a public debate with critique as a necessary correction; secondly this public debate should take place in the initial phases of new technologies; and thirdly, this public debate should be organized deliberately and specifically with non-experts, namely with the population which has to bear the consequences of the technologies."[44]

GIVING FUTURE GENERATIONS A VOICE

The proposal to organize these public debates with non-experts is important. "In risk issues, no one is an expert," writes Ulrich Beck, "or everyone is an expert...."[45] And he adds: "First, people must say farewell to the notion that administrations and experts always know exactly, or at least better, what is right and good for everyone: demonopolization of expertise."[46] But even in this strategy, in which politicians, scientists, captains of industry, and the population discuss the introduction of innovations and share their responsibility for far-reaching decisions, one even more important stakeholder is missing—the future generations. Should they not be represented, in one way or another, if one agrees that we need a "sense of justice, respectively a sense of fairness, which rejects living at the expense of the children and grandchildren."[47]

The necessity to give a voice to future generations has led to interesting initiatives. In Israel, for instance, the parliament had from 2001 to 2006 a Commissioner for Future Generations.[48] In 2016 Wales followed this example,[49] while, since October 2017, the British parliament has an All-Party Parliamentary Group for Future Generations. This Group presents itself on its website as follows: "We raise awareness of long-term issues, explore ways to internalize longer-term considerations into decision-making processes, and create space for cross-party dialogue on combating short-termism in policy-making." [50] The group organized in November 2020 an event on the "Consequences of Covid-19 for Future Generations." There are also local initiatives. Since 2015, for instance, residents of the Japanese town of Yahaba (population 27,000) take part in the project *Future Design*. This project is presented as

> "A unique model of political decision-making where they are invited to public meetings to discuss plans for their town's future. They start as themselves, with the perspective of a current resident. But then—and this is where it gets interesting—they are given colorful ceremonial robes to wear and told to imagine themselves as residents of the town in 2060. It turns out that when they're acting as people from the future, they advocate far more transformative policies, from health care provision to climate change action." [51]

This model is spreading rapidly and was also adopted by Kyoto. These are, indeed, praiseworthy initiatives. However, they don't change the fact that the future generations themselves are absent and cannot express their vision. This is a reason, when making decisions, to be extremely cautious in taking risks and not skate on thin ice.

NOTES

1   "Emerging Systemic Risks in the 21st Century: An Agenda for Action," Paris, OECD, 2003. https://www.oecd.org/gov/risk/37944611.pdf
2   Mark Coeckelbergh, *Human Being @Risk—Enhancement, Technology, and the Evaluation of Vulnerability Transformations* (Dordrecht, Heidelberg, New York, London: Springer, 2013), p. 5.
3   Ulrich Beck, *Was ist Globalisierung?* (Frankfurt am Main: Suhrkamp Verlag, 1998), p. 171.
4   Ulrich Beck, *Risikogesellschaft—Auf dem Weg in eine andere Moderne* (Frankfurt am Main: Suhrkamp Verlag, 1986), p. 37.
5   Anthony Giddens pointed to the fact that "risk" was originally a concept indicating space and only later became a concept indicating time: "The idea of risk appears to have taken hold in the sixteenth and seventeenth centuries and was first coined by Western explorers as they set off on their

voyages across the world. The word 'risk' seems to have come into English through Spanish or Portuguese, where it was used to refer to sailing into uncharted waters. Originally, in other words, it had an orientation to space. Later, it became transferred to time, as used in banking and investment, to mean calculation of the probable consequences of investment decisions for borrowers and lenders." (Anthony Giddens, *Runaway World—How Globalisation is Reshaping our Lives* (London: Profile Books, 2000), pp. 21–22).

6   Hannah Arendt, *The Human Condition* (Chicago and London: The University of Chicago Press, 1958), p. 231.

7   Ibid., pp. 231–32. Arendt expressed the same idea several times. She wrote, for instance, "It is beyond doubt that the capacity to act is the most dangerous of all human abilities and possibilities, and it is also beyond doubt that the self-created risks mankind faces today have never been faced before." (Hannah Arendt, "The Concept of History—Ancient and Modern," in Hannah Arendt, *The Portable Hannah Arendt,* edited and with an introduction by Peter Baehr (New York: Penguin Books, 2000), p. 296.)

8   Joseph S. Nye Jr., *Nuclear Ethics* (New York and London: The Free Press, 1988), p. 71.

9   Gerd Gigerenzer, "Psychologie des Risikos—Wann eine freie Gesellschaft risikokompetente Bürger braucht," *Aus Politik und Zeitgeschichte,* 23–25, June 2020. https://www.bpb.de/shop/zeitschriften/apuz/risikokompetenz-2022/508885/psychologie-des-risikos/

10   The French newspaper *Le Monde* wrote that France, which, with 58 nuclear plants, has after the United States the greatest reactor park of the world, "has today a stock of more than 1,5 million cubic meters radioactive waste, the volume of which will be tripled or quadrupled in the coming decades." The paper explained that "in France … it is the products with high levels of activity or a long life cycle which form the greatest challenge. They represent only 3% of the total stock, but concentrate 99.8% of its radioactivity and will potentially remain very dangerous for health and the environment for hundreds of thousands of years." ("Un débat salutaire sur les déchets nucléaires," Editorial, *Le Monde,* March 9, 2019).

11   Nassim Nicholas Taleb, *Antifragile—Things that Gain from Disorder* (New York: Penguin Books, 2013), p. 6.

12   Ibid.

13   Ibid.

14   This tendency to give disasters, wars, and revolutions *afterwards* a place in a "comforting" historical narrative has also been observed by Fred Halliday. "It is easy," he writes, "from the emplacement of a set of liberal democratic and prosperous countries, from, as it were, the comfort of the OECD armchair, to see the path to contemporary society as a smooth one, and disregard the unfortunate deviations as we went along. It is, of course, quite

inaccurate: the violence of the past—in wars and revolutions—was as much formative of the present as was enlightened, steady progress." (Fred Halliday, *The World at 2000* (Houndmills and New York: Palgrave Macmillan, 2001), p. 144.) Wars don't fit in this progressive, liberal worldview and are therefore often downplayed in the historiography of liberal historians, as Hans Joas emphasizes, who writes: "In the worldview of liberalism, wars and violent internal conflicts must appear as relics of a disappearing epoch, which have not yet been illuminated by the light of the Enlightenment." (Hans Joas, "Der Traum von der gewaltfreien Moderne," in Hans Joas, *Kriege und Werte—Studien zur Gewaltgeschichte des 20. Jahrhunderts* (Weilerswist: Velbrück Wissenschaft, 2000), p. 50.) And Joas continues: "Sharp rejection of violence is in this worldview accompanied by a certain minimalization of its presence." (Ibid., p. 51.)

15   Nassim Nicholas Taleb, *Antifragile—Things that Gain from Disorder,* op. cit., p. 8.

16   James M. Acton and Mark Hibbs, "Why Fukushima was preventable," *The Carnegie Papers,* Washington, D.C., Carnegie Endowment for International Peace, March 2012, p. 1. https://carnegieendowment.org/files/fukushima.pdf

17   Ibid., p. 9.

18   Ibid., p. 2.

19   Nabil Wakim, "On n'a plus besoin de prendre le risque nucléaire—Huit ans après Fukushima, l'ex-patron de l'autorité américaine de sûreté juge que les leçons n'ont pas été tirées," *Le Monde,* March 12, 2019. *The Economist* wrote about a research project at the University of Prague on the question of why natural disasters are so quickly forgotten. The group investigated how far the massive inundations of the river Vltava, which happened a bit less than once per century, led to the construction of houses higher up in the river valley. "In each case, new settlements appeared a significantly higher vertical distance above the river's normal level than settlements built in the same area before the flood, and continued to do so for 25 years (about a generation) after the deluge. By the subsequent generation, however—the grandchildren of the flood's survivors—they started creeping downhill again, closer to the river, and encroaching on the zone of flood risk." The researchers concluded that "to be deterred from placing themselves back in danger, people have to hear disaster tales from eye-witnesses who can convey the visceral emotion of having lived through them." ("When will they ever learn? Memories of natural disasters fade fast. And maybe unnatural ones, too," *The Economist,* April 20, 2019.)

20   Charles Perrow, "Fukushima, risk, and probability: Expect the unexpected," *Bulletin of the Atomic Scientists,* April 1, 2011. https://thebulletin.org/biography/charles-perrow/

21 Lee Clarke, *Worst Cases—Terror and Catastrophe in the Popular Imagination* (Chicago and London: The University of Chicago Press, 2006), p. 3.

22 "Defending Planet Earth: Near-Earth-Object Surveys and Hazard Mitigation Strategies," Report, The National Academy of Science, Washington D.C., 2010, p. 7. https://www.nap.edu/read/12842/chapter/1#xvi

23 http://www.neoshield.eu/ On the website of NEOShield-2 one can read: "What is the threat from NEOs [Near Earth Objects]? NEOs impact the Earth every day! Yes every day! It's therefore not a question if a NEO will hit the Earth, but rather when it will hit and how big will it be!"

24 "How do you stop an asteroid hitting Earth," *The Economist,* July, 4, 2013.

25 Sarah Scoles, "NASA Spacecraft Accomplishes Mission and Smashes Asteroid Into New Orbit." *The New York Times,* October 12, 2022.

26 COP stands for Conference of the Parties (COP) to the United Nations Framework Convention on Climate Change (UNFCCC). These conferences are organized each year. An exception was 2020, when COP26 (in Glasgow) was postponed to 2021, due to the Corona-19 pandemic.

27 Karl Popper considered therefore not the proletariat, but rather the children as the new underdog. On the question of what should be the role of the Left parties, he answered: "The original function of the left was to support the *underdogs,* the most underprivileged. This principle is certainly still valid. What is tiresome is that the left has taken the wrong path and started to lose when, for ideological reasons, she continued to consider the proletariat, the workers, as the *underdogs,* even when they weren't that any longer.... We have to look around and ask ourselves who are the *underdogs.* I argue that the only category which at this moment can be considered as such are the children." (Karl Popper, *La leçon de ce siècle* (Paris: Anatolia Editions, 1993), p. 91.) (Emphasis in the original, MHVH.)

28 Anthony Giddens, *Modernity and Self-Identity—Self and Society in the Late Modern Age* (Stanford: Stanford University Press, 1991), p. 111.

29 Ibid.

30 Some authors already anticipate the negative judgment of future generations about our generation—as, for instance, Tom Chatfield, who does not exclude that they will hate us. (Tom Chatfield, "What our descendants will deplore about us," *BBC,* June 27, 2014.) https://www.bbc.com/future/article/20140627-how-our-descendants-will-hate-us

31 Friedrich Hayek, *The Fatal Conceit—The Errors of Socialism* (London: Routledge, 1990), p. 84.32

32 Hannah Arendt, *The Human Condition,* op. cit., p. 233.

33 Marc D. Hauser, *Moral Minds—How Nature Designed Our Universal Sense of Right and Wrong* (New York: HarperCollins, 2006), p. 8: "Guilt

represents one form of response to a social transgression—a violation of societal norms."

34   One could in this case speak about "guilt" when the researcher consciously and willingly transgresses the security prescriptions.

35   Immanuel Kant, "Idea for a Universal History with a Cosmopolitan Purpose," in Immanuel Kant, *Political Writings,* edited by H. S. Reiss (Cambridge and New York: Cambridge University Press, 1991), p. 44.

36   Max Weber, "Politik als Beruf," in Max Weber, *Schriften 1894–1922,* op. cit., p. 545.

37   Hans Jonas, *Das Prinzip Verantwortung—Versuch einer Ethik für die technologische Zivilisation* (Frankfurt am Main: Suhrkamp Verlag, 1984), p. 23.

38   Ibid., p. 9.

39   Ibid., p. 222.

40   Hannah Arendt, "Collective Responsibility," in Hannah Arendt, *Responsibility and Judgment* (New York: Schocken Books, 2003), p. 147.

41   Paul Ricoeur, "Le concept de responsabilité," in Paul Ricoeur, *Le Juste 1* (Paris: Éditions Esprit, 1995), p. 65.

42   Ibid., p. 68.

43   Ibid.

44   Otfried Höffe, *Sittlich-politische Diskurse—Philosophische Grundlagen, Politische Ethik, Biomedizinische Ethik* (Frankfurt am Main: Suhrkamp Verlag, 1981), p. 211.

45   Ulrich Beck, "The Reinvention of Politics," in Ulrich Beck, Anthony Giddens, Scott Lash, *Reflexive Modernization—Politics, Tradition and Aesthetics in the Modern Social Order* (Cambridge: Polity Press, 1994), p. 9.

46   Ibid., p. 29.

47   Otfried Höffe, *Ist die Demokratie zukunftsfähig?—Über moderne Politik* (Munich: C. H. Beck, 2009), p. 303.

48   Benjamin Möckel, "Zukünftige Generationen—Geschichte einer politischen Pathosformel," *Aus Politik und Zeitgeschichte* (70), 52–53, December 21, 2020, p. 38.

49   Future Generations Commissioner for Wales. https://www.futuregenerations.wales/

50   All-Party Parliamentary Group For Future Generations. https://www.appg-futuregenerations.com/

51   Roman Krznaric, "How to be a good ancestor," *The Boston Globe,* October 30, 2020. https://www.bostonglobe.com/2020/10/30/opinion/how-be-good-ancestor/

CHAPTER 14

EXPLORING THE FUTURE I:
THE ROLE OF UTOPIAS AND DYSTOPIAS

In order to assume responsibility for future generations we have to anticipate the future. But *can* we anticipate the future? The desire to know the future is as old as humanity. Man, gifted with reason, projects himself in time. He knows that he has a past and that—if all goes well— a new day will come tomorrow. How many "tomorrows" there will be he doesn't know, but one thing he knows for certain—one day he will die. He knows that this is his own, personal future and the future of all mortal beings. Death is the final perspective, but between birth and death a lot can happen, and human curiosity is particularly concerned with this personal trajectory. That said, man's curiosity is engaged by not only his personal future, but also that of the group to which he belongs. This group can be his family, his tribe, his nation, or mankind as a whole. In all these cases the time perspective changes because the future of the group doesn't stop with the death of the individual. The group existed before the present generation and will live on long after the present generation has disappeared.

THE UTOPIAN VISIONS OF THOMAS MORE, TOMMASO CAMPANELLA, FRANCIS BACON, AND JULES VERNE

In the course of history man has developed a range of methods for peering into the future. One of these methods are the fantasies about the future created by writers, poets, and philosophers. If these fantasies are optimistic and positive, they are called utopias; if they are pessimistic and negative, they are called dystopias. Both have a modest pretention. The authors of these narratives don't pretend to be clairvoyant, nor to dispose of secret knowledge about the future. Their fantasies remain purely personal visions of what the future could look like. They reflect the hopes and fears of their generation. It is striking that in the sixteenth and seventeenth centuries these narratives were often projected not in time, but in space. They are not yet projected into a future epoch, but are described as contemporaneous societies, recently discovered by explorers in far-off exotic locations. The most well-known of these literary-philosophical fantasies is Thomas More's *Utopia*. The title comes from the Greek οὐ τόπος (ou topos), meaning literally "no place." Thomas More (1478–1535) published "Utopia" in 1516, one year before Martin Luther put his 95 Theses on the church door of Wittenberg and 24 years after Columbus discovered America. It was a time of upheaval and great societal change, which finally brought More to the scaffold. His "Utopia" is the expression of the high expectations he and his contemporaries had of the future.

The inhabitants of Utopia, which is located on an island in the recently discovered New World, are rather modern. In a time when monarchy was the prevailing regime, their state is a republic and, moreover, democracy is already developed: the Utopians have indirect elections and the towns have elected mayors. In Utopia there is a six-hour working day, because "they don't wear people out, though, by keeping them hard at work from early morning till late at night, like cart-horses."[1] This short working day is possible because the women also work. Regarding its political organization, working hours, and labor participation, Utopia comes close to our twenty-first-century norms. The Utopians are also generous: "One seventh of their total exports to any country go as a free gift to the poor—the rest they sell at reasonable prices."[2] Not only does this policy remind one of the modern welfare state and of modern development aid, but it exceeds ours in generosity. Of course, there are from our point of view also negative aspects to More's Utopia. Sex before marriage is strictly forbidden and is punished with a lifelong imposed celibacy; there is no private property; luxury goods are taboo; there is no privacy; and one needs passes to travel within the country. In More's ideal state, equality and solidarity clearly have priority over personal freedom.

One century after More's *Utopia*, Tommaso Campanella (1568–1639) published *La Città del Sole* (1623), the "City of the Sun."

Campanella was a Dominican monk from Calabria (the "toe" of Italy's boot), who wrote the book during his 27 years of imprisonment after the Spanish authorities, who ruled in the south of Italy, had accused him of a conspiracy against the Spanish state. Like Thomas More, Campanella also emphasizes the great transformations that are taking place during his time. "More history has happened in the world in the past hundred years," he writes, "than in the 4000 years before, and more books have been published in these hundred years than in the preceding 5000 [years]."[3] He speaks about the "the surprising inventions of the magnet, the art of printing, and firearms, which are a sign of the unification of the world."[4] Campanella's utopia is clearly inspired by Thomas More. On his imaginary island, too, there is no private property and people work only four hours per day—even less than in More's Utopia. Their abundant leisure time offers the inhabitants the opportunity to study throughout their lives—a *lifelong learning* which looks quite modern. But this is not all, because, he continues, "you should know this—that they have invented the art of flying, which is something we don't have in our part of the world and they expect to acquire an eye-glass with which they can observe hidden stars and a hearing instrument with which they can listen to the harmony of the movements of the planets."[5] Campanella's remark that the inhabitants of his utopian Sun City have invented the art of flying is certainly a sign of a visionary glance into the future, but he is not completely original. In 1488 Leonardo da Vinci (1452–1519) had already made sketches of aircraft. Other ideas put forward by Campanella are rather dystopian, such as his eugenist ideas. Procreation in his Sun City is regulated by the state in order to build a strong and beautiful race. State functionaries chose the best moments for copulation, based on astrological data. Repeated homosexual activity is punished with capital punishment, and children are taken away from their mothers and placed in community houses. As in More's Utopia, Campanella's ideal world of the future is a world in which people don't work a lot and in which emphasis is placed on social equality. However, the fact that this ideal world is founded on an authoritarian state, which meddles in the most intimate affairs of the citizens, is not considered as a problem.

In the same year that Campanella publishes his "Sun City," Francis Bacon (1561–1626) wrote down his vision in *The New Atlantis,* another blueprint for a utopian society called Bensalem, which was located on an exotic island west of America. In the book, which was published posthumously in 1627, Bacon developed his technologically inspired vision. The inhabitants of the island are adepts of experimental science in which they have made considerable progress. They have, for instance, invented a "water of paradise," an elixir which prolongs life. They can also speed up the flowering of plants and manipulate the size of fruits and animals. They benefit from cold stores, skyscrapers, and water power. It is interesting that almost everything that Bacon described has become reality. This is also true for another visionary, Jules Verne (1828–1905) who, two centuries later, let the main characters of his novels travel to the moon, dive deep under the sea in submarines, and travel around the world in eighty days. It seems to be easier to forecast technological progress than to anticipate social and political changes.

The scientific and technological progress which was so loudly praised by Bacon would some centuries later also show its downside. New technologies were used to produce more and better food, travel faster, improve hygiene and health care, and embellish life in general: however, weapon systems were also improved. Alfred Nobel, the inventor of dynamite, had hoped that his invention would make war impossible. His hope was in vain. The invention of the nuclear bomb and the hydrogen bomb, which put the destructive power of dynamite into the shade, led to the same hope. "A frightening coincidence of fatalism and the will to progress now dominates all thinking about progress in history," writes Karl Löwith. "Progress has been imposed on us; it has become our fate."[6]

THE TWENTIETH-CENTURY DYSTOPIAS OF ALDOUS HUXLEY, GEORGE ORWELL, AND JOHN MAYNARD KEYNES

In the twentieth century the time for optimistic views of the future seemed to be over, if we are to believe two authors: Aldous Huxley (1894–1963) and George Orwell (1903–1950), who included their own experience in their visions of the future. Huxley's *Brave New World,* published in 1932,[7] and Orwell's *Nineteen Eighty-Four,* published in

1949,[8] are both prototypes of the modern dystopia. They make clear how the optimism of the past made way for pessimism and concern about the future. Aldous Huxley's point of departure is the technological progress which, in his time, was exemplified by so-called "Fordism"—the dull, deadening production-line work which subjects the worker to the rhythm of a machine—a system that some years later would be ridiculed by Charlie Chaplin in his movie *Modern Times*. In Huxley's dystopia, set in the year 2540, also called 632 AF (After Ford), Huxley depicts a world society ruled by ten World Controllers, in which babies are produced in test tubes outside the uterus. Dependent on the food they receive, five classes are bred, of which the most intelligent become the leaders. It is a society in which efficiency prevails, people are not allowed to engage in permanent relationships, and the citizens are kept satisfied with con- sumerism and tranquilizers.

While Huxley's dystopia is rather a reaction to the extreme capital- ism and "Fordism" in which people become part of a machine, Orwell's inspiration for writing *Nineteen Eighty-Four* comes rather from Stalin's totalitarian state in the Soviet Union. Orwell depicts a future Great Britain which is part of a global empire, called Oceania. This superstate is ruled by the "Party." The party leader is Big Brother, who does not tolerate independent thinking. The "Ministry of Truth" takes care that no one deviates from the official party line, helped by the thought police. In this future state there is no privacy; Big Brother and his helpers can continually observe the citizens at home, as well as in public spaces, and children are encouraged to denounce their parents if they express sub- versive opinions.

A third author, John Maynard Keynes, is not known as someone who wrote about utopias or dystopias. However, I think that he also deserves to be mentioned here. In his essay, titled "Economic Possibilities for our Grandchildren," (1930) he warned that our technological progress could have unexpected downsides.

> "Let us, for the sake of argument, suppose," he wrote, "that
> a hundred years hence we are all of us, on the average,
> eight times better off in the economic sense than we are

today.... Now it is true that the needs of human beings may seem to be insatiable. But they fall into two classes—those needs which are absolute in the sense that we feel them whatever the situation of our fellow human beings may be, and those which are relative in the sense that we feel them only if their satisfaction lifts us above, makes us feel superior to, our fellows. Needs of the second class ... may indeed be insatiable ... but this is not so true of the absolute needs."[9]

Keynes continued: "I draw the conclusion that, assuming no important wars and no important increase in population, the *economic problem* may be solved, or at least within sight of solution, within a hundred years."[10] However, will mankind be happy with the dramatic increase in leisure time this would bring? Keynes doubts that this will be the case. Not happiness, but rather unhappiness will be the result. "Why," he asks, "is this so startling?" And he answered:

"If the economic problem is solved, mankind will be deprived of its traditional purpose.... Must we not expect a general 'nervous breakdown'?... To those who sweat for their daily bread leisure is a longed-for sweet—until they get it.... There is no country and no people, I think, who can look forward to the age of leisure and of abundance without a dread.... It is a fearful problem for the ordinary person, with no special talents, to occupy himself.... To judge from the behavior and the achievements of the wealthy classes today in any quarter of the world, the outlook is very depressing."[11]

For Keynes a future society in which mankind would be largely freed from the necessity to work for the satisfaction of its immediate needs would be a source of boredom and depression. He clearly disagreed with Marx's famous dictum that "the realm of freedom actually begins only where labour which is determined by necessity and mundane considerations ceases."[12]

ARE UTOPIAS AND DYSTOPIAS USEFUL?

Utopias and dystopias reflect the hopes and fears of their authors. They reflect the positive and negative tendencies which they observe in their own societies. These tendencies are projected into the future or described as existing societies in exotic locations. Their prognostic capacity is variable, as well as the way in which they evaluate certain developments. Thomas More and Campanella, living in an agricultural, pre-industrial world with long working days, both predict a reduction of the working day, which they welcome. Huxley, on the contrary, is rather looking to the *quality* of work and the dull and deadening character it has acquired under modern "Fordism." Both More and Campanella, living in authoritarian, feudal societies, seem to have no problems with a lack of privacy and a government which meddles in the most intimate affairs of the citizens, such as procreation and their sexual lives. For Huxley and Orwell, living in modern, individualistic societies, this is a nightmare.

One can question the usefulness of utopias and dystopias, these caricatural exaggerations of trends which the authors observe in their own times. However, we should not forget that these visions, apart from their literary interest, also have a societal function. Just as a dystopia is a warning, the utopia is an encouragement. The German philosopher Ernst Bloch, who wrote a three-volume study on utopias and the principle of hope, forged the concept of "concrete utopias." A concrete utopia was, according to him, "the unity of hope and knowledge of the process."[13] "The solid dream," he explained, "relates actively to what historically stands before the door and is being more or less prevented [from happening].... It is its function ... to deliver the forms and contents which have already developed in the womb of contemporary society."[14] And he continued, "The personal dream also contains a tendency of its time *and of the coming time* expressed in images...."[15] According to Bloch the author of a utopian vision discovers in his own society tendential possibilities which, if they are made into deliberate goals, can be realized "when the time is ripe." The Polish philosopher Leszek Kolakowski has expressed the same idea as follows: "The utopia is the aspiration to have changes which 'in reality' cannot be realized by direct action, which lie outside the predictable future and which one cannot compute in advance."[16] However, according to him we need these utopian dreams to create a better future, because "the existence of the utopia as utopia is the clear precondition for the possibility for the utopia to stop being a utopia."[17] A utopia is a dream about a possible future, and one needs these dreams to make this future come true. The same applies, *mutatis mutandis,* to the dystopia. The author of the dystopia identifies in his society tendential dangers for the well-being of the people, and he hopes that by describing and exaggerating these dangers his forecast will become a *self-denying prophecy.* The utopia, as well as the dystopia, appeal to the actions of people, urging them not to wait passively, but to take action in order to shape their own future and the future of their descendants. Both the utopia and the dystopia rely on tendencies which are present in society and which in the former are valued positively and, in the latter, negatively. An important question, naturally, is whether these "tendencies" are really present in society or whether they are the product of pure fantasy. On this, opinions will differ. The main question which remains is, do we *need* utopias? The American sociologist David Riesman leaves no doubt. He wrote: "A revival of the tradition of utopian thinking seems to me one of the important intellectual tasks of today."[18]

KARL POPPER AND RALF DAHRENDORF
AS CRITICS OF UTOPIAS

However, not everyone is convinced of the positive function of utopias. Karl Popper, for instance, is rather skeptical. "I consider what I call Utopianism an attractive and, indeed, an all too attractive theory," he writes, "for I also consider it dangerous and pernicious. It is, I believe, self-defeating, and it leads to violence."[19] The fact that utopias can lead to violence is, according to Popper, caused by the fact that they often take on the character of religions. And this is even more the case when— as in Marxism—such a utopian society of the future is not presented as a moral imperative, but as the result of a necessary process. The future communist society resembles the Christian kingdom of God at the end of times. Both are a question of belief. For Popper, even without this supposed necessity, utopias are dangerous. "Since we cannot determine the ultimate ends of political actions scientifically or by purely rational methods," he writes, "differences of opinion concerning what the ideal state should be like cannot always be smoothed out by the method of argument. They will at least partly have the character of religious differences. And there can be no tolerance between these different Utopian religions."[20] "However benevolent its ends," he concludes, "it does not bring happiness, but only the familiar misery of being condemned to live under a tyrannical government."[21] For these reasons Popper prefers to renounce utopias completely. "Work for the elimination of concrete evils," he says, "rather than for the realization of abstract goods."[22] Popper is supported by Ralf Dahrendorf. "Utopia is one of the casualties of the twentieth century," he writes. "Not only can it not be found, but the attempt to create it leads to disaster, totalitarianism, and war at its worst."[23] Another critic of utopias is the French-Romanian philosopher Emil Cioran, who asks: "What is the cause of so much naivete or so much stupidity?"[24] And he answers: "Misery is in fact the great support of the utopian, the material on which he works, the substance with which he feeds off his ideas ... the poorer you are, the more you use your time and energy to change everything—in your thoughts, for nothing."[25]

However, for Jürgen Habermas such critiques are exaggerated. He is disappointed about the fact that "critique of utopianism, the writing on the wall of Jacobinism, falsely pillories the so-called inevitable association of utopia with terror."[26] So, what should we think? Are utopias useful or are they the harbinger of future terror? Popper's and Dahrendorf's unrestrained condemnation of utopianism is understandable, because they witnessed how in the Soviet Union the realization of Marx's utopian "classless society" resulted in Stalin's gulag and mass murders. Robespierre's Terror period during the French Revolution is also often mentioned in this context. Robespierre tried to realize the utopian ideal of a society of equal individuals, a noble idea for which he deemed it necessary to send his adversaries to the guillotine. Political utopias can quickly become dangerous. In this context it is interesting to listen to Eric Hobsbawm, a British historian who, in 1932, as a young man, became a member of the Communist Party of Great Britain. He remained a member even after Khrushchev had exposed Stalin's crimes in 1956. Why didn't he follow the example of many colleagues who left the party?

"The problem isn't wanting a better world," he said, "it is believing in the utopia of a perfect world. Liberal thinkers are right when they point out that one of the worst things about not only communism, but all the great causes, is that they are so great that they justify all sacrifices, whether imposed on oneself or on others. This liberal argument is valid when it claims that only those with moderate expectations of the world can avoid inflicting terrible evils and suffering on it. Yet I cannot help feeling that humanity couldn't function without great hopes and absolute passions, even when these experience defeat, and it becomes clear that human action cannot eliminate human unhappiness."[27]

Hobsbawm concedes that the belief in utopias can inflict "terrible evils" and that only those with moderate expectations can avoid inflicting these evils. However, he insists that humanity cannot function "without great hopes and absolute passions." Does this mean that mankind cannot do without these great abstract ideals, these "great hopes and absolute passions?" Hobsbawm is right that great hopes and dreams can stimulate people to seek challenges and formulate new goals. In the same vein John Rawls pleads for a *realistic* utopia. "Is Realistic Utopia a Fantasy?" he asks. And he answers: "Some seem to think that this idea is a fantasy, particularly after Auschwitz. But why so? I wouldn't deny either the historical uniqueness of the Holocaust, or that it could somewhere be repeated."[28] But does this mean the end of utopian thinking? Rawls continues:

"Yet we must not allow these great evils of the past and present to undermine our hope for the future of our society as belonging to a Society of liberal and decent Peoples around the world. Otherwise, the wrongful, evil, and demonic conduct of others destroys us too and seals their victory. Rather, we must support and strengthen our hope by developing a reasonable and workable conception of political right and justice applying to the relations between peoples."[29]

As long as dreams are concrete, specific, and restricted to a certain field of action, they can be useful sources of inspiration. However, one should avoid these dreams crystallizing into all-embracing, closed, deterministic, dogmatic, quasi-religious systems. The Leninist variant of Marxism, for instance, was such a closed system.

THE NEED FOR "MINI-UTOPIAS"

I think that we should not be afraid to cherish dreams that may be labeled utopian, but on four conditions:

1   that these dreams are realistic,
2   that they are not grandiose, but modest and respect the human scale,
3   that they can be realized in one's lifetime or in the lifetime of the next generation,
4   that they resist the temptation to announce an imminent transformation of human nature.

This means that instead of developing great, abstract "science fiction" visions of a new society projected into a distant future, one should rather develop "mini-utopias" with a clearly defined scope, which foster collective action. The last condition mentioned above: that human dreams about a better future should resist the temptation to announce an imminent transformation of human nature, is also important. Marx, for instance, dreamed of a "new man" who would emerge in communist society. This "new man" was a moral, altruistic human being, who would spontaneously work for the common interest. However, when in Stalinist Russia this idea was put in practice, the result was different. Marx's "new man" was transformed into the much-touted Stakhanov worker, the extremely productive model worker who tirelessly worked for the totalitarian, exploitative Soviet state. Dreams about a future "new man" who is supposed to possess extraordinary moral qualities are not only unrealistic, but outright dangerous, because they neglect man's aggressive and selfish instincts.

Alexander Hamilton, one of the Founding Fathers of the United States, did not fall into this trap. Hamilton's utopia was the construction of a democratic republic of continental dimension, a project that—in his time—can be called "utopian" because it was never tried before in human history. However, Hamilton had no illusions about human nature. Unlike Marx, he didn't think that his political project would change human nature and he criticized the naïve theory that commercial republics, such as the United States, would necessarily be more peaceful than monarchies.

> "Has it not, on the contrary" he argued, "invariably been found that momentary passions, and immediate interests, have a more active and imperious control over human conduct than general or remote considerations of policy, utility, or justice? Have republics in practice been less addicted to war than monarchies? Are not the former administered by *men* as well as the latter? Are there not aversions, predilections, rivalships, and desires of unjust acquisitions that affect nations as well as kings? Are not popular assemblies frequently subject to the impulses of rage, resentment, jealousy, avarice, and of other irregular and violent propensities?"[30]

Hamilton's utopia was an independent, democratic republic, called the United States of America. This utopia was realized during his lifetime. But he had no illusions that this new republic would change human nature, nor that it would herald an era of general goodwill and benevolence.

ROBERT NOZICK'S MULTIPLE UTOPIAS

How can one save utopia as a perspective for the living generation, as well as for future generations, but avoid its eventual negative consequences? In his book *Anarchy, State, and Utopia* Robert Nozick proposed an original solution. He argued that my utopia doesn't necessarily coincide with your utopia: "The best of all possible worlds for me will not be that for you. The world, of all those I can imagine, which I would most prefer to live in, will not be precisely the one you would choose."[31] This is the problem, mentioned by Popper, of differences of vision which can develop into religious wars. Nozick mentions the names of very different people, such as Picasso, Buddha, Elizabeth Taylor, Einstein, and Frank Sinatra. "Is there really *one* kind of life which is best for each of these people? Imagine all of them living in any utopia you've ever seen described in detail."[32] According to him no single utopia would be acceptable for everyone without exception. "Utopia will consist of utopias, of many different and divergent communities in which people lead different kinds of lives under different institutions. Some kinds of communities will be more attractive to most than others; communities will wax and wane."[33] However, what is essential is that "... no one can *impose* his own utopian vision upon others."[34] With this condition Nozick satisfies the criticisms of Popper and Dahrendorf. His model is a model of *trial and error,* which he calls a *filtering process.* This process works as follows:

> "People try out living in various communities, and they leave or slightly modify the ones they don't like (find defective). Some communities will be abandoned, others will struggle along, others will split, others will flourish, gain members, and be duplicated elsewhere."[35]

Nozick's model is one of "let a hundred flowers bloom." Let people organize their own utopian society based on their common ideals and then wait and see how it is working out. His model is clearly inspired by the American "subculture structure" in which citizens are accustomed to organizing their own communities and the state—as a "minimal state"—is kept at a distance. A utopia imposed by politics or the state is rejected.

This kind of utopianism probably meets the criticisms of Popper and Dahrendorf, but the problem is that this proposal seems overly inspired by an American model that no longer exists. In modern history America has been the promised land for many European religious sects that were being persecuted in their own country. They migrated to America where they were completely free to live according to their own ideas and ideals. This led to local or regional mini-societies according to the model, described by Nozick.[36] But can this model still be realized in the twenty-first century? We no longer live in the seventeenth, eighteenth, or nine-teenth century. The power of the central state has increased massively, restricting the space for local utopian experiments, which would seem to be possible exclusively at the state level. This brings us back to the criticisms of Popper and Dahrendorf, that nothing is more dangerous than a state which formulates utopian goals. Should we therefore give up, forever and definitively, our utopian fantasies and dreams for the future? After the *démasqué* of the communist utopia and the decline of social-democratic and neoliberal societal models, is there no place left for new ideals and new ideas which can enthuse people? One of the slogans of the French student movement of May 1968 was: "Soyez réalistes, demandez l'impossible" (Be realistic, demand the impossible). Demanding the impossible was anything but realistic. It leads to a blunt refusal by the authorities on the one hand and a sterile repetition of demands that cannot be realized on the other hand.

Each utopia involves a critique of the existing situation. However, as Fred Halliday wrote: "A responsibility of critique has to be matched by a responsibility of plausibility."[37] The goals of a utopian movement have to be plausible, which means realizable. Something may seem improbable at this moment in time, but that need not be the case later on: what counts is what is in principle *possible*. "Two centuries ago," writes Halliday, "the abolition of slavery in the Americas was improbable, but possible: it happened."[38] In the same way one can argue that fifty years ago the emancipation and acceptance of homosexual men and women was improbable. It was improbable, but possible. And it also happened. The slogan "Demand the impossible," on the other hand, is potentially dangerous, because a revolutionary regime may try to realize the impossible with violence and intimidation. It is therefore important to steer a middle course between blind and unrealistic utopianism on the one hand and an exaggerated sterile "realism" on the other hand. The English historian E. H. Carr rightly remarked that

"The antithesis of utopia and reality can in some aspects be identified with the antithesis of Free Will and Determinism. The utopian is necessarily voluntarist: he believes in the possibility of more or less radically rejecting reality, and substituting his

utopia for it by an act of will. The realist analyses a predetermined course of development which he is powerless to
change.... The utopian, fixing his eyes on the future, thinks in
terms of creative spontaneity: the realist rooted in the past in
terms of causality. All healthy human action, and therefore all
healthy thought, must establish a balance between utopia and
reality, between free will and determinism."[39]

We don't need large panoramas and detailed blueprints of an ideal
future society. What we need is the development of many "mini-utopias"
which improve the world—not only for ourselves, but also for the well-
being of future generations.

NOTES

1   Thomas More, *Utopia*, (Harmondsworth: Penguin, 1971), p. 76.
2   Ibid., p. 85.
3   Tommaso Campanella, *La Città del Sole* (Milan: Feltrinelli, 1983), p. 76.
4   Ibid.
5   Ibid.
6   Karl Löwith, "Das Verhängnis des Fortschritts," in Erich Burck (ed.), *Die Idee des Fortschritts—Neun Vorträge über Wege und Grenzen des Fortschrittsglaubens* (Munich: Beck Verlag, 1963), p. 37.
7   Aldous Huxley, *Brave New World* (Harmondsworth: Penguin Books, 1962).
8   George Orwell, *Nineteen Eighty-Four* (Harmondsworth: Penguin Books, 1967).
9   John Maynard Keynes, "Economic Possibilities for our Grandchildren," *The Nation and Athenaeum,* October 11 and 18, 1930.
10   Ibid.
11   Ibid.
12   Karl Marx, *Capital,* Volume 3 (New York: International Publishers, 1977), p. 820.
13   Ernst Bloch, *Das Prinzip Hoffnung,* Volume 2 (Frankfurt am Main: Suhrkamp Verlag, 1968), p. 727.
14   Ibid.
15   Ibid., p. 556. (My emphasis, MHVH.)
16   Leszek Kołakowski, "Het begrip 'links'," in Leszek Kołakowski, *De mens zonder alternatief* (Amsterdam: Moussault's Uitgeverij NV, 1968), p. 133.

17 Ibid., p. 134.
18 David Riesman, "Observations on Community Plans and Utopia," in David Riesman, *Individualism Reconsidered* (New York: Doubleday and Company, Ltd., 1955), p. 67.
19 Karl R. Popper, "Utopia and Violence," in Karl R. Popper, *Conjectures and Refutations—The Growth of Scientific Knowledge* (London and Henley: Routledge and Kegan Paul, 1976), p. 358.
20 Karl R. Popper, op. cit., p. 359. Bruce Ackerman seems to refer to the same phenomenon, writing: "If revolutionary renewal succeeds, political mobilization will subside, for the collective revolutionary achievement empowers most people to explore their differences, rather than their commonalities." (Bruce Ackerman, *The Future of Liberal Revolution* (New Haven and London: Yale University Press, 1992), p. 27.)
21 Karl Popper, op. cit., p. 360.
22 Ibid., p. 361.
23 Ralf Dahrendorf, "Towards the Twenty-First Century," in Michael Howard and Wm. Roger Louis (eds.), *The Oxford History of the Twentieth Century* (Oxford and New York: Oxford University Press, 1998) p. 342.
24 E. M. Cioran, *Histoire et utopie* (Paris : Gallimard, 1960), p. 99.
25 Ibid., p. 101.
26 Jürgen Habermas, "Die Krise des Wohlfahrtsstaates und die Erschöpfung utopischer Energien," in Jürgen Habermas, *Die neue Unübersichtlichkeit* (Frankfurt am Main : Suhrkamp Verlag, 1985), p. 162.
27 Eric Hobsbawm, *On the Edge of the New Century,* in conversation with Antonio Polito (London: Little, Brown and Company, 2000), p. 161.
28 John Rawls, *The Law of Peoples* (Cambridge, Mass., and London: Harvard University Press, 1999), pp. 19–20.
29 Ibid., p. 22.
30 Alexander Hamilton, Federalist Paper No. 6, in Alexander Hamilton, James Madison, John Jay, *The Federalist Papers* (New York, Ontario, London: The New American Library, 1961), p. 56.
31 Robert Nozick, *Anarchy, State, and Utopia* (New York: Basic Books, 1974), p. 298.
32 Ibid.
33 Ibid., p. 312.
34 Ibid.
35 Ibid., p. 316.
36 Cf. David Riesman, "Observations on Community Plans and Utopia," op. cit., p. 69: "In the rough and ready America of the last century ... the country itself seemed to be a functioning utopia to peoples elsewhere, and it was the scene of most of the utopian experiments of the period...."
37 Fred Halliday, *The World at 2000,* op. cit., p. 142.

38 Ibid.
39 E. H. Carr, *The Twenty Years' Crisis 1919–1939 – An Introduction to the Study of International Relations,* with a new introduction by Michael Cox (Houndmills: Palgrave Macmillan, 2001), p. 12.

CHAPTER 15

EXPLORING THE FUTURE II: KONDRATIEV'S "LONG WAVE" THEORY: DOES IT HAVE PREDICTIVE VALUE?

In order to take responsibility for future generations we need to make projections of the future. This can be done by exploring historical trends. If history is a cyclical process, it is easier to make predictions. In this case the main problem is to make accurate estimates of the length of the different cycles. According to Turchin and Nefedov, two authors who analyzed secular cycles of economic expansion, stagflation, crisis, and depression in England, France, Russia, and Ancient Rome,

> "In general, different social processes operate at a variety of temporal scales. The shorter scales include daily, weekly, monthly, and annual cycles. Beyond that we have human generations, processes occurring on the time scale of centuries (including secular cycles), and longer-term phenomena such as social and biological evolution."[1]

These authors explained cycles, ranging from 120 to 335 years, by demographic factors. However, it would be speculative to ascribe a predictive function to this theory with its long, secular cycles. A better example is a shorter cyclical theory: the "long wave" theory developed by Nikolay Kondratiev (1892–1938).[2] Kondratiev was a brilliant Russian economist who, in October 1917, at the age of 25, became deputy minister for food supply in the last government of the moderate socialist Alexander Kerensky. This government lasted only a few days, because in the same month the October Revolution broke out and the Bolsheviks came to power. In the three following years of "War Communism" the Bolshevik government expropriated private businesses, nationalized the industry, and introduced the forced requisition of food products from the peasantry. When this policy led to famine and economic chaos, Lenin adopted in 1921 the New Economic Policy (NEP), which, in fact, was not so new. It reintroduced capitalist elements into the Soviet economy. Kondratiev, who in 1920 had founded the Institute for Business Cycle Research, was a protagonist of the New Economic Policy and helped develop the first of the Soviet Five-Year Plans.

KONDRATIEV AND THE CYCLICAL CHARACTER OF MODERN CAPITALIST ECONOMY

However, it is for another reason that Kondratiev would become famous. He had observed that Western capitalist economies followed an approximately 50-year cycle of crisis, recovery, prosperity, and downturn. Kondratiev's vision was not completely original. Two Dutch socialist economists, Jacob van Gelderen and Salomon de Wolff, had developed similar ideas before him.[3] At that time these ideas were still unorthodox—particularly in the young Soviet Union. The communist dogma was that the capitalist system would necessarily break down and be replaced by a communist society. Kondratiev's "long wave" theory, however, implicitly acknowledged capitalism's vitality. Although capitalist economies went through times of crisis, he argued, these crisis periods were followed by periods of recovery. In Kondratiev's theory capitalism was not on the verge of collapse, but still had a future. "Kondratieff, under attack from Marxists around him," wrote Joshua Goldstein, "elaborated his theory within a traditional Marxist framework."[4] However, his caution would not save him. Suspected of "bourgeois" ideas, Kondratiev was arrested in 1930. In 1931 he was tried and sentenced to eight years in prison.

"Alexander Solzhenitsyn described the campaign waged against Kondratiev by the Soviet regime as painting him as a 'future Prime Minister.' Kondratieff was certainly a key player in any opposition that might have developed after

1928, one that Stalin felt was absolutely necessary to discredit."[5]

In 1938, during Stalin's Great Purge, Kondratiev, forty-six years old, was executed. But his theory survived. In an article, titled "The Long Waves in Economic Life," published in 1935, Kondratiev explained how, since the French Revolution, three long waves had succeeded each other of which the first two had been completed. Each wave was characterized by a period of economic growth and price inflation, followed by a collapse of prices, leading to a crisis.

> "The upswing first long wave embraces the period from 1789 to 1814," he wrote, "i.e., 25 years; its decline begins in 1814 and ends in 1849, a period of 35 years. The cycle is, therefore, completed in 60 years. The rise of the second wave begins in 1849 and ends in 1873, lasting 24 years.... The decline of the second wave begins in 1873 and ends in 1896, a period of 23 years. The length of the second wave is 47 years. The upward movement of the third wave begins in 1896 and ends in 1920, its duration being 24 years. The decline of the wave, according to all data, begins in 1920.... We conclude, therefore, that three great cycles are present in the movement of the price level during the period since the end of the 1780's, the last of which is only half completed."[6]

Kondratiev was not dogmatic and did not present his findings as an established truth. "We think," he wrote, "that, on the basis of the available data, the existence of long waves of cyclical character is very probable."[7] It is no surprise that the authors of the Great Soviet Encyclopedia of 1929 called his theory "wrong and reactionary."[8] But Western economists were also skeptical and Kondratiev's long wave theory was much criticized in academic circles. Paul Samuelson, for instance, called the long wave theory "science fiction."[9] Another author who expressed his initial doubts was Brian Berry, a professor of political economy at the University of Texas.

"I had not intended to work on long waves," he wrote. "Like many of you, I was taught to view the topic with suspicion. Too many 'long wavers' have insufficient regard for the soundness of evidence. At the fringe are crackpots and mystics, charlatans who play on people's fears by writing popular books proclaiming an imminent economic Armageddon—not particularly savory company to be associated with, even peripherally."[10] "Once provoked, however," he continued, "my research led me to resolve a number of important questions about the rhythmic upswings and downturns of prices and economic growth and the clocklike timing of turning-point crises in American development.... I discovered that there *is* something to the long-wave idea...."[11]

DIFFERENT EXPLANATIONS OF KONDRATIEV'S LONG WAVES

There *was,* indeed, something to Kondratiev's long wave theory. And it was telling that his theory, which was almost forgotten after the Second World War, suddenly made a glorious come-back in the 1970s, when the long post-war boom period came to an end. A depressed economy, apparently, provided fertile soil for the reemergence of his ideas. The economic development seemed to confirm his theory. According to Kondratiev the downturn of the last cycle began in 1920, which means that the end of the downturn would be reached around the year 1945, when a new upswing would begin. Kondratiev could not predict the Second World War, but he accurately predicted the end of the downturn and the beginning of the upswing. According to his theory the upswing would start after 1945. This is what happened. The period between 1945 and 1975 are the years of an unprecedented economic growth, called *Les Trente Glorieuses* (The Glorious Thirty Years) by the French. This prolonged boom period was unique, and economists enthused that—thanks to Keynesian politics—bust-boom cycles would have become a phenomenon of the past. Despite the downturn of the 1970s, this was still in 1997 the conviction of Gordon Brown, the British Chancellor of the Exchequer, who declared that "the British economy of the future must be built not on the shifting sands of boom and bust, but on the bedrock of prudent and wise economic management for the long term."[12] In 2008—only a few years later—this self-assured hubris would be shaken by the Great Recession, the deepest recession on record since the 1930s. Kondratiev had written that "the waves are not of exactly the same length, their duration varying between 47 and 60 years."[13] Like the first wave (1789–1849) the fourth wave of 1945–2008 was one of the longer ones. Kondratiev seemed to have won definitively.

But had he? Because despite its *prima facie* plausibility and its apparent confirmation by the facts, Kondratiev's theory had a major flaw. This was that his long wave theory was not really a theory. It was rather an *observation*, based on the analysis of several statistical time series in France, Great Britain, the United States, and—in a lesser degree—Germany, making use of the index numbers of wholesale prices, rates of interest, wages, and the production and consumption of coal and pig iron. However, the reason *why* these prices moved upward and downward was not explained, and Kondratiev did not pretend he could. "We had no intention of laying the foundations for an appropriate theory of long waves," he wrote.[14] After him economists came up with various explanations. One of these was a monetary explanation, assuming a parallel development of prices and the total stock of monetary gold.[15] However, this would make the development of prices dependent on an external factor, such as the discovery of new gold fields. Because the discovery of gold fields is a matter of chance, it contradicts the possibility of regular waves.

Another theory established a causal link between Kondratiev's price waves and waves of investment. There are two different kinds of investment: first, replacement investments, which are investments to replace existing capital goods such as old machines and buildings which have become obsolete, and, second, investments in innovations. The problem with the first kind of investments—also called "echo investments"[16]— is that they normally don't take the form of waves. They are made continuously—except after a war when the industrial base of a country has been destroyed and, in a huge effort, it has to be rebuilt from scratch. This led some theorists to link the Kondratiev waves to the occurrence of wars. Joshua Goldstein, for instance, analyzed 119 wars between 1495 and 1973, and observed in the period 1600–1800 "four regularly recurring war peaks.... These peaks are spaced about fifty years apart and are followed by two more peaks (around 1870 and around 1915), also spaced about fifty years apart...."[17] Was the occurrence of major wars with time intervals of about fifty years the ultimate explanation of the Kondratiev waves? It is not certain, because Goldstein, who defended this theory, had to admit that "only the final, World War II, does not fit the pattern, following too closely after the World War I peak."[18] Jack Levy, who analyzed the same data, concluded that "there are no hints of any cyclical pattern in either the occurrence of war or in any of its other dimensions. For each of the war indicators, the highest peaks in war as well as the periods of no war appear to be scattered at random."[19] It seems, therefore, that Goldstein's attempt to link the Kondratiev waves to a regular, fifty-year pattern of wars is too speculative to accept.

JOSEPH SCHUMPETER'S INNOVATION CYCLES

A quite different approach was taken by Joseph Schumpeter, who explained the Kondratiev waves by investment waves made for industrial innovation.[20] In his book *Business Cycles,* published in 1939, he stressed the importance of new inventions which triggered new investments. A keyword, used by him, was "railroadization."[21] The invention of the steam locomotive in the nineteenth century led to the development of a transcontinental railroad system: a completely new means of transport which would deeply transform the economy. At the beginning of the twentieth century the combination of two other new inventions—the internal combustion engine and the automobile—would lead to the next big investment wave. Schumpeter stressed the fact that these innovations and their industrialization were the work of "new men" and that these investment waves were accompanied by a process of "creative destruction"—the decline of old production methods and the destruction of machines and buildings which had become obsolete. Schumpeter explained his theory as follows:

> "If we glance at those long waves in economic activity....
> Each of them consists of an 'industrial revolution' and the

absorption of its effects. For instance, we are able to observe statistically and historically … the rise of such a long wave toward the end of the 1780s, its culmination around 1800, its downward sweep and then a short recovery ending at the beginning of the 1840s. This was the Industrial Revolution dear to the heart of textbook writers. Upon its heels, however, came another such revolution, producing another long wave that rose in the forties, culminated just before 1857 and ebbed away to 1897, to be followed in turn by the one that reached its peak about 1911 and is now in the act of ebbing away. These revolutions periodically reshape the existing structure of industry by introducing new methods of production—the mechanized factory, the electrified factory, chemical synthesis, and the like; new commodities, such as railroad service, motor cars, electrical appliances; new forms of organization … while these things are being initiated we have brisk expenditure and predominating "prosperity" … and while those things are being completed and their results pour forth we have elimination of antiquated elements and predominating 'depression.'"[22]

IS TECHNOLOGICAL INNOVATION SLOWING DOWN?

The significance of technological and economic innovations for investment waves is today widely accepted. Does this mean that Schumpeter succeeded in his attempt to explain the Kondratiev waves by these innovation waves? Walt Rostow was not convinced. "Schumpeter's effort to use the dynamics of innovation to explain Kondratiev's long cycles was only partially successful," he wrote.[23] Rostow criticized Schumpeter, because "the railroad expansion in the 1840s, in Britain and the American northeast, was accompanied by relatively stagnant or falling prices,"[24] which was contrary to Kondratiev's theory that the upward cycle was characterized by inflationary growth. However, one could for a moment give Schumpeter the benefit of the doubt, because the proof of the pudding is in the eating and the ultimate litmus test for the validity of Schumpeter's interpretation was the question of whether his theory had predictive power. The question was whether the Industrial Revolution and the subsequent "railroadization" were completely unique events or parts of a series of events which would repeat themselves at fifty-year intervals in the future. Schumpeter had no doubt: innovation waves would be repeated, because they were essential for the development of the capitalist economy.

In recent years, however, doubts have emerged as to whether later innovation waves can compete with Schumpeter's favorite examples of the nineteenth century "railroadization" or the introduction of the automobile in the beginning of the twentieth century. The observation that the pace of change and innovation has slowed down was, for instance, made by Jonathan Huebner, who wrote that "the rate of innovation reached a peak in the nineteenth century and then declined throughout the twentieth century even with higher levels of education, major advances in science, and the invention of the computer."[25] This author argued "that a higher proportion of the innovations in recent years are simply improvements in existing technologies as opposed to the higher proportion of fundamental new technologies developed in the nineteenth century."[26] He concluded that "the evidence presented indicates that the rate of innovation reached a peak over a hundred years ago and is now in decline ... the pace of technological development will diminish with each passing year."[27] Huebner wrote this in 2005. Had he missed some important innovations? Not really. He mentioned the computer, and in 1992 the smartphone had already been invented. He wrote his article three years before Tesla launched its first electric car, but equally this innovation could be labeled "an improvement in existing technologies."

The same observation, that technological progress had stalled, was made seven years later by the British historian Niall Ferguson, who wrote,

"The harsh reality is that, from the vantage point of 2012, the next twenty-five years (2013–38) are highly unlikely to see more dramatic changes than science and technology produced in the last twenty-five (1987–2012).... The achievements of the last twenty-five years were not especially impressive compared with what we did in the preceding twenty-five years, 1961–89 (for example, landing men on the moon). And the technological milestones of the twenty-five years before that, 1935–60, were even more remarkable (such as splitting the atom)."[28]

Nine years later the mood had not become more optimistic. David Brooks, for instance, wrote in the *New York Times:*

"If you were born in 1900 and died in 1970, you lived from the age of the horse-drawn carriage to the era of a man on the moon. You saw the widespread use of electricity, air-conditioning, aviation, the automobile, penicillin, and so much else. But if you were born in 1960 and lived until today, the driving and flying experience would be safer, but otherwise the same, and your kitchen, aside from the microwave, is basically unchanged."[29]

Another author, Tyler Cowen, wrote in the same vein:

"The period from 1880 to 1940 brought numerous major technological advances to our lives. The long list of new developments include electricity, electric lights, powerful motors, automobiles, airplanes, household appliances, the telephone, indoor plumbing, pharmaceuticals, mass production, the typewriter, the tape recorder, the phonograph, and radio, to name just a few, with television coming at the end of that period … agriculture saw the introduction of the harvester, the reaper, and the mowing machine, and the development of highly effective fertilizers...."[30] However, he continued: "Today, in contrast, apart from the seemingly magical internet, life in broad material terms isn't so different from what it was in 1953.... Life is better and we have more stuff, but the pace of change has slowed down compared to what people saw two or three generations ago."[31]

One does not need to be a prophet to predict that innovation waves will continue to take place in the future. However, will these innovation waves always accurately follow the fifty-to-sixty-year rhythm predicted by Kondratiev and Schumpeter? One may doubt it. Solomou wrote: "The critical question that remains unanswered, beyond circular reasoning, is ... why the major innovational bunching should occur cyclically every fifty years or so."[32] Solomou argued that "it would be surprising to observe an unchanged long-wave growth path"[33] and he accused Kondratiev and Schumpeter of a "historicist perspective." The question of whether the existence of the Kondratiev wave has been "proven" is therefore far from being answered. Kondratiev had observed two and a half waves. Schumpeter linked these waves to respectively the Industrial Revolution, the "railroadization," and the introduction of the automobile. However, it is far from certain that future innovation waves will have the same impact or will come at the same time intervals. Paul Samuelson, who had earlier called the Kondratiev waves "science fiction," wrote later—more cautiously— "whether these long waves are simply historical accidents due to chance gold discoveries, inventions, and political wars, it is still too soon to say."[34] Such a cautious approach seems to be the appropriate attitude. It is too early to adopt uncritically the Kondratiev/Schumpeter paradigm. It is equally too early to reject it right away. The chance that these waves will succeed each other indefinitely, however, appears dim. It seems, therefore, that accepting Kondratiev's theory is mainly a question of *belief* as, for instance, is the case for the British historian Eric Hobsbawm, who writes: "And if you believe, as I still do, in Kondratev's [sic] theory of long waves...."[35] According to Pitirim Sorokin (1889–1968), the founder of the sociology department at Harvard,

> "The existence of ever-repeating identical cycles, whether in the evolution of the whole world or in the history of mankind, is not proved. Consequently the corresponding theories of identical cycles are likely to be in error. The existence of definite, steady, and eternal trend in historical and social change has not been proved either. All attempts to establish the existence of such a tendency have failed. Among hundreds of such trends, formulated by various authors, I do not know a

single one which, after a careful, scientific scrutiny could be said to have scientific validity."[36]

That opinion is shared by Isaiah Berlin, who deserves to be quoted at length:

"One of the deepest of human desires is to find a unitary pattern in which the whole of experience, past, present and future, actual, possible and unfulfilled, is symmetrically ordered ... From the days of Herder and Saint-Simon, Hegel and Marx, to those of Spengler and Toynbee and their imitators, claims have been made widely varying in degree of generality and confidence, to be able to trace a structure of history (always *a priori* for protests to the contrary), to discover the one and only true pattern into which alone all facts will be found to fit. But this is not, and can never be, accepted by any serious historian who wishes to establish the truth as it is understood by the best critics of his time, working by standards accepted as realistic by his most scrupulous and enlightened fellow workers. For he does not perceive one unique schema as the truth—the only real framework in which alone the facts truly lie; he does not distinguish the one real, cosmic pattern from false ones, as he certainly seeks to distinguish real facts from fiction. The same facts can be arranged in many patterns, seen from many perspectives, displayed in many lights, all of them equally valid, although some will be more suggestive or fertile in one field than in another...."[37]

Berlin warns historians (but not only these) against the "obsession by a given pattern" which "causes a given writer to interpret the facts too artificially, to fill the gaps in his knowledge too smoothly, without sufficient regard to the empirical evidence."[38] Mankind seems, indeed, to have an inborn urge to find repeating patterns in history, enabling him to predict and plan the future. However, he should be careful not to make too hasty judgments and jump too quickly to conclusions.

NOTES

1   Peter Turchin and Sergey A. Nefedov, *Secular Cycles* (Princeton: Princeton University Press, 2009), p. 25.
2   Kondratiev's name is also spelled Kondratieff—particularly, but not only, in older publications. We will use the new spelling.
3   Jacob van Gelderen developed these ideas in an article, published in 1913, titled "Springtide—Reflections on Industrial Development and Price Movements," (Original title, published under the pseudonym J. Fedder: "Springvloed—Beschouwingen over industriële ontwikkeling en prijsbeweging," *De Nieuwe Tijd,* 1913). https://core.ac.uk/reader/6787204 Sam de Wolff's book *Het economisch getij: bijdrage tot de verklaring van het conjunctuurverschijnsel* (The economic tide: a contribution to the explanation of the business cycle phenomenon) was published in 1929. Kondratiev denied that he would have been influenced by these two Dutch theorists. In an article, published in English in 1935, he wrote: "I arrived at the hypothesis concerning the existence of long waves in the years 1919–21.... Only at the beginning of 1926 did I become acquainted with S. de Wolff's article 'Prosperitäts- und Depressionsperioden' ... De Wolff in many points reaches the same results as I do. The works of J. van Gelderen, which de Wolff cites and which have evidently been published only in Dutch, are unknown to me." (N. D. Kondratieff, "The Long Waves in Economic Life," *The Review of Economic Statistics,* Volume XVII, No. 6, November 1935, p. 115.) The text is available at https://www.cannonfinancial. com/uploads/main/Long-Waves-in-Economic-Life.pdf
4   Joshua Goldstein, *Long Cycles: Prosperity and War in the Modern Age* (New Haven: Yale University Press, 1988), p. 27.
5   Vincent Barnett, *Kondratiev and the Dynamics of Economic Development* (London: Palgrave Macmillan, 1998), p. 189.
6   N. D. Kondratieff, "The Long Waves in Economic Life," op. cit., pp. 106–07.
7   Ibid., p. 115.
8   Quoted in Benoît Tonglet, "Les cycles Kondratieff : une philosophie critique," *Innovations,* 2004/1 No. 9.
9   Quoted in Joshua Goldstein, *Long Cycles: Prosperity and War in the Modern Age,* op. cit., p. 21.
10 Brian J. L. Berry, *Long-Wave Rhythms in Economic Development and Political Behavior* (Baltimore and London: The Johns Hopkins University Press, 1991), p. 1.
11 Ibid.
12 Deborah Summers, "No return to boom and bust: what Brown said when he was Chancellor," *The Guardian,* September 11, 2008.

13 N. D. Kondratieff, "The Long Waves in Economic Life," op. cit., p. 107.

14 Ibid., p. 115.

15 J. Tinbergen, "Kondratiev Cycles and So-Called Long Waves," *Futures,* August 1981, p. 259.

16 Ibid., p. 260.

17 Joshua Goldstein, *Long Cycles: Prosperity and War in the Modern Age,* op. cit., p. 239.

18 Ibid.

19 Jack S. Levy, *War in the Modern Great Power System* (Lexington, Kentucky: The University of Kentucky Press, 1983), p. 137.

20 Apart from the Kondratiev wave, Schumpeter distinguished two other waves: the Kitchin wave and the Juglar wave. The Kitchin wave was a 3.3 year commodity cycle and the Juglar cycle was a 7-to-11 year business cycle. According to Schumpeter three Kitchin cycles occurred within each Juglar cycle and six Juglars within a Kondratiev cycle.

21 Joseph A. Schumpeter, *Business Cycles: A Theoretical, Historical, and Statistical Analysis of the Capitalist Process* (New York and London: McGraw-Hill, 1939), pp. 325–51.

22 Joseph A. Schumpeter, *Capitalism, Socialism, and Democracy* (New York and London: Harper & Brothers Publishers, 1947), pp. 67–68.

23 Walt Rostow, "Kondratieff, Schumpeter, and Kuznets: Trend Periods Revisited," *The Journal of Economic History,* 35 (4), 1975, p. 721.

24 Ibid.

25 Jonathan Huebner, "A possible declining trend for worldwide innovation," *Technological Forecasting & Social Change,* 72 (2005), p. 981.

26 Ibid., p. 983.

27 Ibid., p. 985.

28 Niall Ferguson, *The Great Degeneration—How Institutions Decay and Economies Die* (London and New York: Penguin, 2014), pp. 148–49.

29 David Brooks, "Get ready for greater technology," *The New York Times,* February 18, 2021.

30 Tyler Cowen, "The Great Stagnation—How America Ate All the Low-Hanging Fruit of Modern History, Got Sick, and Will (Eventually) Feel Better," London, Penguin e-Special, January 25, 2011.

31 Ibid.

32 Solomos Solomou, *Phases of Economic Growth, 1850–1973: Kondratieff Waves and Kuznets Swings* (Cambridge and New York: Cambridge University Press, 1990), p. 8.

33 Ibid., p. 9.

34 Paul A. Samuelson, *Economics* (New York: McGraw-Hill, 1980), p. 241.

35 Eric Hobsbawm, *On the Edge of the New Century,* In Conversation with Antonio Polito, op. cit., p. 3.

36 Pitirim A. Sorokin, "A Survey of the Cyclical Conceptions of Social and Historical Process," *Social Forces,* Volume 6, No. 1, September 1927, p. 39.
37 Isaiah Berlin, *Historical Inevitability* (London, New York, Toronto: Oxford University Press, 1955), pp. 69–70.
38 Ibid., p. 70.

CHAPTER 16

HOMO HISTORICUS
AND HIS WISH TO KNOW THE FUTURE:
A CALL FOR MODESTY

When we assume responsibility for future generations, we need to anticipate the future, and if not "the future" as such, then at least future trends. Is this possible? Interesting is Kant's critical comment on man's ability to predict the future. Predicting, he wrote, was the "*a priori* possible representation of the things that have to come." And he asked: "But how is a history *a priori* possible?" "Answer: when the soothsayer himself creates the things he is predicting."[1] Kant didn't believe in the magical abilities of prophets and fortune tellers. The only way a supposed prophet could become a real prophet was, according to him, when the prophet was the actor of a *self-fulfilling prophecy.* The prophet predicts what he himself is causing to happen. This means that according to Kant's reasoning the only ones who could predict the 9/11 terrorist attacks on the Twin Towers in New York and the Pentagon in Washington were its initiators: Bin Laden and the terrorists who hijacked the planes. However, even they could not be sure whether these attacks would be successful.

PREDICTING THE FUTURE:
A ROLE FOR THE HISTORIAN?

Kant's skepticism is a healthy antidote against unrealistic expectations about man's clairvoyant capabilities. It is clear that professional historians, who don't claim to possess special psychic gifts, nor pretend to be in contact with supernatural forces, approach the future differently. In the first place their real profession is not the study of the future, but the study of the past. They do this from a contemporary scientific interest. Not the future, but the present and the past are therefore the two poles between which the activity of the historian oscillates. Does this mean that the future remains outside his scope? Strictly speaking, yes. One does not expect him to develop great visions of the future. Because such visions are built on speculation and what one expects from the historian is not speculation, but rational analysis, based on facts. "Cobbler, stick to your last," one could say. But do historians always stick to their last— the study of phenomena of the past? Not always, because the temptation is sometimes (too) great. One might imagine the historian as someone who is standing before a broad river, looking upstream and observing how the river behaves at different locations: how sometimes the water is flowing faster, flooding the river banks and inundating the land outside, then goes through flat land in which the water stagnates. He follows the stream until it arrives right in front of him. Will he not be curious about what will happen afterwards, downstream, when the river has passed by? Even more so when people, who consider him to be an expert, ask him for his opinion or advice? Of course, the temptation will be great. And maybe he is right to give in and try—although tentatively and hesitantly—to give an answer to their questions. David Staley, a historian, wrote: "While we have traditionally applied our skills to the study of the past, historians could, with only minimal intellectual adjustment, face the other temporal direction and fruitfully explore the future."[2] He is right. Historians certainly have a role to play. In this context, a proposal made by Niall Ferguson and Graham Allison is interesting.

> "It is sometimes said," they wrote, "that most Americans live in 'the United States of Amnesia.' Less widely recognized is how many American policy makers live there too." And they continued: "To address this deficit, it is not enough for a president to invite friendly historians to dinner, as Obama has been known to do. Nor is it enough to appoint a court historian, as John F. Kennedy did with Arthur M. Schlesinger Jr. We urge the next president to establish a White House Council of Historical Advisers."[3]

This new Council, they said, would mirror "the Council of Economic Advisers, established after World War II." The authors wrote that it was time for "a new and rigorous 'applied history,'" analyzing precedents and historical analogues. They explained that applied historians "would take a current predicament and try to identify analogues in the past."[4] At the same time these authors warned: "To be sure, historical analogies are easy to get wrong."[5] The new Council should also be asked to develop counterfactuals, asking "what if" questions, such as: what would have happened if President Obama had enforced the "red line" against the Assad regime after its use of chemical weapons? Also, more general questions could be treated, such as: "Is the US in decline?" Unfortunately, this proposal did not fall on fertile ground. The authors published it just before the election of Donald Trump, a man unwilling to take advice and absolutely devoid of historical knowledge or historical curiosity. However, their proposal to create a Council of Historical Advisers, tasked to provide essential historical insights to policy makers, remains relevant. Their knowledge of the past could inform politicians how to act to avoid setbacks and catastrophes in the future. Expert advice by professional historians to politicians could improve political decision making—particularly in foreign policy. Should only historians be asked to develop scenarios of the future? Not necessarily. In this respect an initiative of the French Ministry of Defense is interesting. The Ministry asked about ten authors of science fiction to imagine how the future would look like in the period 2030–2060. The group, called "Red Team,"[6] assisted by scientific and military experts, presented in December 2020 two scenarios, which will nourish the army's strategic thinking.[7]

SOME STRIKING PREDICTIONS

One must admit historians—but not only these—make sometimes striking predictions. Let us give some examples. Alexis de Tocqueville, who is undoubtedly one of the greatest political scientists of the nineteenth century, pronounced on January 27, 1848, as a member of the French Parliament, a speech in which he warned that a new revolution was imminent:

> "For the first time in fifteen years," he said, "I feel a certain fear of the future; and what proves that I am right is that I am not the only one who has this impression: I think that I can ask all who listen to me and that all will answer me that in the regions they represent a similar impression exists; that the people feel overwhelmed by a certain malaise, a certain fear; that, maybe for the first time in sixteen years, the feeling, the intuition of instability, this feeling which precedes revolutions, which often announces these, which sometimes lets them arise, that this feeling exists to a great extent in the country."[8]

And Tocqueville continued: "Don't you feel, by a kind of instinctive intuition that cannot be analyzed, but which is certain, that the ground is shaking again in Europe? Don't you feel ...—what will I say?—a revolutionary wind which is in the air?"[9] The revolution, predicted by Tocqueville, was indeed "in the air": only some weeks later his prediction came true, when, on 22 February 1848, the revolution broke out. Note that Tocqueville in his speech did not refer to a scientific analysis of the situation, but to "a kind of instinctive intuition that cannot be analyzed." However, with this instinctive intuition he perfectly grasped the situation.

Another example of a striking prediction is the case of the Dutch historian Jan Romein, who, in a book which was published in 1938, predicted the Second World War and considered that the years 1936 and 1937 constituted a "foreplay" of this war.

> "One should not consider it as a failure when I speak about a 'foreplay' of the next world war, when this eventually doesn't come soon, because in the first place it can always come later and in the second place, even if it wouldn't come, the word 'foreplay' only expresses this: yes, certainly, that I expect that it will come, but that this expectation expresses, as such, nothing else than that I observe tendencies, which, if nothing stands in the way, in a near or further future are leading to it."[10]

Note how extremely cautiously this author expresses himself, saying
that if the war doesn't come in the short term, as he expects, it can always
arrive later, and even if it doesn't come later, he, nevertheless "observes
tendencies, which, if nothing stands in the way, in the near or further future lead to it." Romein was right and his prediction materialized one
year later. What is important here is that Romein did not refer to his intuition, but to "tendencies" which he observed, which means that he
refers to a scientific analysis of the situation made by him in his quality
of a professional historian. He showed himself convinced of the correct-
ness of his analysis, writing that the tendencies he observed would "in
a near future lead to it" on the condition that "nothing stands in the way."
Romein pointed to the importance of causal processes in history and he
presumed—rightly—that these causal chains are not only effective in
the past but continue to have an impact in the future.

A similar prediction that the Second World War was imminent was
made by Jean Monnet, a French top diplomat who, after the war, would
become one of the "Fathers of Europe." In his Memoirs Monnet tells
about his stay in 1935 in the United States, where he was sent as a special
envoy of the French government.

> "On a day in September 1935 we were eating at Murnane's
> on Long Island," writes Monnet, "when Foster Dulles came
> with the news of the anti-Jewish laws Hitler wanted to intro-
> duce in Germany. 'The man who is capable to do that,' I said
> to my friends, 'will also start a war. The spirit of discrimina-
> tion and superiority knows no limits.' If this episode remained
> engraved in my memory, different from many others which I
> have forgotten, it is because it was the moment on which I
> realized that Nazism would necessarily lead to war, like a ty-
> phoon wreaks havoc."[11]

Note that Monnet made his prediction as early as 1935—even *before*
Hitler reoccupied the Rhineland, annexed Austria, and invaded Czecho-
slovakia. Monnet's causal chain was based on the *immorality* of Hitler's
regime: if the Nazis were capable of trampling on fundamental human
rights and started to persecute the Jews, then they were not only capable

of starting a war, but war would be a necessary consequence.

Another interesting example is the American historian Arthur Schlesinger Jr., who developed a cyclical theory of American history based on the replacement of generations. This cyclical theory enabled him to predict important changes in American politics. Like Albert O. Hirschman, Schlesinger observed an alternation of periods in which private or public action prevailed. This alternation led to recurring political changes.

> "In the twentieth century," he wrote, "this alternation has taken place at thirty-year intervals: on the public-activism side, for example, Theodore Roosevelt and the Progressive Era in 1901, Franklin D. Roosevelt and the New Deal in 1933, John F. Kennedy and the New Frontier in 1961. There is no mystery about the periodicity. Thirty years is roughly the span of a generation, and the generational succession has been the mainspring of the cycle. If the thirty-year rhythm held, the 1992 election was scheduled to bring about a swing toward affirmative action. That indeed appeared to take place with the victory of the children of Kennedy—Bill Clinton and Al Gore—just as thirty years earlier the incoming Kennedy generation had been the children of Franklin Roosevelt, and thirty years before that the incoming FDR generation had been the children of Theodore Roosevelt and Woodrow Wilson."[12]

The book in which Schlesinger developed this cyclical theory was originally published in 1968. In the Foreword of the 1999 edition, quoted above, he expressed his satisfaction that his theory was confirmed in the early 1990s by the election of Bill Clinton. The question was, what would happen next? Would Schlesinger's cyclical theory[13] also hold up in the twenty-first century? Twenty-eight years later his theory seemed—again—to be confirmed when, on November 3, 2020, Joe Biden was elected President. Like Kennedy Biden considered himself a "child of Franklin Roosevelt." "In the weeks before taking office," wrote *The New York Times,* "President Biden and his aides spent time digging into books

about Franklin D. Roosevelt, both biographies and volumes exploring
Roosevelt's iconic first 100 days, on the theory that no president since
then has taken office with the country in a crisis quite so grave."[14] President Biden shared with Roosevelt his transformative fervor. In the first
ten days of his presidency Biden signed about 45 executive orders,
which was "the fastest start of any president since Roosevelt."[15]

I had also, myself, the dubious pleasure of predicting an event which
later actually took place. In the concluding chapter of my book *Putin's
Wars—The Rise of Russia's New Imperialism,* which was published in
the first months of 2014, I wrote:

> "If Ukraine were to opt for deeper integration into the Euro-
> pean Union, a Georgian scenario could not be excluded, in
> which the Kremlin could provoke riots in Eastern Ukraine or
> the Crimea, where many Russian passport holders live. This
> would offer Russia a pretext for intervening in Ukraine in
> order 'to protects its nationals' and dismember the country.
> Unfortunately, such a scenario cannot be excluded."[16]

This text was written in the beginning of 2013, one year before the
Russian aggression took place. However, it could be read as a blueprint
for what would happen next. In February 2014 pro-Russian militias and
Russian soldiers dressed up as "polite green men" occupied the Ukrainian regions of Crimea and Donbas. In March the Crimea was annexed
after a fake referendum. Referring to my prediction, Craig Nieman
wrote: "The authors' great accuracy in his projection is attributable to
his analysis of Russian strategic culture and a study of Russia's national
strategy as it previously applied to their Chechen and Georgian wars."[17]
He was right. I didn't possess some secret predictive powers, nor was I
personally briefed by the Kremlin. However, this does not mean that my
prediction was plucked out of the air. As in the case of Jan Romein, who
accurately predicted the outbreak of the Second World War, my prediction was based on concrete facts: the fact that in 2008 Russia had already
waged a war against Georgia, Putin's repeated remarks that Ukraine
"was not a real country," and the principles of Russian foreign policy,
formulated by President Medvedev in August 2008, which mentioned

the principle of "protecting the lives and dignity of our citizens, *wherever they may be*," which left the door open for military adventures throughout Russia's "neighborhood." What I observed in 2013 was a Russian willingness and readiness to intervene and to annex parts of Ukraine. It only needed the right pretext—the toppling of the pro-Russian Ukrainian President Yanukovych during the Maidan Revolution—to be put into practice.

MAKING SMALL HOLES IN THE RAWLSIAN VEIL OF IGNORANCE

By identifying causal patterns—or, as in Schlesinger's case: by identifying cyclical trends—the historian hopes to leave pure speculation behind. Causal patterns and returning cycles are *structured* processes. These processes develop according to a certain logic. In the case of causal patterns, this is the causal nexus: "*if* A, then B." In the case of cyclical trends this is: "*after* A comes B, and after B comes C (or reappears A)."

> "Cosmic history...," writes Robert MacIver, "fulfills its endless processing in accordance with laws that are eternally operative, each successive stage being the necessary sequel of the stage before. When we turn to human history, though its scale is utterly insignificant in the cosmic frame, we obtain a close-up of how the future is made in the present in ways that may be partly predictable and in ways that no knowledge of the past enables us to predict."[18]

MacIver is confident that the future is "partly predictable." What does this mean? This means that the historian—but also the sociologist or political scientist—doesn't have to be satisfied with the observation that the future is completely hidden behind a Rawlsian *veil of ignorance,* but that he can try to make small holes in this veil—enabling himself to catch a glimpse of the future, however restricted that glimpse might be.

FORECASTING AND THE PROBLEM
OF "SYSTEM BREAKS"

But how should the historian proceed? His method is to deconstruct reality into a number of smaller areas and explore whether in these small areas there exist tendencies and patterns which can be extrapolated to the future. Extrapolation will be more difficult in some fields, such as culture, fashion, and even politics, than in the field of economics, technology, or demography. The American sociologist Daniel Bell, who in his book *The Coming of Post-Industrial Society* (first edition 1973) had made an attempt at "social forecasting," warned that forecasting on the basis of extrapolation of tendencies doesn't always work.

> "The foundation of all forecasting is some form of extrapolation—the effort to read some continuing tendency from the past into a determinate future. The most common, and deceptive, technique is the straight projection of a past trend plotted on a line or curve. Linear projections represent the extension of a regular time series—population, or productivity, or expenditures—at a constant rate. The technique has its obvious difficulties. Sometimes there are 'system breaks.'"[19]

These "system breaks" take place when suddenly the tempo of a certain tendential growth or decline changes and the predicted development doesn't take place. Bell gives the example of agricultural productivity in the United States: "If one had computed agricultural productivity from the mid-1930s for the next twenty-five years at the rate it had followed for the previous twenty-five, the index (using 1910 as a base) would in 1960 have been about 135 or 140, instead of the actual figure of 400."[20] The introduction of new methods in agriculture, especially mechanization and the use of fertilizer and pesticides led to a change in the growth curve and made earlier forecasts obsolete. One may expect that modern genetically modified treatment techniques which will lead to greater, better, and more frequent harvests, will again lead to such a system break. Making prognoses for the future—even for developments in small, specialized areas—remains therefore a tricky affair, even for those who dispose of the most detailed data.

ATTENTION: FORECASTING DREAM SCENARIOS CAN IMPEDE THEIR REALIZATION

With the provisos mentioned above, one can argue that making small holes in the Rawlsian *veil of ignorance* is in principle possible. However, the question is whether people are satisfied with these modest "mini-predictions" of future developments in certain areas—even if they prove to be correct. Maybe the holes which these predictions make in the veil of ignorance are too small to satisfy man's desire to know the future. That may be the reason for the success of those authors who have fewer scruples, and who paint great panoramas of the future. Apparently, people want to dream. But rather than dreaming one should listen to Reinhart Koselleck's warning: "Often it is the case—and that is also a lesson from history—that the naïve desirability of a coming situation impedes its realization."[21] Marx's naïve, utopian wish to create a "classless society" didn't lead to a classless society, but to a totalitarian society of powerless citizens. The less far-reaching ideals, the "mini-utopias" of the social-democrats, had a greater long-term positive effect than the utopian dreams of Marx and his followers. Speculative projections of the future can therefore be potentially dangerous. The adage for the work of a historian is, *stick to the facts*. This adage is also valid for historians and social scientists who want to get a glimpse into the future. They should be aware that even the trends and patterns which they have discovered often cannot be extrapolated in a linear way. The future can only be explored in a limited way. It is a huge, unknown continent—for some a land of hope, for others an inhospitable land full of apocalyptic threats.

A SOCIOLOGY OF THE FUTURE?

Predicting the future should not be considered as a purely intellectual game for creative minds. There exist compelling reasons for scholars to be engaged in thinking about the future. The main reason is that our technological reach into the future is steadily increasing and that future generations will be affected by the decisions we are taking today. Cynthia Selin pleads therefore for a "sociology of the future." "Exploring the future tense provides a means of taking responsibility for what is to come," she writes.[22] She observes that "processes of discovery and invention in the natural sciences and the translation of such knowledge into commodities are faster than our ability to safely regulate or make sense of the new social dynamics engendered by such processes."[23] Trying to predict the future and developing different scenarios is therefore not a game. In our technologically advanced world it has become a necessity. Because our future is not "given"; as a *human* future it is increasingly the object of our intervention and modulation. We can develop different scenarios of the future and if in one of these scenarios future generations are overly exposed to unnecessary risk we can decide and *should* decide *not* to develop certain technologies or impose strict regulations.

NOTES

1   Immanuel Kant, "Der Streit der Fakultäten," Zweiter Abschnitt, in Immanuel Kant, *Schriften zur Anthropologie, Geschichtsphilosophie, Politik und Pädagogik 1, Werkausgabe Volume XI* (Frankfurt am Main: Suhrkamp Verlag, 1977), p. 351.

2   David Staley, *History and Future: Using Historical Thinking to Imagine the Future* (Lanham, MD: Lexington Books, 2010), p. 2.

3   Graham Allison and Niall Ferguson, "Why the U.S. President Needs a Council of Historians," *The Atlantic,* September 2016.

4   Ibid.

5   Ibid.

6   https://redteamdefense.org/

7   Anne Chemin, "Les auteurs de science-fiction transformés en prophètes," *Le Monde,* November 20, 2021.

8   Alexis de Tocqueville, "L'Annonce de la révolution de 1848," in Alexis de Tocqueville, *Textes essentiels,* Anthologie critique par J.-L. Benoît (Paris : Havas Poche, 2000), p. 349.

9   Ibid., p. 352.

10 Dr. Jan Romein, *Machten van dezen tijd – 1936–1937* (Amsterdam: Wereldbibliotheek, 1938), p. 7.

11 Jean Monnet, *Erinnerungen eines Europäers,* with an Introduction by Helmut Schmidt (Munich: Deutscher Taschenbuch Verlag, 1980), p. 149.

12   Arthur M. Schlesinger Jr., *The Cycles of American History,* Foreword to the Mariner Edition of 1999, op. cit., p. vii.

13   Schlesinger was not the first to develop this cyclical theory. The sociologist Pitirim Sorokin already mentioned it in an article, published in 1927, writing: "Dominating political parties and governmental policy and other social phenomena have a cycle of thirty to thirty-three years. This span of time, about one generation, is one of the natural units of the historical period." (Pitirim Sorokin, "A Survey of the Cyclical Conceptions of Social and Historical Process," *Social Forces,* Volume 6, No. 1, September 1927, p. 37.)

14   Peter Baker, "Copying Roosevelt, Biden Wanted a Fast Start. Now Comes the Hard Part," *The New York Times,* January 30, 2021 (updated February 2, 2021).

15   Ibid.

16   Marcel H. Van Herpen, *Putin's Wars—The Rise of Russia's New Imperialism* (Lanham, MD.: Rowman & Littlefield, 2014), p. 247.

17   Craig Nieman, "Deterrence and Engagement: A Blended Strategic Approach to a Resurgent Russia," Joint Forces Staff College, Norfolk, VA, April 4, 2016.

18   R. M. MacIver, *The Challenge of the Passing Year—My Encounter with Time,* op. cit., p. 110.

19   Daniel Bell, *The Coming of Post-Industrial Society—A Venture in Social Forecasting* (New York: Basic Books, Inc., 1976), p. 201.

20   Ibid.

21   Reinhart Koselleck, "Lernen aus der Geschichte Preußens ?" in *Vom Sinn und Unsinn der Geschichte,* op. cit., p. 173.

22   Cynthia Selin, "The Sociology of the Future: Tracing Stories of Technology and Time," *Sociology Compass,* 2/6, 2008.

23   Ibid.

CHAPTER 17
COULD THE END OF THE SOVIET UNION BE PREDICTED?

Is the future a completely closed book or have visionary individuals the ability to catch a glimpse of the future, even if this glimpse remains modest and restricted? We have seen that even the Enlightenment philosophers took care not to make precise predictions. From the background of their optimistic philosophy of history they were convinced that the world was already moving in the right direction and that humanity in the future would enjoy increasing happiness. However, what exactly that future world would look like, they didn't know and did not pretend to know. The Enlightenment philosophers were conscious of the vagaries of history, which often takes strange and unexpected turns. However, even if the *moment,* the *form,* and the *actors* of an historical event cannot exactly be predicted, does this mean that some events cannot be predicted? Take, for example, the end of communism and the demise of the Soviet Union: both events were, certainly, totally unexpected, but were they also completely unpredictable?

PROPHETS OF THE IMMINENT SOVIET COLLAPSE

As a matter of fact, for a long time Western economists had been predicting that the Soviet economy would increasingly stagnate, so that in the long run this model of society was not viable. They were convinced that this would ultimately lead to a crisis. These prophets proved to be right. The stagnation of the Soviet economy led to *perestroika,* Gorbachev's reform policy. In 1983—two years before Gorbachev became General Secretary—the American historian Arthur Schlesinger wrote: "But there is enough to the reality of Soviet troubles to lead even the ideologues in

Washington to conceive Soviet Russia as a nation at once so robust that it threatens the world and so frail that a couple of small pushes will shove its ramshackle economy into collapse."[1] Whilst perestroika in a certain sense could have been predicted, this was not the case with the geopolitical consequences, such as the demise of the Soviet Union—although some visionary individuals had also predicted this. One of the first was the Russian dissident Andrei Amalrik who, in 1970, published the pamphlet "Will the Soviet Union Survive until 1984?"[2] The pamphlet was considered as the wishful thinking of an opponent of the regime rather than as a serious scientific analysis. In 1976—six years after Amalrik's publication—the French author Emmanuel Todd wrote: "If the apparatchiks want to make the USSR into a developed country, then they should accept the partial or complete decoupling of the Baltic republics, of Central Asia, and the Caucasus. It is also possible that Ukraine will claim some liberties for itself."[3] Some pages later Todd announced—almost triumphantly—"End of the USSR?"[4] This prediction was, of course, partly historical speculation. But this speculation was based on some hard economic facts. Two authors who equally predicted the demise of the Soviet Union were Vladimir Solovyov and Elena Klepikova. In 1987—four years before the Soviet Union collapsed—they wrote:

> "We also have to take into account the contradictory nature of the multinational conglomerate that is the Soviet Union, which can be kept within the framework of the empire only by force, since in that empire an ethnic minority (the Russians) rules a great majority of vassal peoples (in a ratio of 140 million to 250 million, if we include Eastern Europe, Mongolia, and Afghanistan). The ailing Soviet economy needs democratic reforms at all costs; yet they imperil the empire, since they inevitably lead to disturbances on its outskirts, and in the end may bring about its collapse. Instead of strengthening the country, Gorbachev's reforms, however limited, are shaking its very foundation."[5]

When the Soviet Union finally disintegrated the news was acclaimed in the West, although the euphoria was tempered by the fear that the Soviet nuclear arsenal could end up in the wrong hands. The general feeling was that the West had "won" the Cold War. However, in reality the West had "won" nothing. Russia had lost its colonial empire, as had happened before with the other European powers. The general feeling of euphoria was best expressed in the famous article "The End of History," written by the American political scientist Francis Fukuyama (which, by the way, was published before the demise of the Soviet Union). "What we may witnessing," wrote Fukuyama, "is not just the end of the Cold War … but the end of history as such, that is, the end point of mankind's ideological evolution and the universalization of Western liberal democracy as the final form of human government."[6] To announce the "end of history," as if with the "conversion" of the Soviet leaders to the principles of liberal democracy "the final form of human government" would be achieved, was of course an outrageous interpretation of the events. According to Fukuyama the world had finally become "rational"—as in Hegel's philosophy of history—and a higher form of development could not be imagined. This was not only an ahistorical blocking of the future, but it was also premature. Fukuyama's prediction that liberal democracy would be "the final form of human government" was immediately challenged—not only in Russia where soon an authoritarian regime would be reinstalled, but equally in the US and Europe, where populist parties and populist leaders emerged.[7]

The British historian Paul Kennedy warned: "The Western democracies might be unwise to assume that the collapse of the "evil empire" is going to be an unqualified advantage to themselves."[8] Kennedy, author of *The Rise and Fall of the Great Powers,* [9] spoke from his own experience as a historian. The decline of the great powers, as described and analyzed by him, was often accompanied by wars and revolutions. Not Fukuyama's self-satisfied euphoria, but Kennedy's warning holds up thirty years later. In Russia liberal democracy has become a faraway dream, the economy has developed into a bureaucratic state kleptocracy, and the country conducts an aggressive, revisionist foreign policy which has already led to a war in Chechnya and two wars with neighboring countries. Both Kennedy and Fukuyama assume that in history there are tendencies operating. For Fukuyama this is apparently a Hegelian, teleological philosophy of progress. For Kennedy this is the experience that the decline of great empires is often accompanied by wars and violence.

DO HISTORICAL TENDENCIES EXIST? THE JANUS-FACED CHARACTER OF HUMAN HISTORY

This brings us—again—to the question of whether "historical tendencies," which point to the future, exist. This seems undeniably the case. Just imagine that there didn't exist historical tendencies; world history would be reduced to a series of random facts, without coherence and without any logic. One may object that there are also completely unpredictable events which can still give a decisive turn to history. Yes, indeed, that is also the case. Human history is apparently characterized by two opposite phenomena: the first is the absolute unpredictability of certain events, the second is a predictability of some tendencies. Human history has, therefore, a double, two-sided, Janus-faced character. We humans live each day with this tension between predictability and unpredictability. This was also the case with the demise of the Soviet Union. That the Soviet economy in the long run would miss the train of the third industrial revolution and would increasingly stagnate was a tendency that was clear to any informed observer. However, the *moment* at which the crisis would erupt and the exact *form* it would take, were unknown. That a crisis was imminent, however, was clear. It was the *personality* of Gorbachev, the Soviet leader—a completely unpredictable historical fact—which would determine the specific turn the crisis was to take. Gorbachev's decision not to repress the movement for independence in the Baltic republics opened the way towards a peaceful disintegration of the Soviet Union.

THE FIRST WORLD WAR AND *THUCYDIDES'S TRAP*

Another example of this Janus-faced character of human history is the outbreak of the First World War. The underlying trend which caused this war was the rise of the German Empire as a new great power in Europe and the growing rivalry between this geopolitical newcomer on the one hand and the old, established powers France, England, and Russia, on the other. The American political scientist Graham Allison has coined the term *Thucydides's Trap* for the historical tendency that the rise of a new power can lead to increased international rivalry—analogous to the situation in ancient Greece, described by the Athenian historian Thucydides, where the rise of Athens led to the animosity of Sparta and resulted in the Peloponnesian War (431–404 before our era) between both city states.

> "The complexity of causation in human affairs," wrote Allison, "has vexed philosophers, jurists, and social scientists. In analyzing how wars break out, historians focus primarily on proximate, or immediate causes.... Proximate causes for war are undeniably important. But the founder of history believed that the most obvious causes for bloodshed mask even more significant ones. More important than the sparks that lead to war, Thucydides teaches us, are the structural factors that lay its foundations: conditions in which otherwise manageable events can escalate with unforeseeable severity and produce unimaginable consequences."[10]

The direct triggers for the First World War were two accidental and unforeseeable events: the murder of the Austrian Archduke Franz Ferdinand on June 28, 1914, in Sarajevo, on the one hand, and the decision of Tsar Nicholas II to mobilize the Russian army against the central powers (Germany, Austria-Hungary, the Ottoman Empire, and Bulgaria). In a more distracted period this would not have led to a world war. It was the structural causes—a power change in Europe in favor of newcomer Germany—which allowed the situation to become poisoned.

The extrapolation of historical "tendencies," however, is not without danger. Allison has applied the *Thucydides's Trap* for instance to the present relationship between the United States and China. China's rise as an economic and military superpower, making it a potential rival of the United States, resembles greatly the situation in ancient Greece or the situation in Europe in 1914. However, one should take care not to consider these tendencies as "necessary laws of history" from which one cannot escape. Because in that case the tendency becomes a *self-fulfilling prophecy* in which the prophecy influences human action. In his book Allison tries rather to change the Thucydides' Trap into a *self-denying prophecy*. The last part of his book is titled "Why war is not inevitable," and he gives twelve guidelines for peace. In the meantime, the Thucydides' Trap syndrome has become an important subject of discussion in the United States with defenders and critics regarding the pertinence of this historical trend. Henry Kissinger who, as Nixon's national security adviser, initiated the Western opening up to China and made the subsequent rise of China possible, is somewhat optimistic. He emphasizes that "China's foreign policy aimed primarily for a peaceful international environment (including good relations with the United States)...."[11] Robert Kagan, on the contrary, is less optimistic. "Every day the Chinese military prepares for a possible war with the United States over Taiwan," he writes. "It is a war the Chinese government would like very much to avoid but believes may someday be unavoidable."[12] Will the Thucydides' Trap also be applicable to the China-US rivalry, or will both powers find some way of getting along with each other? History will tell which of the two is right.

THE ROLE OF HISTORICAL ACCIDENTS

Historical accidents are the opposite of historical tendencies: they are the erratic twists of fate, the unexpected and unpredictable events which change the world out of the blue, as a total surprise—like the assassination of President Kennedy on November 22, 1963. The generation alive at that time know exactly where they were and what they were doing at the very moment that they heard the news—myself included. The same is true of another event: the attack by Al Qaeda on the Twin Towers of the World Trade Center in New York on September 11, 2001. Unpredictable and capricious events like these suddenly give a new twist to history. One might ask, for instance, whether the American involvement in the war in Vietnam, which began under Kennedy, would have taken on such proportions if Kennedy had *not* been murdered. And without 9/11, would America have started wars in Iraq and Afghanistan? One may doubt it. The election of the populist Donald Trump as American president in November 2016 was equally such a capricious twist of history, which seemed to signal the beginning of a new era. This tension between predictability and unpredictability presents a great challenge for historians who want to interpret their own times and draw lines into the future. Unpredictable events are the *awkward facts of history* which interrupt smooth narratives, based on the extrapolation of tendencies, and often completely undermine them. However, history is not a pure sequence and accumulation of capricious and random events, but also a process in which one can observe clear trends and tendencies. It is this quality of the historical process which makes it sometimes possible to catch a glimpse of the future.

NOTES

1   Arthur Schlesinger Jr., "Foreign Policy and the American Character," *Foreign Affairs*, Volume 62, No. 1, Fall 1983, p. 7.

2   Andrei Amalrik, *Will the Soviet Union Survive Until 1984?* (New York: Harper & Row, 1970).

3   Emmanuel Todd, *La chute finale – Essai sur la décomposition de la sphère soviétique* (Paris: Éditions Robert Laffont, 1976), p. 316.

4   Ibid., p. 320.

5   Vladimir Solovyov and Elena Klepikova, "Postscript 1987," in Vladimir Solovyov and Elena Klepikova, *Inside the Kremlin* (London: W.H. Allen & Co Plc, 1988), pp. 291–92.

6   Francis Fukuyama, "The End of History," *The National Interest,* No. 16, Summer 1989, p. 3. Fukuyama's "end of history" philosophy is only a modern variant of the Enlightenment's philosophy of progress. This philosophy even flourished in the dark days of the interbellum, as the French philosopher Georges Gusdorf reminds us. "Until the war of 1939–1945," he writes, "the common opinion on the market place of university philosophy was in favor of a moderate rationalism which embraced with enthusiasm the progress of scientific knowledge and of technical efficiency. Science and wisdom, truth and value would necessarily go together; humanity, having become adult and endowed with an enlightened intelligence should succeed to solve the international problems, as well as the social conflicts.... The triumph of the arbitrary, naked violence, tyranny was unthinkable; the emergence of the cosmopolitan city of the just, of democracy in spirit and in reality imposed Itself quite naturally...." (Georges Gusdorf, "Situation spirituelle de notre temps," in Georges Gusdorf, *Le crépuscule des illusions – Mémoires intempestifs* (Pari s: La Table Ronde, 2002), pp. 16–17.)

7   On populism see Marcel H. Van Herpen, *The End of Populism—Twenty Proposals to Defend Liberal Democracy* (Manchester: Manchester University Press, 2021).

8   Paul Kennedy, *Preparing for the Twenty-First Century* (London: Fontana Press, 1994), first published 1993, p. 249.

9   Paul Kennedy, *The Rise and Fall of the Great Powers—Economic Change and Military Conflict from 1500 to 2000* (New York: Random House, 1987).

10   Graham Allison, *Destined for War: Can America and China Escape Thucydides's Trap?* (Boston and New York: Houghton, Mifflin, Harcourt: 2017), p. xiv.

11   Henry Kissinger, *On China* (London and New York: Penguin, 2012), p. 490.

12   Robert Kagan, *The Return of History and the End of Dreams* (New York: Alfred A. Knopf, 2008), p. 34.

CHAPTER 18

CONCLUSION

A main characteristic of human life is the fact that humans live in time. Of course, one might say that animals also live in time: animals are born, they live, procreate, and die, and all this supposes a certain duration. A fly can live for some days, a dog for fourteen years, and a turtle for one hundred years. But the difference is that for animals, time remains something external: they live *in* time, but they don't *experience* time like humans do. Humans live in time and experience time. Without this time dimension human life would no longer be human. This time dimension is a challenge, as well as a curse. It is a challenge because humans set goals for themselves: they make projects. The word "project" implies a future dimension. It comes from the Latin word *proicere,* which means "throwing something forward"—into an unknown future. Humans know that they are mortal and that time is in limited supply. This encourages them to "use" the time which is at their disposal in an efficient way.

However, time is not only an opportunity and a challenge. It is also a curse, because many things simply "happen"—these are the things and events over which one has no control: one can become ill, one can lose one's job in an economic crisis, or—worse—a war breaks out. The human time dimension is therefore a generator of hope, as well as of fear. It is true that animals can show behavior which resembles hope and fear. When one shows a dog a sausage he will wag his tail in expectation, and if he meets an aggressive dog he will run away. However, the time span of a dog's hope and fear is extremely short: it is immediate. The dog will neither look forward to the next summer holiday, nor stay awake at night because he fears meeting the aggressive dog again.

HANNAH ARENDT AND OUR
"MARCH INTO THE FUTURE"

It is this double character of the human time dimension—being a generator of hope and fear—which influences man's attitude towards history. He wants to learn lessons from history to avoid negative experiences repeating themselves, and he wants to take a glimpse into the future to assuage his fears and to feed his hopes. History, as a science, is therefore more than most other sciences bound up with the human condition. Karl Marx, who is mainly known as a philosopher and an economist, was aware of this when he wrote in *The German Ideology*: "We know only one science, the science of history."[1] Man is constantly living on the dividing line between past and future. He may be inclined to forget the past, longing for a benign amnesia in which the past is no longer haunting him. However, as Tocqueville warned: "Since the past has ceased to throw its light upon the future, the mind of man wanders in obscurity."[2] The importance of the past is also emphasized by Hannah Arendt, who wrote: "Not only the future … but also the past is … a force, and not … a burden man has to shoulder and of whose dead weight the living can or even must get rid in their march into the future."[3]

The past is, indeed, a force, as Hannah Arendt argued, but on the condition that we don't make ourselves illusions, either by depicting the past as some mythical "golden age" or, on the contrary, as a dark period of primitive and ignorant barbarism. Although historians will never be able to exactly reproduce the past, they should try to come as close as possible to historical reality by painstakingly sticking to the facts. It is only by a truthful and realistic representation of past events that one will be able to learn from history and make it possible for the present generation to take history's lessons to heart. Hannah Arendt spoke, tellingly, about man's "march into the future." Marching into the future is different from walking or—worse—limping into the future. To *march* into the future, one has to be confident that—whatever may happen—one can overcome unexpected obstacles and problems and that one is able, more or less, to shape the future.

This confidence is a modern phenomenon. In Ancient Greece and Rome this confidence was lacking. For the Greeks the future was in the hands of the three *Moirai*, goddesses who determined human destinies—

in particular their misery and suffering. In Rome these three goddesses were called *Parcae*. The modern confidence and self-assurance that one could *march* into the future emerged only in the second half of the eighteenth century with the optimistic Enlightenment philosophy. The Enlightenment period was followed by an unprecedented surge of innovation which brought the train, electricity, the telephone, the automobile, and the plane. This outburst of creativity seemed to confirm the Enlightenment optimism about the future. Predictions about the year 2000, made in the beginning of the twentieth century, envisioned many new innovations. "Futurists of the early 1900s predicted an incredible boom in technology that would transform human lives for the better. In fact, many of those predictions for the future in which we live weren't far off, from the proliferation of automobiles and airplanes to the widespread transmission of information."[4]

THE PREDICTION OF ALEXANDER GRAHAM BELL

Exemplary is a speech, delivered in February 1917 by Alexander Graham Bell (1847–1922), the inventor of the telephone, in which he reminded his audience that "we progress from candles to electricity in one lifetime":

> "I, myself," said Bell, "am not so very old yet, but I can remember the days when there were no telephones. I remember, too, very distinctly when there were no automobiles here. There were thousands of horses, and Washington, in the summer time, smelled like a stable. There were plenty of flies, and the death rate was high. Now, it is very interesting and instructive to look back over the various changes that have occurred and trace the evolution of the present from the past. By projecting these lines of advance into the future, you can forecast the future, to a certain extent, and recognize some of the fields of usefulness that are opening up to you."[5]

Despite his optimism, Alexander Graham Bell was not naive. More than half a century before the Club of Rome would publish its report

"The Limits of Growth," he already told his audience that "in relation to coal and oil, the world's annual consumption has become so enormous that we now are actually within measurable distance of the end of the supply. What shall we do when we have no more coal or oil?"[6] And he formulated already possible solutions, pointing to "tidal and wave power (which we have not yet learned to utilize), and the employment of the sun's rays directly as a source of power."[7] These early signs of doubt concerning the emerging carbon economy did not undermine the prevailing optimism about the benefits of modern technology. Criticism, if it emerged, took rather the form of satirical representations of the mind-numbing repetitiveness of Fordist factory life as shown, for instance, by Charlie Chaplin in his memorable role as a factory worker employed on an assembly line in the 1936 comedy film *Modern Times*.

Although technological innovation has brought much progress, and even the most optimistic eighteenth-century Enlightenment philosophers wouldn't believe their eyes if they could see the modern world with its planes and cars, its nuclear energy, moon landings, and huge megalopolises. Later generations were less convinced that man's march into the future was a smooth and easy walk. Hannah Arendt pointed to the ambiguous, double-edged character of technological progress when in 1954, at the height of the Cold War, she wrote:

> "In Europe today, the development, possession, and threatened use of atomic weapons by the United States is a primary fact of political life. Europeans have, of course, engaged in the now familiar debates about the soullessness of a country dominated by modern technology, the monotony of the machine, the uniformity of a society based upon mass-production, and the like for many years. But today the matter has gone much beyond that. The intimate connection between modern warfare and a technicalized society has become obvious to everybody, and as a result large segments of the population—and not only the intellectuals—are passionately opposed to, and afraid of, technological progress and the growing technicalization of our world."[8]

Innovations could bring new benefits, she argued, as well as new dangers. Atomic energy was a case in point. It could be used as a source of clean energy, as well as a weapon of mass destruction which could annihilate human life. The American historian Arthur Schlesinger Jr. wrote:

> "I had always supposed that, with the nuclear genie out of the bottle, the prospect of the suicide of the human race would have a sobering effect on those who possessed the tragic power to initiate nuclear war. For most of the nuclear age this supposition has been roughly true.... [But] I no longer have much confidence in the admonitory effect of the possession of nuclear weapons. The curse of ideology is that as it impoverishes our sense of reality, it impoverishes our imagination, too. It enfeebles our capacity to visualize the Doomsday horror. It inhibits us from confronting the awful possibility we can no longer deny: the extermination of sentient life on this planet."[9]

In the same vein the philosopher Thomas Nagel wrote:

> "The widespread willingness to rely on thermonuclear bombs as the ultimate weapon displays a cavalier attitude toward death that has always puzzled me. My impression is that whatever they may say, most of the defenders of these weapons are not suitably horrified at the possibility of a war in which hundreds of millions of people would be killed. This may be due to monumental lack of imagination, or perhaps to a peculiar attitude toward risk which leads to the discounting of probabilities of disaster substantially below 50 percent. Or it may be a mechanism of defensive irrationality that appears in circumstances of aggressive conflict."[10]

These authors emphasized—rightly—the danger that modern man runs the risks of becoming the victim of a human quality and a human defect: his technological genius on the one hand and his lack of imagination on the other. The British physicist Stephen Hawking (1942–2018) went so far as to advise humans to leave earth to avoid the risk of being annihilated by nuclear war or climate change,[11] while in 2020 Barry McCaffrey, the principal arms control negotiator with Russia during the Strategic Arms Reduction Treaty (START I), wrote that we had "ten years until Armageddon" because of the growing nuclear threat.[12] Historical optimism had given way to gloom, and mankind increasingly had the feeling of having become Goethe's sorcerer's apprentice, who famously complained: *"The spirits I summoned, I can't rid of them."*[13]

MODERN TECHNOLOGY AND FEAR OF THE FUTURE: DO WE SUFFER FROM A "SORCERER'S APPRENTICE" SYNDROME?

The feeling of having been betrayed by the lofty promises of "technological progress" is not only linked to global warming or the possibility of an imminent nuclear war. Let us take, for instance, the Internet. In 1950 no one could predict that some decades later this new medium would be invented, nor could one imagine its far-reaching consequences. When the Internet arrived it was welcomed as an almost magical new medium which made it possible to connect with the world. Comfortably sitting in your armchair at home you had access to a wealth of information. This new, interconnected world, from which in principle no one was excluded, seemed to herald the advent of a new, egalitarian utopia, called the "information society." Expectations were high. Wouldn't the free flow of information, characteristic of liberal-democratic societies, undermine authoritarian and illiberal regimes which would become increasingly unable to control information? Although there was no direct link with China's opening up and the demise of the Soviet Union, these two events seemed to confirm this positive trend. The euphoria increased with the advent of social media which made it possible to be friends with unknown people all over the world. A world without borders, with free information and international bonds of friendship, seemed within reach.

Thirty years later those utopian dreams have completely vanished. It is true, the Internet *did* change the world, but quite differently from what one expected. The new world in which we woke up was a world of cyberattacks, dark net, fake news, hate speech, and conspiracy theories. As a result of the growth of electronic commerce, retail shops in city centers closed, making these centers less attractive. Cyberbullying led to an increase of suicides among adolescents.[14] The Internet also became a geopolitical battleground for hostile powers. Hacking the computers of ministries, governments, and political parties in foreign countries and interfering in elections became an integral part of a new kind of warfare, called "hybrid warfare." Because these attacks were most of the time anonymous, the instigators could claim *plausible deniability,* a phenomenon which, in fact, stimulated this kind of attack. However, these negative developments should not obscure the positive sides of this innovation. The Internet *did* promote the free flow of information, created new services, made online transactions possible, and facilitated automation. This positive side of the Internet became particularly clear during the Covid-19 lockdowns, when it facilitated working from home and prevented the economy from coming to a standstill.

New innovations can and will have unpredictable consequences: positive as well as negative. Artificial intelligence (A.I.) is another example of a much-touted innovation. Artificial intelligence has many benefits. It is not only essential for the development of self-driving cars, but it is also a useful tool for monitoring known criminals, logging in to online accounts, or securing devices like phones and laptops. However, although A.I. has been marketed as a completely safe system for self-driving cars, the reality is different.

"Despite its abilities," wrote *The New York Times,* "Autopilot does not remove responsibility from the driver. Tesla tells drivers to stay alert and be ready to take control of the car at all times.... But many experts worry that these systems, because they enable drivers to relinquish active control of the car, may lull them into thinking that their cars are driving themselves. Then, when the technology malfunctions or cannot handle a situation, drivers may be unprepared to take control."[15]

Another problem is that A.I. could easily become an instrument in the hands of authoritarian regimes to control their populations. In an article, titled *The Panopticon Is Already Here,* Ross Andersen warned, for instance, that the Chinese government

> "wants to build an all-seeing digital system of social control, patrolled by precog (sic) algorithms that identify potential dissenters in real time…. In the near future every person who enters a public space could be identified instantly, by AI matching them to an ocean of personal data, [such as] travel records, friends and associates, reading habits, purchases— to predict political resistance before it happens."[16]

Andersen warned that China, which, within the next decade could become the global leader in A.I. technology, could export its know-how to other countries, a development which "could shift the balance of power between the individual and the state worldwide."[17] According to Kay Firth-Butterfield, the head of artificial intelligence and machine learning at the World Economic Forum, "We need to ask if the use of A.I. will benefit humans and the planet."[18] She argued that "we will need some sort of regulation for things like facial recognition and cases where A.I. impinges on people's rights and liberties…." Fundamental aspects of this regulation should include "transparency, accountability, privacy and explainability about what you're doing with data." She added that "companies should definitely have an A.I. ethics officer, as well as an ethics statement."[19] A.I. could not only have dire consequences for the citizen's freedom and privacy. Another problem is that facial recognition algorithms, developed and used in the United States, tend to misidentify people of color which makes it more likely that the police, using facial recognition systems, arrest the wrong person.[20] A report commissioned by the European Parliament mentioned other problems, such as automated content removal by technology companies to fight hate speech, which would be "a dangerous trend, given the limited competence of machine learning to understand tone and context. Automated content removal risks censorship of legitimate speech."[21] A.I. will also change modern warfare. "A.I. technology has the potential to transform warfare to the same, or perhaps even greater, extent than the advent of nuclear weapons, aircraft, computers and biotechnology."[22] The reason is that it tends to replace human decision-making, which raises many legal and ethical questions. "One concern is that automated weapon systems that exclude human judgment could violate international Human Law, and threaten our fundamental right to life and the principle of human dignity. A.I. could also lower the threshold of going to war, affecting global stability."[23] Sometimes A.I. is compared with Pandora's Box. Irving John Good, a British mathematician who was one of the cryptologists working alongside Alan Turing at Bletchley Park during World War II, wrote:

> "Let an ultra-intelligent machine be defined as a machine that can far surpass all the intellectual activities of any man, however clever. Since the design of machines is one of these intellectual activities, an ultra-intelligent machine could design even better machines, there would then unquestionably be an 'intelligence explosion,' and the intelligence of man would be left far behind. Thus the first ultra-intelligent machine is the last invention that man need ever make, provided that the machine is docile enough to tell us how to keep it under control."[24]

This "empire of the machines," which has the potential to subjugate humans, seems to be, for the moment, science fiction. However, it reveals the extent of unease the present generation feels about this innovation.

HOW CAN WE PUT THE GENIE BACK IN THE BOTTLE?

So, what should be done? According to one author, when developing innovations we have three choices: "No regulation at all, some regulation, and banning."[25] However, is it as simple as that? Is it possible to ban a new technology when it promises huge economic benefits or when other countries are already actively developing the new technology—including hostile governments which plan to use it in their military, making existing defense systems increasingly obsolete? Is this choice realistic?

Even more so, when your own country, in this case the United States, is a leader in A.I.-related research? A.I., touted for its promise to create a dream world full of self-driving cars, will also bring self-driving tanks and killer robots. "The robotics field, at least for the military, is going through a very extreme uptick of interest in the Pentagon. A lot of things that were distant future are rapidly accelerating," said Kevin Mills, associate director for ground vehicle robotics at the U.S. Army Tank Automotive Research Development and Engineering Center.[26] This trend is confirmed by Michael O'Hanlon, a defense expert who, in a paper forecasting change in military technology for the period 2020–2040, called the projected advances concerning the use of artificial intelligence and robotics "revolutionary."[27] In a Position Report, published in May 2021, the International Committee of the Red Cross (ICRC) warned that autonomous weapon systems could undermine international humanitarian law, writing that "new rules are needed to clarify and specify how IHL [International Humanitarian Law] applies to AWS [autonomous weapon systems] … new legally binding rules would offer the benefits of legal certainty and stability."[28]

Will it be possible to limit and regulate the use of these weapons? The National Commission on Artificial Intelligence, established by the U.S. Congress, leaves some doubt. In its Final Report one can read:

> "Even with the right artificial intelligence (AI)-ready technology foundations in place, the U.S. military will still be at a battlefield disadvantage if it fails to adopt the right concepts and operations to integrate AI technologies.… The Department of Defense (DoD) should not be a witness to the AI revolution in military affairs, but should deliver it with leadership from the top, new operating concepts, relentless experimentation and a system that rewards agility and risk."[29]

One gets the impression that a new technology, once it has been invented and developed, is unstoppable and that the negative consequences for present and future generations tend to be underestimated or ignored, which enhances the scary feeling that we are not so much the creators of modern technology as its hostages. A report from the UN Panel of

Experts on Libya, published in 2021, is the writing on the wall. According to the report an autonomous drone operated by A.I. would in March 2020, without any humans controlling, have "hunted down and remotely engaged" soldiers fighting for general Khalifa.[30] "The age of autonomous warfare has arrived," wrote Arthur Holland Michel, a defense expert, who emphasized that this strike "should galvanize efforts to do something about autonomous weapons."[31] Indeed. But the question is what exactly should be done in order to avoid being crushed under the wheels of the juggernaut of technological innovation.

"PLAYING GOD" WITH THE GENETIC CODE

Manipulating the genetic code by genetic engineering is another new, revolutionary technology. The good news is that this process of "editing" the human genome by cutting and pasting DNA at specific spots enables us to cure hereditary diseases by replacing a "bad" gene by a "good" gene. However, the problem is that this technology cannot only be used to cure diseases and improve health, but also for more far-reaching objectives such as creating people with stronger muscles, better memories, and faster brains. So-called "transhumanists" consider this new technology a means to improve humanity and to create "superhumans" who are above the natural norm. The American philosopher Michael Sandel points to

> "The danger of creating two classes of human beings: those with access to enhancement technologies, and those who must make do with their natural capacities. And if the enhancements could be passed down the generations, the two classes might eventually become subspecies—the enhanced and the natural."[32]

A similar concern is expressed by David Masci, an editor at Pew Research Center, citing critics who say, "transhumanism could very well create an ever wider gap between the haves and have-nots and lead to new kinds of exploitation or even slavery."[33] This dystopian future is, for instance, envisioned in films like *Gattaca*, in which non-genetically-enhanced humans are considered "invalid."

The emergence of a new class society, based on the availability or respectively non-availability of gene editing, may seem far-fetched. But is it? At a conference organized in December 2015 by the National Academy of Sciences in Washington D.C., about 500 researchers, ethicists, and others urged the scientific community to hold off editing embryos for now, arguing that we do not yet know enough to safely make changes that can be passed down to future generations.[34] This declaration did not come too early, because in 2018 He Jiankui, a researcher at the Southern University of Science and Technology in Shenzhen, China, announced that he had created the world's first gene-edited babies. The twin girls were given the pseudonyms Lulu and Nana. The researcher said he had done the gene editing to protect the babies from getting infected with the AIDS virus. The news sparked global outrage—not only because it was opening the door for "designer babies," but particularly because no one knew whether this kind of gene-editing would be safe for the babies and their eventual offspring. In 2019 He Jiankui was put on trial and sentenced to three years in prison.[35] The *MIT Technology Review* called He's work "a graphic demonstration of attempted gene editing gone awry. Two living human beings, and potentially their descendants too, will bear the consequences."[36] Not only the scientific community was shocked. "The extraordinary wave of genomic-engineering innovation...," wrote Carolyn Brokowski, "has sparked worldwide scientific and ethical uncertainty. Great concern has arisen across the globe about whether heritable genome editing should be permissible in humans—that is, whether it is morally acceptable to modify genomic material such that the 'edit' is transferable to future generations."[37] Another author spoke about "the perils of playing god."[38]

The mass media rushed to cover this sensitive topic. The BBC published an article with the alarming title: "New technologies may have already introduced genetic errors to the human gene pool. How long will they last? And how could they affect us?"[39] The article mentioned "the many surprises in the field," such as "rabbits altered to be leaner that inexplicably ended up with much longer tongues." The argument that man should not be playing god is as old as humanity. It can not only be found in the ancient Greek myth of Prometheus who stole the fire from the gods and gave it to humanity, but also in the Bible story of Adam and

Eve, who earned God's wrath by eating from the tree of knowledge. Science and religious belief have always been at odds. When the first *in vitro* fertilizations took place, these were equally attacked as "unnatural" and even today they are presented in the Christian press as attempts "to force God's hand."[40] We should not block scientific progress. However, the risks for future generations implied in "gene editing" are too great to be neglected. Therefore, we need not only an open discourse that addresses the concerns of the public, but also clear rules which tightly regulate what is allowed. In civil society there are signs of a growing awareness of the problem. In Britain, for instance, *Human Genetics Alert,* an NGO, was founded. On its website one can read that "We are not opposed to genetic research.... However, we are opposed to some developments, such as genetic discrimination, cloning and inheritable ('germ line') genetic engineering of human beings."[41] Professor Sigrid Graumann, a member of the German Ethics Council, questioned, in the same vein, "whether human embryos are worthy of protection and the rights of future persons and generations belong to the most controversial questions of bioethics."[42]

HISTORY AND RESPONSIBILITY: SURVIVING IN A DYSTOPIAN WORLD

A.I. and gene editing are only two examples of technological innovations which evoke questions about our moral responsibility for future generations. We are confronted with a new situation, which the sociologist Ulrich Beck described as "organized irresponsibility."[43] "We are prisoners of a rationality," wrote Beck, "which is on the verge of turning into its opposite."[44] He observed that "confidence in progress is certainly still the dominant ... attitude, because it confirms what happens anyway."[45] However, mankind, rather than making deliberate choices, seems increasingly at the mercy of anonymous forces, a situation for which, according to him, the social sciences are also to blame: "Sociology is just as 'apocalypse blind' as society.... The question what the imminent self-destruction means for society, its institutions, its self-understanding and its notion of progress, for the judicial, scientific, and economic system, for politics and culture, has been criminally neglected by the social sciences."[46] Beck warned that "due to the fact that progress and the possibility of destruction go hand in hand, the second half of this [20th] century is not only different from the first phase of industrialism … but also from *all* … cultures and epochs of human history."[47] We are facing a totally new situation: the possibility of the destruction of the human race—not by some unknown external cause, but by the very faculty which enabled the human race to develop: his intelligence.

Clearly national governments and parliaments, as well as international organizations such as the United Nations, have a role to play. But shouldn't ordinary citizens also have a say? Ulrich Beck proposes to place the ultimate responsibility for making choices about the development of new technologies into the hands of the citizens. He pleads in this context for the introduction of a "technological citizenship." By developing alternatives this new kind of citizenship would enable "an escape from the global autonomous system of technological innovations."[48] This "technological citizenship," he explains, could emerge in a society,

> "which organizes debates on the consequences of technical and economic developments *before* the key decisions are taken. The burden of proof concerning future risks and dangers would be imposed on those who are causing these and no longer on the potential or actual victims or persons at risk…."[49]

Beck is certainly right that public debates should be organized on the consequences of important technological innovations before their implementation. However, his suggestion that the persons who are responsible for an innovation should prove the possible damage their project might cause, seems to be counterintuitive. It is like asking a suspect to present arguments for his own condemnation. The initiators and promoters of technological innovations are not only small high-tech start-ups, but often multinational companies and governments. These do not only possess the expert knowledge about a new technology, but they often have significant financial, economic, political, and military stakes in the project. One cannot expect that they will provide exhaustive and reliable information on the downsides of a project. However, Beck is right that the decision on the introduction of new technologies cannot be left exclusively to experts and economic stakeholders. If the risks are carried by the whole population, including future generations, it is reasonable that a public debate will take place before their introduction.

How should these debates be organized? One could think about a model, developed by James Fishkin, who proposed to organize "deliberative polls" in which a few hundred randomly selected citizens participate. According to Fishkin,

> "The idea is simple. Take a national random sample of the electorate and transport those people from all over the country to a single place. Immerse the sample in the issues, with carefully balanced briefing materials, with intensive discussions in small groups, and with the chance to question competing experts and politicians. At the end of several days of working through the issues face to face, poll the participants in detail. The resulting survey offers a representation of the considered judgments of the public—the views the entire country would come to if it had the same experience of behaving more like ideal citizens immersed in the issues for an extended period."[50]

This doesn't mean that parliaments and governments transfer their regulatory powers to these citizens' assemblies. It *does* mean that parliaments and governments should take the conclusions of these assemblies into account. A model that resembles Fishkin's proposal was applied in France, where, in 2019 and 2020, a "Citizens' Convention on Climate" was organized. It was the first time that a panel, representative of the diversity of the French population, was directly involved in the preparation of a law.[51] The Convention brought together 150 people, all drawn by lot, who received information from different experts before the debates. Their task was to prepare draft laws and the French President had committed to submitting these proposals either to a referendum, to a vote in Parliament, or to direct implementation. The Convention was organized in 7 sessions, the first of which took place on 4-5-6 October 2019 and the last on 19-20-21 June 2020. Although this Convention did not discuss technological innovations, it could be a model to be emulated. Certainly, it will be rare that new technologies will be banned altogether for the reasons explained above—particularly for reasons of international economic competition or great power rivalry.[52] However, these debates are likely to enhance awareness of the risks associated with the introduction of technological innovations and thereby promote regulatory efforts—on a national, as well as on an international level. In these debates there is not only a role to play for technical experts, but equally for historians and social scientists who can point to eventual ethical and societal consequences of innovations. Although it is not their task to predict the future, they can help develop different future scenarios which consider how not only the actual generation, but also future generations may be affected by decisions which are taken today.

As Edmund Burke famously observed: society "becomes a partnership not only between those who are living, but between those who are living, those who are dead and those who are to be born."[53] Will the new, increased responsibility for past and future generations, which comes on top of our responsibility for our own generation, prove to be too heavy a burden for our generation? It is too early to tell. But we should not forget that this responsibility is the price we must pay for our freedom, the most precious human quality, as Stephen Jay Gould reminds us:

"*Homo sapiens* ranks as a 'thing so small' in a vast universe, a wildly improbable evolutionary event, and not the nub of universal purpose. Make of such a conclusion what you will. Some people find the prospect depressing. I have always regarded such a view of life as exhilarating—a source of both freedom and consequent moral responsibility. We are the offspring of history and must establish our own paths in this most diverse and interesting of conceivable universes—one indifferent to our suffering, and therefore offering us maximal freedom to thrive, or to fail, in our own chosen way."[54]

NOTES

1   Karl Marx and Friedrich Engels, "Die deutsche Ideologie," in *Marx Engels Werke* Volume 3 (Berlin: Dietz Verlag, 1969), p. 18.
2   Quoted in Hannah Arendt, *Between Past and Present* (New York: Penguin, 1977), p. 6.
3   Ibid., p. 10.

4   Claudia Geib, "Does Life in 2018 Live up to What We Predicted a Century Ago?" *Futurism,* April 1, 2018.

5   Alexander Graham Bell, "Some of the Problems Awaiting Solution," An address to the graduating class of the McKinley Manual Training School, Washington, D.C., February 1, 1917 (revised for the National Geographic Magazine), *National Geographic Magazine,* Volume 31, No. 2.

6   Ibid.

7   Ibid.

8   Hannah Arendt, "Europe and the Atom Bomb," in Hannah Arendt, *Essays in Understanding 1930–1954, Formation, Exile, and Totalitarianism* (New York: Schocken Books, 1994), p. 418.

9   Arthur Schlesinger, Jr., "Foreign Policy and the American Character," op. cit., p. 13.

10   Thomas Nagel, "Birth, Death, and the Meaning of Life," in Thomas Nagel, *The View from Nowhere,* op. cit., p. 230.

11   Peter Kotecki, "Stephen Hawking: Humans need to leave Earth or risk being annihilated by nuclear war or climate change," *Business Insider,* October 18, 2018. https://www.businessinsider.fr/us/stephen-hawking-humans-leave-earth-or-be-annihilated-2018-10

12   Barry McCaffrey, "10 years until Armageddon: The nuclear threat grows," *Seattle Times,* October 29, 2020. https://www.seattletimes.com/opinion/10-years-until-armageddon-the-nuclear-threat-grows/

13   Johann Wolfgang Goethe, "The sorcerer's apprentice" (Der Zauberlehrling), translated by Richard Stokes. https://www.oxfordlieder.co.uk/song/4163

14   I have analyzed this phenomenon in my book *The Rise of the Shame Society—America's Change from a Guilt Culture into a Shame Culture* (Lanham, MD., and London: Lexington Books, 2022).

15   Cade Metz, "How safe are systems like Tesla's Autopilot? No one knows," *The New York Times,* June 9, 2022.

16   Ross Andersen, "The Panopticon Is Already Here," *The Atlantic,* September 2020. https://www.theatlantic.com/magazine/archive/2020/09/china-ai-surveillance/614197/

17   Ibid.

18   Ellen Rosen, "We need to ask if the use of A.I. will benefit humans," Interview with Kay Firth-Butterfield, *The New York Times,* March 8, 2021.

19   Ibid.

20   Karen Hao, "A US government study confirms most face recognition systems are racist," *MIT Technology Review,* December 20, 2019. https://www.technologyreview.com/2019/12/20/79/ai-face-recognition-racist-us-government-nist-study/

21   "The ethics of artificial intelligence: Issues and initiatives," *European*

Parliament Research Service Scientific Foresight Unit (STOA), Brussels, March 2020, p. 15. https://www.europarl.europa.eu/RegData/etudes/STUD/2020/634452/EPRS_STU(2020)634452_EN.pdf

22   Ibid., p. 63.

23   Ibid., p. 64.

24   Ersel Aker, "Artificial Intelligence: Key to the Future or Pandora's Box?" *SmartWeek,* July 7, 2016. https://www.smartweek.it/artificial-intelligence-key-to-the-future-or-pandoras-box/

25   Thorin Klosowski, "Facial Recognition Is Everywhere. Here's What We Can Do About It," *The New York Times,* July 15, 2020.

26   Quoted in Robert Wall, "Armies Race to Deploy Drone, Self-Driving Tech on the Battlefield," *The Wall Street Journal,* October 29, 2017.

27   Michael E. O'Hanlon, "Forecasting change in military technology," *Brookings,* September 2018, p. 5. https://www.brookings.edu/wp-content/uploads/2018/09/FP_20181218_defense_advances_pt2.pdf

28   "ICRC Position on Autonomous Weapon Systems," *ICRC,* Geneva, May 12, 2021, p. 11.

29   "National Security Commission on Artificial Intelligence—Final Report," NSCAI, Washington, D.C., March 2021, p. 77.

30   "Final Report of the Panel of Experts on Libya established pursuant to Security Council resolution 1973 (2011)," *Security Council,* March 8, 2021, p, 17. https://undocs.org/S/2021/229

31   Arthur Holland Michel, "Libya's UAV Strike Should Galvanize Efforts to Do Something About Autonomous Weapons," *Defense One,* June 2, 2021. https://www.defenseone.com/ideas/2021/06/libyas-uav-strike-should-galvanize-efforts-autonomous-weapons/174449/

32   Michael J. Sandel, "The Case Against Perfection—What's wrong with designer children, bionic athletes, and genetic engineering," *The Atlantic,* April 2004.

33   David Masci, "Human Enhancement—The Scientific and Ethical Dimensions of Striving for Perfection," *Pew Research Center,* September 23, 2020._https://www.pewresearch.org/science/2016/07/26/human-enhancement-the-scientific-and-ethical-dimensions-of-striving-for-perfection/

34   Ibid.

35   Rob Stein, "Chinese Scientist He Jiankui Sentenced To 3 Years In Prison For Editing Human Genes," *NPR,* December 30, 2019. https://www.npr.org/2019/12/30/792456775/chinese-scientist-he-jiankui-sentenced-to-3-years-in-prison-for-editing-human-ge?t=1623838492591&t=1623916236174

36   Kiran Misunuru, "Opinion: We need to know what happened to CRISPR twins Lula and Nana," *MIT Technology Review,* December 3, 2019. https://www.technologyreview.com/2019/12/03/65024/crispr-baby-twins-lulu-and-nana-what-happened/

37 Carolyn Brokowski, "Do CRISPR Germline Ethics Statements Cut It?" *The CRISPR Journal,* 1 (2), April 1, 2018. https://www.ncbi.nlm.nih.gov/ pmc/articles/PMC6694771/

38 Larry G. Locke, "The Promise of CRISPR for Human Germline Editing and the Perils of 'Playing God,'" *The CRISPR Journal,* 3 (1), February 2020. https://www.ncbi.nlm.nih.gov/pmc/articles/PMC7047104/

39 Zaria Gorvett, "New technologies may have already introduced genetic errors to the human gene pool. How long will they last? And how could they affect us?" *BBC,* April 12, 2021. https://www.bbc.com/future/article/20210412-the-genetic-mistakes-that-could-shape-our-species

40 "A Christian understanding of in vitro fertilization," *Ministry Magazine,* July 2012.

41 http://www.hgalert.org/

42 Sigrid Graumann, "Ende des Schicksals? Genomeditierung in der Medizin," *Aus Politik und Zeitgeschichte,* 72, 34–35/2022, August 2022, p. 22.

43 Ulrich Beck, *Gegengifte—Die organisierte Unverantwortlichkeit* (Frankfurt am Main: Suhrkamp Verlag, 1988), p. 96.

44 Ibid.

45 Ibid., p. 106.

46 Ibid., p. 128.

47 Ibid.

48 Ulrich Beck, *Was ist Globalisierung? Irrtümer des Globalismus—Antworten auf Globalisierung,* op. cit., p. 170.

49 Ibid.

50 James S. Fishkin, *The Voice of the People—Public Opinion & Democracy* (New Haven and London: Yale University Press, 1997), p. 162.

51 The mandate of the Convention was "to define a series of measures that will allow to achieve a reduction of at least 40% in greenhouse gas emissions by 2030 (compared to 1990) in a spirit of social justice." Website of the Convention https://www.conventioncitoyennepourleclimat.fr/en/

52 An exception is the international Biological and Toxin Weapons Convention which was signed on 10 April 1972 and entered into force on 26 March 1975. The Treaty bans biological and chemical weapons by prohibiting their development, production, acquisition, transfer, stockpiling, and use.

53 Edmund Burke, *Reflections on the Revolution in France* (London: Dent, 1971), p. 93.

54 Stephen Jay Gould, *Rocks of Ages—Science and Religion in the Fullness of Life* (New York: Ballantine Books, 2002), pp. 206–07.

BIBLIOGRAPHY

Aarons, Victoria, and Alan L. Berger. *Third-Generation Holocaust Representation: Trauma, History, and Memory* (Evanston, IL: Northwestern University Press, 2017).

Abel, Olivier. "La responsabilité incertaine," *Esprit,* No. 206, November 1994.

Abeling, Joris. *Teloorgang en wederopstanding van de Nederlandse monarchie (1848–1898)* (Amsterdam: Prometheus, 1996).

Ackerman, Bruce. *The Future of Liberal Revolution* (New Haven and London: Yale University Press, 1992).

Allison, Graham. *Destined for War: Can America and China Escape Thucydides's Trap?* (Boston and New York: Houghton Mifflin Harcourt, 2017).

Allison, Graham, and Niall Ferguson. "Why the U.S. President Needs a Council of Historians," *The Atlantic,* September 2016.

Amalrik, Andrei. *Will the Soviet Union Survive Until 1984?* (New York: Harper & Row, 1970).

Andrews, Helen. *Boomers—The Men and Women who Promised Freedom and Delivered Disaster* (New York: Sentinel, 2021).

Applebaum, Anne. *Gulag—A History of the Soviet Camps* (London and New York: Allen Lane, 2003).

Arendt, Hannah. *The Origins of Totalitarianism,* Preface to the First Edition (New York and London: Harcourt Brace Jovanovich, 1973).

Arendt, Hannah. "Wahrheit und Lüge in der Politik," in Hannah Arendt, *Denken ohne Geländer – Texte und Briefe,* (Munich and Zurich: Piper, 2010).

_____. "The Concept of History—Ancient and Modern," in Hannah

Arendt, *The Portable Hannah Arendt,* edited and with an introduction by Peter Baehr (New York: Penguin Books, 2000).

_____. "Europe and the Atom Bomb," in Hannah Arendt, *Essays in Understanding 1930—1954, Formation, Exile, and Totalitarianism* (New York: Schocken Books, 1994).

_____. *The Human Condition* (Chicago and London: The University of Chicago Press, 1958).

_____. *Between Past and Present* (New York: Penguin, 1977).

_____. "Collective Responsibility," in Hannah Arendt, *Responsibility and Judgment* (New York: Schocken Books, 2003).

Aron, Raymond. "Du pessimisme historique," in Raymond Aron, *Penser la liberté, penser la démocratie* (Paris: Gallimard, 2005).

Barnett, Vincent. *Kondratiev and the Dynamics of Economic Development* (London: Palgrave Macmillan, 1998).

Bauman, Zygmunt. *Retrotopia* (Cambridge: Polity Press, 2017).

Beardslee, G. William. "The 1832 Cholera Epidemic in New York State—19th Century Responses to *Cholerae Vibrio* (Part 1)," *The Early America Review,* 3 (2), 2000.

Beaufils, Thomas. *Histoire des Pays-Bas—Des origines à nos jours* (Paris: Éditions Tallandier, 2018).

Beck, Ulrich. *Was ist Globalisierung?* (Frankfurt am Main: Suhrkamp Verlag, 1998). —

_____. *Gegengifte—Die organisierte Unverantwortlichkeit,* (Frankfurt am Main: Suhrkamp Verlag, 1988).

_____. *Risikogesellschaft—Auf dem Weg in eine andere Moderne* (Frankfurt am Main: Suhrkamp Verlag, 1986).

_____. "The Reinvention of Politics," in Ulrich Beck, Anthony Giddens, and Scott Lash, *Reflexive Modernization—Politics, Tradition and Aesthetics in the Modern Social Order* (Cambridge: Polity Press, 1994).

Becker, Henk A. *Generations of Lucky Devils and Unlucky Dogs: Strategies for an assertive growing up, active ageing and intergenerational solidarity up to 2030* (Amsterdam: Rozenberg Publishers, 2012).

Bell, Alexander Graham. "Some of the Problems Awaiting Solution," An address to the graduating class of the McKinley Manual Training School, Washington, D.C., February 1, 1917 (revised for the National Geographic Magazine), *National Geographic Magazine,* Volume 31, No. 2.

Bell, Daniel. *The Coming of Post-Industrial Society—A Venture in Social Forecasting* (New York: Basic Books, Inc., 1976).

Berger, Peter L. "The Greening of American Foreign Policy," in Peter L. Berger, *Facing Up to Modernity—Excursions in Society, Politics, and Religion* (Harmondsworth and New York: Penguin Books, 1979).

Berlin, Isaiah. "Winston Churchill in 1940," in Isaiah Berlin, *The Proper Study of Mankind—An Anthology of Essays* (New York: Farrar Straus and Giroux, 1997).

———. *Historical Inevitability* (London, New York, Toronto: Oxford University Press, 1955).

Berry, Brian J. L. *Long-Wave Rhythms in Economic Development and Political Behavior* (Baltimore and London: The Johns Hopkins University Press, 1991).

Bloch, Ernst. *Das Prinzip Hoffnung,* Volume 2 (Frankfurt am Main: Suhrkamp Verlag, 1968).

Bloch, Marc. *Apologie pour l'histoire ou Métier d'historien,* Préface de Jacques Le Goff (Malakoff: Armand Colin, 2018).

Blom, J. C. H., and E. Lamberts. *History of the Low Countries* (New York and Oxford: Berghahn Books, 2006).

Bobbio, Norberto. *Teoria generale della politica* (Turin: Einaudi Editore, 1999).

Boogman, J. C. "Vaderlandse geschiedenis (na de middeleeuwen) in hedendaags perspectief. Enige kanttekeningen en beschouwingen," in J. C. Boogman, *Van spel en spelers—Verspreide opstellen* ('s-Gravenhage: Martinus Nijhoff, 1982).

Borkenau, Dr. F. *The New German Empire* (Harmondsworth: Penguin Books, 1939).

Braudel, Fernand. "Geschichte und Sozialwissenschaften—Die 'longue durée'," in Hans-Ulrich Wehler (ed.), *Geschichte und Soziologie* (Cologne: Kiepenheuer & Witsch, 1976).

_____. *La Méditerranée et le monde méditerranéen à l'époque de Philippe II* (Paris: Armand Colin, 1979).

_____. *A History of Civilizations* (New York and London: Penguin Books, 1995).

Brink, C. O. *Horace on Poetry,* Volume 1, The Ars Poetica (Cambridge: Cambridge University Press, 1963).

Brinton, Crane. *The Anatomy of Revolution* (New York: Vintage Books, 1965).

_____. John B. Christopher, and Robert Lee Wolff. *A History of Civilization—1715 to the Present* (Englewood Cliffs, NJ: Prentice-Hall, 1971).

Burckhardt, Jacob. *Weltgeschichtliche Betrachtungen* (Tübingen: Otto Reichl Verlag, 1949).

Buffon, Bertrand. *Vulgarité et modernité* (Paris: Gallimard, 2019).

Burke, Edmund. *Reflections on the Revolution in France* (London: Dent, 1971).

Buruma, Ian. *Year Zero—A History of 1945* (New York: The Penguin Press, 2013).

Campanella, Thomas. *La Città del Sole* (Milan: Feltrinelli, 1983).

Carlyle, Thomas. *On Heroes, Hero-Worship, & the Heroic in History—Six Lectures* (London: James Fraser, 1841).

Carr, E. H. *The Twenty Years' Crisis 1919–1939 – An Introduction to the Study of International Relations,* With a new introduction by Michael Cox (Houndmills, Basingstoke: Palgrave Macmillan, 2001).

_____. *What is History?* With a new introduction by Richard J. Evans (Houndmills, Basingstoke: Palgrave Macmillan, 2001).

Cassirer, Ernst. *An Essay on Man—An Introduction to a Philosophy of Human Culture* (New Haven and London: Yale University Press, 1968).

Castoriadis, Cornelius. *Domaines de l'homme (Les carrefours du labyrinthe 2)* (Paris: Éditions du Seuil, 1986).

Churchill, Winston. *Great Contemporaries* (London: Thornton Butterworth Ltd., 1937).

Cicero. *De Oratore Libri tres,* With an introduction and notes by Augustus S. Wilkins (Hildesheim, Zurich, and New York: Georg Olms Verlag, 1990).

Cioran, E. M. *Histoire et utopie* (Paris: Gallimard, 1960).

Clarke, Lee. *Worst Cases—Terror and Catastrophe in the Popular Imagination* (Chicago and London: The University of Chicago Press, 2006).

Coeckelbergh, Mark. *Human Being @ Risk—Enhancement, Technology, and the Evaluation of Vulnerability Transformations* (Dordrecht, Heidelberg, New York, London: Springer, 2013).

Colonomos, Ariel. "L'exigence croissante de justice sans frontières—le cas de la demande de restitution des biens juifs spoliés," *Les Études du CERI,* No. 78, July 2001. Condorcet. *Esquisse d'un tableau historique des progrès de l'esprit humain* (Paris: Éditions sociales, 1971).

Constant, Benjamin. "De la perfectibilité de l'espèce humaine," in Benjamin Constant, *Écrits politiques* (Paris: Éditions Gallimard, 1997).

Coquery-Vidrovitch, Catherine. *Enjeux politiques de l'histoire coloniale* (Marseille: Agone, 2009).

Cowen, Tyler. "The Great Stagnation—How America Ate All the Low-Hanging Fruit of Modern History, Got Sick, and Will (Eventually) Feel Better" (London: Penguin e-Special, 2011).

Croce, Benedetto. *Zur Theorie und Geschichte der Historiographie* (Tübingen: J. C. B. Mohr, 1915).

Dahrendorf, Ralf. "Towards the Twenty-First Century," in Michael Howard and Wm. Roger Louis (eds.), *The Oxford History of the Twentieth Century* (Oxford and New York: Oxford University Press, 1998).

De Baets, Antoon. "A Declaration of the Responsibilities of Present Generations Toward Past Generations," *History and Theory,* Issue 43, No. 4, December 2004.

De Kom, Anton. *Wij slaven van Suriname* (Amsterdam and Antwerp: Uitgeverij Atlas Contact, 2021).

De Maistre, Joseph. "Considerations on France," in Joseph de Maistre, *The Works of Joseph de Maistre,* with a new foreword by Robert Nisbet (New York: Schocken Books, 1971).

Derrida, Jacques. "Le siècle et le pardon," in *Foi et savoir suivi de Le Siècle et le Pardon* (Paris: Éditions du Seuil, 2000).

De Tocqueville, Alexis. *De la démocratie en Amérique,* Volume 2 (Paris: Garnier Flammarion, 1981).

_____. "L'Annonce de la révolution de 1848," in Alexis de Tocqueville, *Textes essentiels,* Anthologie critique par J.-L. Benoît (Paris: Havas Poche, 2000).

Diamond, Jared. *Collapse—How Societies Choose to Fail or Succeed* (New York and London: Penguin, 2011).

Driscoll, Dennis J. "The Development of Human Rights in International Law," in Walter Laqueur and Barry Rubin (eds.), *The Human Rights Reader* (New York: New American Library, 1979).

Edmund, June, and Bryan S. Turner. "Global generations: social change in the twentieth century," *The British Journal of Sociology,* Volume 56, Issue 4, November 25, 2005.

Elias, Norbert, and John L. Scotson. *Etablierte und Außenseiter* (Frankfurt am Main: Suhrkamp Verlag, 1993).

"Emerging Systemic Risks in the 21st Century: An Agenda for Action," Paris, OECD, 2003.

Emmer, P. C. *De Nederlandse slavenhandel 1500–1850* (Amsterdam and Antwerp: De Arbeiderspers, 2000).

Erikson, Erik H. *Insight and Responsibility* (New York and London: W. W. Norton & Company, Inc., 1964).

Fanon, Frantz. *Black Skin, White Masks* (London: Pluto Press, 1986).

Ferguson, Niall. *The Great Degeneration—How Institutions Decay and Economies Die,* (London and New York: Penguin, 2014).

_____. "Introduction—Virtual History: Towards a 'chaotic' theory of the past," in Niall Ferguson (ed.), *Virtual History: Alternatives and Counterfactuals* (New York: Basic Books, 1999).

Festinger, Leon, Henry W. Riecken, and Stanley Schachter. *When Prophecy Fails—A Social and Psychological Study of a Modern Group that Predicted the Destruction of the World* (New York: Harper & Row, 1964).

Fichte, Johann Gottlieb. *Die Grundzüge des gegenwärtigen Zeitalters* (Hamburg: Felix Meiner Verlag, 1956).

_____. "Reden and die deutsche Nation," in Fichtes Werke, Volume VII (Berlin: Walter de Gruyter & Co., 1971).

Fischer, David Hackett. *Historians' Fallacies: Toward a Logic of Historical Thought* (New York: Harper & Row, 1970).

Fishkin, James S. *The Voice of the People—Public Opinion & Democracy* (New Haven and London: Yale University Press, 1997).

Flinkenflögel, Willem. *Nederlandse slavenhandel (1621–1803)* (Utrecht and Antwerp: Kosmos – Z & K Uitgevers, 1994).

Foessel, Michaël. *Récidive 1938* (Paris: Presses Universitaires de France, 2019).

Fromkin, David. *A Peace to End All Peace—The Fall of the Ottoman Empire and the Creation of the Modern Middle East* (New York: Henry Holt and Company, 2001).

Fukuyama, Francis. "The End of History," *The National Interest,* No. 16, Summer 1989.

_____. *The Origins of Political Order—From Prehuman Times to the French Revolution* (London: Profile Books, 2012).

Furet, François. *La Révolution en débat* (Paris: Gallimard, 1999).

Gadamer, Hans-Georg. "Angst und Ängste," in Hans-Georg Gadamer, *Über die Verborgenheit der Gesundheit* (Frankfurt am Main: Suhrkamp Verlag, 1994).

Galbraith, John Kenneth. *The Age of Uncertainty* (London: British Broadcasting Corporation, 1977).

Gentile, Emilio. *Qu'est-ce que le fascisme? Histoire et interprétation* (Paris: Gallimard, 2004).

Geyl, Pieter. "Een historicus tegenover de wereld van nu," in Pieter Geyl, *Historicus in de tijd* (Utrecht: Uitgeversmaatschappij W. de Haan N.V., 1954).

_____. "Ongeluksprofeten," in Pieter Geyl, *Historicus in de tijd* (Utrecht: Uitgeversmaatschappij W. de Haan N.V., 1954).

_____. *Verzamelde opstellen, 1* (Utrecht and Antwerpen: Het Spectrum, 1978).

Giddens, Anthony. *Runaway World—How Globalisation is Reshaping our Lives,* (London: Profile Books, 2000).

_____. *Modernity and Self-Identity—Self and Society in the Late Modern Age* (Stanford: Stanford University Press, 1991).

Gide, André. *Journals, Volume 3, 1928–1939* (Urbana and Chicago: University of Illinois Press, 2000).

Gigerenzer, Gerd. "Psychologie des Risikos—Wann eine freie Gesellschaft risikokompetente Bürger braucht," *Aus Politik und Zeitgeschichte,* 23–25, June 2020.

Gilbert, Martin. *Churchill—A Life* (London: Heinemann, 1991).

Gilman, Nils, and Maya Indira Ganesh. "Making Sense of the Unknown," *Berggruen Institute,* July, 2020.

Goebbels, Joseph. "Der Faschismus und seine praktischen Ergebnisse," in Ernst Nolte (ed.), *Theorien über den Faschismus* (Cologne and Berlin: Kiepenheuer & Witsch, 1967).

Goldhagen, Daniel Jonah. *Worse than War—Genocide, Eliminationism, and the Ongoing Assault on Humanity* (New York: PublicAffairs, 2009).

Goldstein, Joshua. *Long Cycles: Prosperity and War in the Modern Age* (New Haven: Yale University Press, 1988).

Gould, Stephen Jay. *Rocks of Ages—Science and Religion in the Fullness of Life* (New York: Ballantine Books, 2002).

Graumann, Sigrid. "Ende des Schicksals? Genomeditierung in der Medizin," *Aus Politik und Zeitgeschichte,* 72, 34-35/2022, August 2022.

Grayling, A. C. "History and Progress in the Twentieth Century," in A. C. Grayling, *Liberty in the Age of Terror—A Defence of Civil Liberties and Enlightenment Values* (London, Berlin, and New York: Bloomsbury, 2009).

Griewank, Karl. *Der neuzeitliche Revolutionsbegriff—Entstehung und Geschichte* (Frankfurt am Main: Suhrkamp Verlag, 1973).

Griffin, Roger. *The Nature of Fascism* (London: Routledge, 1993).

Gruner, Rolf. "Über einige Probleme der historischen Kausalrelation," in *Archiv für Philosophie,* Band 10/1-2, Stuttgart 1960, pp. 107–13.

Gusdorf, Georges. "Situation spirituelle de notre temps," in Georges Gusdorf, *Le crépuscule des illusions—Mémoires intempestifs* (Paris: La table Ronde, 2002).

Habermas, Jürgen. "Die Krise des Wohlfahrtsstaates und die Erschöpfung utopischer Energien," in Jürgen Habermas, *Die neue Unübersichtlichkeit* (Frankfurt am Main: Suhrkamp Verlag, 1985).

Halbwachs, Maurice. *On Collective Memory,* Edited, Translated, and with an Introduction by Lewis A. Coser (Chicago and London: The University of Chicago Press, 1992).

Halliday, Fred. *The World at 2000* (Houndmills and New York: Palgrave Macmillan, 2001).

Hamilton, Alexander, James Madison, and John Jay. *The Federalist Papers* (New York, Ontario, and London: The New American Library, 1961).

Hamon, Hervé, and Patrick Rotman. *Génération – 1. Les années de rêve* (Paris: Éditions du Seuil, 1987).

Hanssen, Léon. *Huizinga en de troost van de geschiedenis* (Amsterdam: Uitgeverij Balans, 1996).

Hauser, Marc D. *Moral Minds—How Nature Designed Our Universal Sense of Right and Wrong* (New York: HarperCollins, 2006).

Hayek, Friedrich. "The Common Sense of Progress, in F. A. Hayek, *The Constitution of Liberty* (London and Henley: Routledge & Kegan Paul, 1976).

_____. *The Fatal Conceit—The Errors of Socialism* (London: Routledge, 1990).

Hegel, G. W. F. "Vorlesungen über die Philosophie der Geschichte," in G. W. F. Hegel, *Werke,* Volume 12 (Frankfurt am Main: Suhrkamp Verlag, 1970).

Held, David, Anthony McGrew, David Goldblatt, and Jonathan Perraton. *Global Transformations—Politics, Economics and Culture* (Stanford, CA.: Stanford University Press, 1999).

Herder, Johann Gottfried. *Auch eine Philosophie der Geschichte zur Bildung der Menschheit* (Frankfurt am Main: Suhrkamp Verlag, 1967).

Herder, Johann Gottfried. *Journal meiner Reise im Jahr 1769* (Stuttgart: Reclam, 1976).

Hirschman, Albert O. *Shifting Involvements—Private Interest and Public Action* (Princeton, NJ: Princeton University Press, 1982).

Hitler, Adolf. *Mein Kampf* (Munich: Verlag Franz Eher Nachfolger, 1933).

Hobbes, Thomas. *Leviathan,* Edited with an Introduction by C. B. Macpherson (Harmondsworth: Penguin, 1972).

Hobsbawm, Eric. *On the Edge of the New Century,* In Conversation with Antonio Polito (London: Little, Brown and Company, 2000).

Höffe, Otfried. *Ist die Demokratie zukunftsfähig?* (Munich: C. H. Beck, 2009).

_____. *Moral als Preis der Moderne—Ein Versuch über Wissenschaft, Technik und Umwelt* (Frankfurt am Main: Suhrkamp Verlag, 1995).

_____. *Sittlich-politische Diskurse—Philosophische Grundlagen, Politische Ethik, Biomedizinische Ethik* (Frankfurt am Main: Suhrkamp Verlag, 1981).

Holsti, K. J. "Governance without Government: Polyarchy in Nineteenth-Century European International Politics," in James N. Rosenau and Ernst-Otto Czempiel (eds.), *Governance without Government: Order and Change in World Politics* (Cambridge and New York: Cambridge University Press, 1998).

Honneth, Axel. "Anerkennung zwischen Staaten," in Axel Honneth, *Das Ich im Wir* (Berlin: Suhrkamp Verlag, 2010).

Horkheimer, Max, and Theodor W., Adorno. *Dialektik der Aufklärung* (Frankfurt am Main: S. Fischer Verlag, 1969).

Huebner, Jonathan. "A possible declining trend for worldwide innovation," *Technological Forecasting & Social Change,* 72, 2005.

Huizinga, Johan. *Geschonden wereld—Een beschouwing over de kansen op herstel van onze beschaving* (Haarlem: H. D. Tjeenk Willink & Zoon N. V., 1945).

Huxley, Aldous. *Brave New World* (Harmondsworth: Penguin Books, 1962).

Iggers, Georg G. *Deutsche Geschichtswissenschaft—Eine Kritik der traditionellen Geschichtsauffassung von Herder bis zur Gegenwart* (Munich: Deutscher Taschenbuch Verlag, 1971).

Jacquet, Jennifer. *Is Shame Necessary? New Uses for an Old Tool* (London: Penguin Books, 2016).

Jaspers, Karl. *Die geistige Situation der Zeit (1931)* (Berlin: Walter de Gruyter & Co., 1971).

_____. "Die Schuldfrage," in Karl Jaspers, *Die Schuldfrage—Für Völkermord gibt es keine Verjährung* (Munich: R. Piper & Co. Verlag, 1979).

Joas, Hans. "Wertegeneralisierung—Die Allgemeine Erklärung der Menschenrechte und die Pluralität der Kulturen," in Hans Joas, *Die Sakralität der Person—Eine neue Genealogie der Menschenrechte* (Berlin: Suhrkamp Verlag, 2015).

_____. "Der Traum von der gewaltfreien Moderne," in Hans Joas, *Kriege und Werte—Studien zur Gewaltgeschichte des 20. Jahrhunderts* (Weilerswist: Velbrück Wissenschaft, 2000).

_____. "Die Modernität des Krieges—Die Modernisierungstheorie und das Problem der Gewalt," in Wolfgang Knöbl and Gunnar Schmidt (eds.), *Die Gegenwart des Krieges* (Frankfurt am Main: Fischer Taschenbuch Verlag, 2000).

Jonas, Hans. *Das Prinzip Verantwortung—Versuch einer Ethik für die technologische Zivilisation* (Frankfurt am Main: Suhrkamp Verlag, 1984).

Kagan, Robert. "The New German Question—What Happens When Europe Comes Apart?" *Foreign Affairs,* Volume 98, No. 3, May/June 2019.

_____. *The Return of History and the End of Dreams* (New York: Alfred A. Knopf, 2008).

Kant, Immanuel. "Idea for a Universal History with a Cosmopolitan Purpose," in Immanuel Kant, *Political Writings,* edited by H. S. Reiss (Cambridge and New York: Cambridge University Press, 1991).

_____. "Der Streit der Fakultäten," Zweiter Abschnitt, in Immanuel Kant, *Schriften zur Anthropologie, Geschichtsphilosophie, Politik und Pädagogik 1, Werkausgabe Volume XI* (Frankfurt am Main: Suhrkamp Verlag, 1977).

Kennan, George F. *Memoirs 1925–1950* (New York: Pantheon Books, 1967).

_____. *American Diplomacy 1900–1950* (Chicago: The University of Chicago Press, 1951).

Kennedy, Paul. *Preparing for the Twenty-First Century* (London: Fontana Press, 1994).

_____. *The Rise and Fall of the Great Powers—Economic Change and Military Conflict from 1500 to 2000* (New York: Random House, 1987).

Kershaw, Ian. "Ghosts of Fascists Past," *The National Interest,* No. 112, March/April 2011.

Keynes, John Maynard. "Economic Possibilities for our Grandchildren (1930)," in John Maynard Keynes, *Essays in Persuasion* (London: Macmillan and Co., 1931).

Kissinger, Henry. *On China* (London and New York: Penguin, 2012).

_____. *World Order—Reflections on the Character of Nations and the Course of History* (London and New York: Penguin, 2014).

Kolakowski, Leszek. "Het begrip 'links'," in Leszek Kolakowski, *De mens zonder alternatief* (Amsterdam: Moussault's Uitgeverij NV, 1968).

Kondratieff, N. D. "The Long Waves in Economic Life," *The Review of Economic Statistics,* Volume XVII, No. 6, November 1935.

Koselleck, Reinhart. "Wiederholungsstrukturen in Sprache und Geschichte," in Reinhart Koselleck, *Vom Sinn und Unsinn der Geschichte - Aufsätze und Vorträge aus vier Jahrzehnten* (Berlin: Suhrkamp Verlag, 2010).

_____. "Lernen aus der Geschichte Preußens," in Reinhart Koselleck, *Vom Sinn und Unsinn der Geschichte—Aufsätze und Vorträge aus vier Jahrzehnten* (Berlin: Suhrkamp Verlag, 2010).

_____. *Kritik und Krise—Eine Studie zur Pathogenese der bürgerlichen Welt* (Frankfurt am Main: Suhrkamp Verlag, 1973).

Kotek, Joël. "Le génocide des Herero, symptôme d'un *Sonderweg* allemand?" *Revue d'Histoire de la Shoah,* 2008/2 (No. 189).

Kreuels, Marianne. *Über den Wert der Sterblichkeit—Ein Essay in analytischer Existenzphilosophie* (Berlin: Suhrkamp Verlag, 2015).

Krupp, Fred, Nathaniel Keohane, and Eric Pooley. "Less Than Zero—Can Carbon-Removal Technologies Curb Climate Change?" in *Foreign Affairs,* Volume 98, No. 2, March/April 2019.

Krznaric, Roman. *The Good Ancestor—How to Think Long-Term in a Short-Term World* (London: Penguin, 2020).

Laqueur, Walter. *Weimar—Die Kultur der Republik* (Frankfurt am Main and Berlin: Ullstein, 1977).

Lasch, Christopher. *The True and Only Heaven—Progress and Its Critics* (New York and London: Norton & Company, 1991).

Leroy, Béatrice. *Les juifs dans l'Espagne chrétienne avant 1492* (Paris: Éditions Albin Michel, 1993).

Lessing, Gotthold. "Die Erziehung des Menschengeschlechts, in *Lessings Werke,* Volume 7 (Leipzig and Vienna: Meyers Klassiker Ausgaben, no year).

Lévinas, Emmanuel. "La responsabilité pour autrui," in Emmanuel Lévinas, *Éthique et infini* (Paris: Fayard, 1982).

Levy, Jack S. *War in the Modern Great Power System* (Lexington, KY: The University of Kentucky Press, 1983).

Löwith, Karl. "Das Verhängnis des Fortschritts," in Erich Burck (ed.), *Die Idee des Fortschritts—Neun Vorträge über Wege und Grenzen des Fortschrittsglaubens* (Munich: Beck Verlag, 1963).

_____. *Weltgeschichte und Heilsgeschehen—Die theologischen Voraussetzungen der Geschichtsphilosophie* (Stuttgart and Berlin: Kohlhammer Verlag, 1967).

Mann, Thomas. "The German Republic," in Anton Kaes, Martin Jay, and Edward Dimendberg (eds.), *The Weimar Republic Sourcebook* (Berkeley and London: University of California Press, 1994).

Mannheim, Karl. *Man and Society in an Age of Reconstruction—Studies in Modern Social Structure* (London and Henley: Routledge & Kegan Paul, 1980).

_____. "Das Problem der Generationen," *Kölner Vierteljahresheft für Soziologie,* 7 (1928).

Marx, Karl. "Grundrisse. Einleitung zur Kritik der politischen Ökonomie," in Karl Marx and Friedrich Engels, *Marx Engels Werke,* Volume 13 (Berlin: Dietz Verlag, 1974).

_____. "Der 18. Brumaire des Louis Bonaparte," in Karl Marx and Friedrich Engels, *Marx Engels Werke,* Volume 8 (Berlin: Dietz Verlag, 1960).

_____, and Friedrich Engels. "Die deutsche Ideologie," in *Marx Engels Werke,* Volume 3 (Berlin: Dietz Verlag, 1969).

_____.*Capital,* Volume 3 (New York: International Publishers, 1977).

Masci, David. "Human Enhancement—The Scientific and Ethical Dimensions of Striving for Perfection," *Pew Research Center,* September 23, 2020.

McCarthy, Daniel. "Did Liberalism Fail?" *The National Interest,* No. 156, July/August 2018.

Meadows, Donella H., Dennis L. Meadows, Jørgen Randers, and William W. Behrens III. *The Limits to Growth—A Report for the Club of Rome's Project on the Predicament of Mankind* (Washington, D.C.: Potomac Associates, 1972).

Meinecke, Friedrich. "Kausalitäten und Werte in der Geschichte," in *Historische Zeitschrift,* Volume 137, No. 2, 1928.

_____. *Die Entstehung des Historismus* (Munich: R. Oldenbourg Verlag, 1965).

Metternich. *Memoirs of Prince Metternich 1773–1815,* Book I. Materials for the History of my Public Life 1773– 1815, edited by Prince Richard Metternich (New York: Charles Scribner's Sons, 1880).

Miegel, Meinhard, and Stefanie Wahl. *Das Ende des Individualismus— Die Kultur des Westens zerstört sich selbst"* (Munich and Landsberg am Lech: Verlag Bonn Aktuell, 1993).

Milza, Pierre. *Les fascismes* (Paris: Éditions du Seuil, 2001).

Möckel, Benjamin. "Zukünftige Generationen—Geschichte einer politischen Pathosformel," *Aus Politik und Zeitgeschichte* (70), 52–53, December 21, 2020.

Monnet, Jean. *Erinnerungen eines Europäers,* with an Introduction by Helmut Schmidt, (Munich: Deutscher Taschenbuch Verlag, 1980).

More, Thomas. *Utopia* (Harmondsworth: Penguin, 1971).

Münkler, Herfried and Marina. *Abschied vom Abstieg—Eine Agenda für Deutschland* (Berlin: Rowohlt, 2019).

Mussolini, Benito. "Trenchocracy," in Roger Griffin (ed.), *Fascism* (Oxford and New York: Oxford University Press, 1995).

Nagel, Thomas. "Birth, Death, and the Meaning of Life," in Thomas Nagel, *The View from Nowhere* (New York and Oxford: Oxford University Press, 1989).

Neiman, Susan. "Von den Deutschen lernen? – Essay," *Aus Politik und Zeitgeschichte,* October 1, 2021.

Nieman, Craig. "Deterrence and Engagement: A Blended Strategic Approach to a Resurgent Russia," Joint Forces Staff College, Norfolk, VA, April 4, 2016.

Nietzsche, Friedrich. "Vom Nutzen und Nachteil der Historie für das Leben," (Unzeitgemässe Betrachtungen, Zweites Stück), in Friedrich Nietzsche, *Werke,* Volume I (Munich: Carl Hanser Verlag, 1977).

_____. "Menschliches, Allzumenschliches—Ein Buch für freie Geister," Volume I, in Friedrich Nietzsche, *Werke,* Volume I (Munich: Carl Hanser Verlag, 1977).

_____. "Also sprach Zarathustra," in Friedrich Nietzsche, *Werke,* Volume II (Munich: Carl Hanser Verlag, 1977).

Nisbet, Robert. "History and Sociology," in Robert A. Nisbet, *Tradition and Revolt—Historical and Sociological Essays* (New York: Vintage Books, 1970).

Nozick, Robert. *Anarchy, State, and Utopia* (New York: Basic Books, 1974).

Nye Jr., Joseph S. *Nuclear Ethics* (New York and London: The Free

Press, 1988). O'Hanlon, Michael E. "Forecasting change in military technology," *Brookings,* September 2018.

Orwell, George, *Nineteen Eighty-Four* (Harmondsworth: Penguin Books, 1967).

_____. *Notes on Nationalism* (London and New York: Penguin Books, 2018).

Pelizäus, Helga, and Jana Heinz. "Stereotypisierungen von Jung und Alt in der Corona-Pandemie," *Aus Politik und Zeitgeschichte* (70), 52-53/2020, December 21, 2020.

Pareto, Vilfredo. *Trattato di sociologia generale,* Volume primo (Milano: Edizioni di Comunità, 1981).

Parfit, Derek. *Reasons and Persons* (Oxford and New York: Oxford University Press, 1987).

Paulhac, François. *Les accords de Munich et les origines de la guerre de 1939* (Paris: Librairie J. Vrin, 1988).

Petrov, Nikita. "Don't Speak, Memory—How Russia Represses Its Past," *Foreign Affairs,* Volume 97, No. 1, January/February 2018.

Polanyi, Karl. *The Great Transformation—The Political and Economic Origins of Our Time,* with an Introduction by R. M. MacIver (Boston: Beacon Press, 1957).

Popper, Karl. *La leçon de ce siècle* (Paris: Anatolia Editions, 1993).

_____. "Utopia and Violence," in Karl R. Popper, *Conjectures and Refutations—The Growth of Scientific Knowledge* (London and Henley: Routledge and Kegan Paul, 1976).

Rawls, John. *The Law of Peoples* (Cambridge, MA, and London: Harvard University Press, 1999).

Rice, Condoleezza. "The Making of Soviet Strategy," in Peter Paret (ed.), *Makers of Modern Strategy—From Machiavelli to the Nuclear Age* (Princeton, NJ: Princeton University Press, 1986).

Rickert, Heinrich. *Die Probleme der Geschichtsphilosophie—Eine Einführung* (Heidelberg: Carl Winters Universitätsbuchhandlung, 1924).

Ricoeur, Paul. *Memory, History, Forgetting* (Chicago: The University of Chicago Press, 2006).

_____. "Le concept de responsabilité," in Paul Ricoeur, *Le Juste 1* (Paris : Éditions Esprit, 1995).

Riesman, David. "Observations on Community Plans and Utopia," in David Riesman, *Individualism Reconsidered* (New York: Doubleday and Company, Ltd., 1955).

_____. *The Lonely Crowd—A Study of the Changing American Character,* with Nathan Glazer and Reuel Denney (New Haven and London: Yale University Press, 1978).

Romein, Dr. Jan. *Machten van dezen tijd—1936–1937* (Amsterdam: Wereldbibliotheek, 1938).

Rosanvallon, Pierre. *Pour une histoire conceptuelle du politique* (Paris: Éditions du Seuil, 2003).

Roseman, Mark. (ed.). *Generations in Conflict— Youth revolt and generation formation in Germany 1770-1968* (Cambridge and New York: Cambridge University Press, 1995).

Rosenberg, Charles. *The Cholera Years: The United States in 1832, 1849, and 1866* (Chicago and London: The University of Chicago Press, 1987).

Rostow, Walt. "Kondratieff, Schumpeter, and Kuznets: Trend Periods Revisited," *The Journal of Economic History,* 35 (4), 1975.

Roudinesco, Élisabeth. *Soi-même comme un roi—Essai sur les derives identitaires* (Paris: Seuil, 2021).

Rummel, R. J. *Death by Government* (New Brunswick and London: Transaction Publishers, 2004).

Samuelson, Paul A. *Economics* (New York: McGraw-Hill, 1980).

Sandel, Michael J. "The Case Against Perfection—What's wrong with designer children, bionic athletes, and genetic engineering," *The Atlantic,* April 2004.

Sartre, Jean-Paul. *L'être et le néant—Essai d'ontologie phénoménologique* (Paris: Éditions Gallimard, 1943).

Schäfer, Liane. "Wem gehört die Vergangenheit? Generationenbrüche im deutschen Erinnern," *Aus Politik und Zeitgeschichte* (70), 52–53, December 21, 2020.

Scheler, Max. "Mensch und Geschichte," in Max Scheler, *Philosophische Weltanschauung* (Bern and Munich: Francke Verlag, 1968).

Schlesinger Jr., Arthur. "Foreign Policy and the American Character," *Foreign Affairs,* Volume 62, No. 1, Fall 1983.

_____. *The Cycles of American History* (Boston and New York: Houghton Mifflin Company, 1999).

Schlink, Bernhard. "Epilog: Die Gegenwart der Vergangenheit," in Bernhard Schlink, *Vergangenheitsschuld und gegenwärtiges Recht* (Frankfurt am Main: Suhrkamp Verlag, 2002).

Schmidt, Helmut, and Fritz Stern. *Unser Jahrhundert—Ein Gespräch* (Munich: Verlag C.H. Beck, 2010).

_____. *Ausserdienst—Eine Bilanz* (Munich: Siedler Verlag, 2008).

_____. "Ansprache in Auschwitz-Birkenau, Gehalten am 23. November 1977," in Helmut Schmidt, *Der Kurs heisst Frieden* (Düsseldorf and Vienna: Econ Verlag, 1979).

Schumpeter, Joseph A. *Business Cycles: A Theoretical, Historical, and Statistical Analysis of the Capitalist Process* (New York and London: McGraw-Hill, 1939).

_____. *Capitalism, Socialism, and Democracy* (New York and London: Harper & Brothers Publishers, 1947).

Selin, Cynthia. "The Sociology of the Future: Tracing Stories of Technology and Time," *Sociology Compass* 2/6, 2008.

Servigne, Pablo, and Raphaël Stevens. *Comment tout peut s'effondrer— Petit manuel de collapsologie à l'usage des générations présentes* (Paris: Éditions du Seuil, 2015).

Servigne, Pablo, Raphaël Stevens, and Gauthier Chapelle. *Une autre fin du monde est possible—Vivre l'effondrement (et pas seulement y survivre)* (Paris: Éditions du Seuil, 2018).

Shils, Edward *Tradition,* (Chicago: The University of Chicago Press, 1981).

Sichrovsky, Peter, *Schuldig geboren—Kinder aus Nazifamilien* (Cologne: Kiepenheuer & Witsch, 1987).

Simmel, Georg. *Die Probleme der Geschichtsphilosophie—Eine erkenntnistheoretische Studie* (Leipzig: Verlag Duncker & Humblot, 1902).

_____. "Deutschlands innere Wandlung—Rede, gehalten in Straßburg, November 1914," in Georg Simmel, *Gesamtausgabe,* Volume 16 (Frankfurt am Main: Suhrkamp Verlag, 1999).

Skvortsov, L. V., *Istoriya i Anti-Istoriya—kritike metodologii burzhuaznoy filosofii istorii* (Moscow: Politizdat, 1976).

Solomou, Solomos. *Phases of Economic Growth, 1850–1973: Kondratieff Waves and Kuznets Swings* (Cambridge and New York: Cambridge University Press, 1990).

Solovyov, Vladimir, and Elena Klepikova. *Inside the Kremlin* (London: W. H. Allen & Co Plc, 1988).

Sorel, Georges. *Les illusions du progrès* (Paris: Marcel Rivière, 1927).

Sorokin, Pitirim A. "A Survey of the Cyclical Conceptions of Social and Historical Process," *Social Forces,* Volume 6, No. 1, September 1927.

Spencer, Herbert. *The Man Versus the State* (Indianapolis: Liberty Classics, 1981).

Spengler, Oswald. *Der Untergang des Abendlandes,* Band 1, reprint of original (Altenmünster: Jazzybee Verlag Jürgen Beck, no year).

_____. *Jahre der Entscheidung: Deutschland und die weltgeschichtliche Entwicklung* edited by Frank Lisson, (Graz: Ares Verlag, 2007).

Spruyt, Hendrik. *Ending Empire: Contested Sovereignty and Territorial Partition* (Ithaca: Cornell University Press, 2005).

Staley, David. *History and Future: Using Historical Thinking to Imagine the Future* (Lanham, MD: Lexington Books, 2010).

Starobin, Paul. "Guilty Conscience," *The National Interest,* Number 170, November/December 2020.

Stern, Fritz. *Kulturpessimismus als politische Gefahr—Eine Analyse nationaler Ideologie in Deutschland* (Stuttgart: Klett-Cotta, 2018).

Strauß, Franz-Josef. *Deutschland Deine Zukunft* (Stuttgart: Seewald Verlag, 1975).

Strauss, Leo. "Natural Right and the Historical Approach," in *The Review of Politics,* Volume XII, 1950.

Strauss, William, and Neil Howe. *Generations—The History of America's Future, 1584 to 2069* (New York and London: Harper Perennial, 1991).

Streeck, Wolfgang. *Gekaufte Zeit—Die vertagte Krise des demokratischen Kapitalismus* (Berlin: Suhrkamp Verlag, 2013).

Taguieff, Pierre-André. *Du progrès* (Paris: Librio, 2001).

Taleb, Nassim Nicholas. *Antifragile—Things that Gain from Disorder* (New York: Penguin Books, 2013).

Taylor, A. J. P. *The First World War* (London and New York: Penguin, 1966).

Tilly, Charles. *Credit & Blame* (Princeton and Oxford: Princeton University Press, 2008).

Tinbergen, J. "Kondratiev Cycles and So-Called Long Waves," *Futures,* August 1981.

Todd, Emmanuel. *La chute finale—Essai sur la décomposition de la sphère soviétique* (Paris: Éditions Robert Laffont, 1976).

Tonglet, Benoît. "Les cycles Kondratieff: une philosophie critique," *Innovations,* 2004/1 No. 9.

Troeltsch, Ernst. *Protestantism and Progress—A Historical Study of the Relation of Protestantism to the Modern World* (Boston: Beacon Press, 1958).

Turchin, Peter, and Sergey A. Nefedov. *Secular Cycles* (Princeton: Princeton University Press, 2009).

Turgot. "Tableau philosophique des progrès successifs de l'esprit humain," in *Œuvres,* Volume I (Paris: Éditions Schelle, 1913), Reprint Glashütter im Taunus, 1972.

Van Doorn, J. A. A. *Indische lessen: Nederland en de koloniale ervaring* (Amsterdam: Bert Bakker, 1995).

––––––. "Lotgenoten en hun ontvankelijkheid," in J. A. A. van Doorn, *Gevangen in de tijd—Over generaties en hun geschiedenis* (Amsterdam: Boom, 2002).

Van Herpen, Marcel H. *The Rise of the Shame Society—America's Change from a Guilt Culture into a Shame Culture* (Lanham, MD and London: Lexington Books, 2022).

_____. *The End of Populism—Twenty Proposals to Defend Liberal Democracy* (Manchester: Manchester University Press, 2021).

_____. *Putin's Wars—The Rise of Russia's New Imperialism* (Lanham, MD: Rowman & Littlefield, 2014).

_____. *Putinism—The Slow Rise of a Radical Right Regime in Russia* (Houndmills and London: Palgrave Macmillan, 2013).

_____. *Marx en de mensenrechten—Politiek en ethiek van Rousseau tot Marx* (Weesp: Het Wereldvenster, 1983).

_____. "Rousseau en de 'Sturm und Drang'—De vroegste receptie van Rousseau's cultuurkritiek in Duitsland," *De Gids,* 142, 1979.

Van Oostrum, Duco. "De adem der vrijheid. Wij slaven van Suriname als literatuur," in Anton de Kom, *Wij slaven van Suriname* (Amsterdam and Antwerp: Uitgeverij Atlas Contact, 2021).

Van Weezel, Natascha. *De derde generatie—Kleinkinderen van de Holocaust* (Amsterdam: Uitgeverij Balans, 2015).

Viveret, Patrick. "Le pouvoir, l'expertise, la responsabilité," in Monique Vacquin (ed.), *La responsabilité—La condition de notre humanité* (Paris: Éditions Autrement, 1994).

Voltaire. *Philosophical Diary,* edited and translated by Theodore Besterman (London and New York: Penguin, 2004).

_____. *Candide,* Introduction by Philip Littell (New York: Boni and Liveright, Inc., 1918).

Von Mutius, Bernhard. "Geschwindigkeit und Flexibilität," in Peter Kemper and Ulrich Sonnenschein (eds.), *Globalisierung im Alltag* (Frankfurt am Main: Suhrkamp Verlag, 2002).

Vuckovic, Nadja. "Qui demande des réparations et pour quels crimes?" in Marc Ferro, *Le livre noir du colonialisme – XVIe – XXIe siècle: de l'extermination à la repentance* (Paris : Robert Laffont, 2003).

Wallace-Wells, David. *The Uninhabitable Earth: Life After Warming* (New York: Tim Duggan Books, 2019).

Weber, Max. "Die protestantische Ethik und der 'Geist' des Kapitalismus," in Max Weber, *Schriften—1894–1922,* selected by Dirk Kaesler (Stuttgart: Alfred Kröner Verlag, 2002).

_____. "'Kirchen' und 'Sekten'," in Max Weber, *Schriften 1894–1922,* selected by Dirk Kaesler (Stuttgart: Alfred Kröner Verlag, 2002).

_____. "Politik als Beruf," in Max Weber, *Schriften 1894–1922,* selected by Dirk Kaesler (Stuttgart: Alfred Kröner Verlag, 2002).

Weitz, Eric D. *Weimar Germany—Promise and Tragedy* (Princeton and Oxford: Princeton University Press, 2009).

Wesseling, Henri. *Le partage de l'Afrique 1880–1914* (Paris: Denoël, 1996).

Wesseling, H. L., "Heeft Afrika een geschiedenis?" in H. L. Wesseling, *De draagbare Wesseling* (Amsterdam: Prometheus, 2002).

_____. "Fernand Braudel, historicus van de lange duur," in H. L. Wesseling, *Vele ideeën over Frankrijk – Opstellen over geschiedenis en cultuur* (Amsterdam: Uitgeverij Bert Bakker, 1988).

_____. "Schuld en boete," in H. L. Wesseling, *Daverende dingen dezer dagen* (Amsterdam: Prometheus, 2018).

Winkler, Heinrich August. *Geschichte des Westens—Von den Anfängen in der Antike bis zum 20. Jahrhundert* (München: C. H. Beck, 2010).